DAKOTA IN EXILE

IOWA AND THE MIDWEST EXPERIENCE

Series editor, William B. Friedricks,
Iowa History Center at Simpson College

DAKOTA IN EXILE

✳ THE UNTOLD STORIES OF CAPTIVES ✳
IN THE AFTERMATH OF THE
U.S.-DAKOTA WAR

LINDA M. CLEMMONS

Foreword by Robert V. Hopkins Jr.

UNIVERSITY OF IOWA PRESS ✳ IOWA CITY

University of Iowa Press, Iowa City 52242

Copyright © 2019 by the University of Iowa Press

www.uipress.uiowa.edu

Printed in the United States of America

Printed on acid-free paper

Library of Congress Cataloging-in-Publication Data

Names: Clemmons, Linda M., 1969– author.

Title: Dakota in exile : the untold stories of captives in the aftermath of the U.S.-Dakota war / Linda M. Clemmons.

Description: Iowa City : University of Iowa Press, [2019] | Series: Iowa and the Midwest experience | Includes bibliographical references and index.

Identifiers: LCCN 2018040172 (print) | LCCN 2019008433 (ebook) | ISBN 978-1-60938-634-4 (ebook) | ISBN 978-1-60938-633-7 (pbk. : alk. paper)

Subjects: LCSH: Dakota War, Minnesota, 1862. | Dakota Indians—History—19th century. | Dakota Indians—Government relations—History—19th century. | Dakota Indians—Social conditions—19th century.

Classification: LCC E83.86 (ebook) | LCC E83.86 .C54 2019 (print) | DDC 973.7—dc23

LC record available at https://lccn.loc.gov/2018040172

Map on page xviii by David Deis, Dreamline Cartography

To Bill, Charlie, Sam, and Ellie

CONTENTS

FOREWORD

The U.S.-Dakota War of 1862 and its aftermath intimately affected my family, especially my great-great-grandparents, Robert and Sarah Hopkins, and their children. Unfortunately, there has not been a lot of talk among our elders about the war or about where we come from. We needed to hide much of our history. It is only recently that I have talked with elder aunts and other family members and have begun to learn this history that had been hidden out of fear.

After the war, our ancestors had to flee to different reservations. My great-great-grandmother arrived in Montana by train. She got off the train in Glasgow on the western side of what is now the Fort Peck Reservation in northeastern Montana. Even though my relatives were Dakota, they settled on the western side, which was Assiniboine, instead of the eastern Sioux side. According to the Dawes Act of 1887, my ancestors had to choose which tribe they belonged to; because they resided on the western side, they became Assiniboine. They were reluctant to talk about their background or the war, because they did not want to be disenrolled if their Dakota heritage became known.

Despite the fact that they had to hide their history, the Hopkins family always knew who they were, and they had the foresight to understand what they needed to do to survive before, during, and in the long years after the war. Today, our elders are finally beginning to talk about the war and its aftermath and to fill in gaps in their history prior to the Dawes Act. This helps families understand where they come from and who they are. In addition to hearing stories from my elders, I have been lucky through my work as the tribal liaison for a large energy company to connect with my *tahans'i*, my relatives, living on the Rosebud, Sisseton, and other reservations.

The aftermath of the war divided my family and forced us to hide our heritage and stories, but we always knew who we were. When we talk about these events and reconnect with family members, it opens our eyes still further and helps us understand where we come from.

Robert V. Hopkins Jr./Flyingshield
Fort Peck Reservation, Montana
July 2018

ACKNOWLEDGMENTS

Over the course of writing this book, I accumulated an extensive list of institutions and people I want to thank. Several institutions provided financial assistance for this project, including two summer grants from Illinois State University and a grant from the State Historical Society of Iowa. Many archives across the country provided access to their extensive collections of primary and secondary sources. I would specifically like to thank the librarians and staff at the Minnesota Historical Society Library, St. Paul, Minnesota; the Center for Western Studies at Augustana University in Sioux Falls, South Dakota; Augustana College in Rock Island, Illinois; the Davenport Public Library in Davenport, Iowa; and Wheaton College in Wheaton, Illinois. Vanette Schwartz and Josh Layden from the Milner Library at Illinois State University tracked down obscure citations and ordered many reels of microfilm for me.

Numerous colleagues at Illinois State University helped me with this project, both at our department's faculty seminars and in the hallways. I would especially like to thank Kyle Ciani for talking me through numerous points during the research and writing process, as well as Ron Gifford and Amy Wood, who offered their expertise on Civil War and late nineteenth-century prisons to help me try to figure out various perplexing issues about the Dakota prison in Davenport. Anthony Crubaugh and now Ross Kennedy, chairs of the Illinois State University History Department, have also been supportive of my work. Marvin Bergman, the editor of the *Annals of Iowa*, and David Rich Lewis, the editor of the *Western Historical Quarterly*, helped improve my research, arguments, and writing style in two published articles based on topics covered in this book. Their critiques and those of their anonymous readers helped me improve the overall project.

Dakota in Exile would not have happened without the support of the University of Iowa Press, especially senior acquisitions editor Ranjit Arab and copy editor Holly Carver. Both believed in this project and saw it through to its completion. I would also like to thank the press's two anonymous readers for the helpful comments that guided my revisions. Of course, any mistakes are entirely my own. David Deis constructed the map.

Aside from a few words, I do not speak or read Dakota. Instead, I have relied on the talents of others, who have shared the gift of translating and publishing some of the letters written by the prisoners held in Davenport. Special recognition must go to Louis Garcia of Tokio, North Dakota, for translating several letters and articles for me, especially obituaries of Robert Hopkins and Catherine Totidutawin. Michael Simon of Sisseton, South Dakota, helped translate an important letter written by Sarah Hopkins and her mother, Catherine Totidutawin. Clifford Canku and Michael Simon have offered an invaluable resource to the public through *The Dakota Prisoner of War Letters*, their translations of fifty letters written by three dozen of the Davenport prisoners.

I cannot thank Robert Hopkins enough for helping me with this project. Bob graciously shared his time and family stories with me and agreed to write the foreword to this book. Without his help and input, the story of Robert Hopkins and his family before and after the war would be incomplete. Pidamaya.

Finally, I would like to thank my husband, Bill Jackson, and our three children, Charlie, Sam, and Ellie, for all their encouragement and inspiration throughout this process. Bill took care of our children while I sat in libraries and my office writing and rewriting. He also helped with research in numerous archives and read multiple drafts of portions of this book. Margaret Clemmons helped me search newspapers and read the manuscript in its entirety. I would like to thank all of them for their love, patience, and support.

PREFACE

During the course of writing this book, several events occurred that made it clear to me that the legacy of the U.S.-Dakota War of 1862 remains relevant and important to study into the present day. First, in 2017, Sam Durant, a non-Dakota artist, created *Scaffold*, a life-size structure that referenced the wooden gallows used to hang thirty-eight Dakota men in Mankato, Minnesota, after the war. The hangings remain to date the largest mass execution on United States soil. Without consulting any Dakota communities, the Walker Art Center in Minneapolis installed the gallows in its outdoor sculpture garden. While Durant intended the structure to be a critique of capital punishment, Dakota protesters decried it as insensitive and harmful because it led them to relive one of the most traumatic events in their history. In a separate incident, in 2018, a sacred pipe from White Dog, a Mdewakanton Dakota executed at the Mankato mass hanging, was put up for auction (see fig. 1). Dakota communities attempted to halt the auction, but to no avail.

Both these incidents ended favorably for the Dakota. The gallows were eventually removed from the sculpture garden. An anonymous donor purchased the pipe for close to $40,000 and returned it to the Dakota Oyate, the Dakota Nation. The fact that both these events took place more than 150 years after the war and the hangings at Mankato illustrates the continuing relevance of many of the themes highlighted in this book, including the objectification and commodification of Dakota for amusement and profit and, above all, their resistance and resilience when faced with the enduring legacy of the war.

FIGURE 1. The sacred pipe (and detail) that White Dog gave to one of his guards just before his execution. Courtesy of Skinner, Inc., skinnerinc.com.

My involvement in this project has followed a rather circuitous path. After publishing my first book, *Conflicted Mission: Faith, Disputes, and Deception on the Dakota Frontier*, in 2014, I wanted to know more. That book examines the contentious relationship between Dakota people and Protestant missionaries in Minnesota. It begins with the missionaries' arrival in the territory in the mid-1830s and ends with a brief account of the U.S.-Dakota War of 1862. Immediately after the book was released, I wanted to dive back into the missionaries' letters and other documents to see what happened to them, their few converts, and Dakota in general after the war ended in 1862. Did the same themes and conclusions I found in the prewar period extend into the postwar period?

When I began researching the postwar period, the project changed—as all projects invariably do—evolving beyond the missionaries and their converts and written sources related to these topics. As I conducted my research, I kept running across references to one Dakota man in particular, Çaske—First-Born Son in Dakota—whom the missionaries later renamed Robert Hopkins. I was already familiar with the Hopkins family because they appeared briefly in my first book, as they were some of the very few Christian converts in the pre-1862 years. After 1862, however, their names showed up with increasing frequency in missionary letters and publications, government documents, and even newspaper articles. As luck would have it, I found an e-mail address for Robert Hopkins's great-great-grandson, Bob Hopkins, who currently lives in Montana. When I reached out to him, he generously shared some of his family stories about Robert and his wife, Sarah, and their children.

When I started writing, I kept returning to Robert Hopkins Çaske and his family because they bridged the gap between my old and my new projects. However, despite the many written and oral sources I located, I could not find enough material to write a full-length biography. More important, because he and his family were part of a small number of literate and Christian Dakota, I was unsure how much of his story was representative of Dakota people's overall experiences. Before the U.S.-Dakota War of 1862, very few Dakota men and women had converted to Christianity, and those who had, like the Hopkins family, faced strong opposition from the majority, who rejected the missionaries' efforts to eliminate their religion and culture through conversion and the adoption of "civilization." Further research showed, however, that their ties to the missionaries did not exempt them from the hardships of the war and its aftermath. Members of the Hopkins family still experienced tremendous suffering—both emotional and physical—and oppression both during and after 1862.

Because of their prominent place in the records as well as their importance as exemplars of various themes that transpired during and after the war, I decided to open each chapter with portions of the Hopkinses' story, which together form a short biography. These opening vignettes provide context to help answer a series of questions. How did government officials, members of the public, and Protestant missionaries view and treat Dakota families in the postwar years? How did Dakota men, women, and children endure execution, imprisonment, exile, and starvation? What role did literacy and

Christianity play in their efforts to survive? Who were the Dakota scouts, and what role did they play in the aftermath of the war? The Hopkins family, like all Dakota, stood at the intersection of these questions and debates as they fought to survive in the postwar years.

These questions were not easy to answer, as the past remains contested ground. I also found it difficult to choose words and language to describe the terrible conditions faced by Dakota families during the four years that followed the war. At the time, journalists, missionaries, government officials, and members of the public brandished words like "heathen," "savage," "uncivilized," and "extermination" with impunity. I decided to use these words in the book only in the context of quotations from the time that appeared in newspaper articles, letters, documents, and speeches in order to explain what the Dakota endured. I acknowledge that repeating these words can cause distress in and of themselves.

I have not attempted to correct grammar, spelling, and punctuation in the many letters, newspaper articles, and other sources that I quote from, although I occasionally insert a letter or word in brackets for clarification. Similarly, I have not standardized the names of the writers and recipients of the letters, using instead the words as they appear on the letters themselves. Thus, we have "Joseph Brown to Gabriel Renville" and "Joseph Brown to 'My dear daughter'" as well as "Stephen Riggs to Mary Riggs" and "Stephen Riggs to 'My Dear Home.'"

Equally confusing to cite were the hundreds of newspapers referenced in this book. In the second half of the nineteenth century, newspapers frequently ceased publication, reformed, and changed names. For example, the Dakota/ English/and Dakota-English language newspaper of the American Board of Commissioners for Foreign Missions had four different incarnations, many published in the same year: *Iapi Oaye*, *Iapi Oaye/The Word Carrier*, the *Word Carrier*, and the *Word Carrier of the Santee Normal Training School*. As another example, the *St. Paul Press* and the *St. Paul Daily Press* were both published at the same time. The changing names and runs of these newspapers added to the often incorrect digital designations (for instance, the newspapers.com search engine listed Davenport's *Daily Democrat and News* as the *Quad-City Times*), which made citing these newspapers tedious.

Another issue presented by the documents was that of proper names: I grappled with what names and spellings to use for Dakota men, women, and children during a time that lacked standardized spellings of Dakota names. Moreover, as part of their larger program of assimilation, government officials and Protestant missionaries replaced Dakota names with English ones. Robert Hopkins Çaske's name illustrates both of these challenges. His Dakota name had divergent spellings depending on the written source, including Chaske, Chaskay, Chaskaydan, and Chaska as well as dozens of other permutations. Also, he was born Çaske, but Protestant missionaries later renamed him Robert Hopkins. I have generally chosen to call him Robert Hopkins or Robert Hopkins Çaske, as that is what he called himself (and signed his letters) throughout most of the period under study. At times, I simply call him Robert and his wife Sarah, especially in the introductions to each chapter, as these pages collectively constitute a more personal biography. Throughout the book, I reference other Dakota men, women, and children using both English and Dakota names, depending on the source quoted or what they generally chose to call themselves. When English names are used, however, it is important to remember that this is but one example of the larger issue of the colonization of Dakota people before and after the war.

On the other hand, I often refer to missionaries by their full names. By 1862, the first generation of Minnesota missionaries had been joined by their children, creating a second generation of missionaries, many of whom shared the same first or last or both names. So for clarity, I tend to use the missionaries' first and last names to distinguish between the first and second generations, all of whom continued to proselytize to the Dakota during this time.

The conflicted history of words and names reflects the larger struggle over how to remember and how to discuss the U.S.-Dakota War of 1862. For Dakota, this book will likely reopen the wounds that remain into the present day. Likewise, many Euro-Americans who have lived in this region for generations may experience discomfort about the actions of their ancestors. Despite the extensive descriptions of suffering, I hope that both Dakota and non-Dakota readers will follow this story to the end. The Dakota's experiences need to be told to and acknowledged by all Americans, because their treatment after 1862 provides an example of the painful history of Native American encounters with the U.S. government, settlers, and missionaries. Unfortunately, the Dakota's story is just one of many.

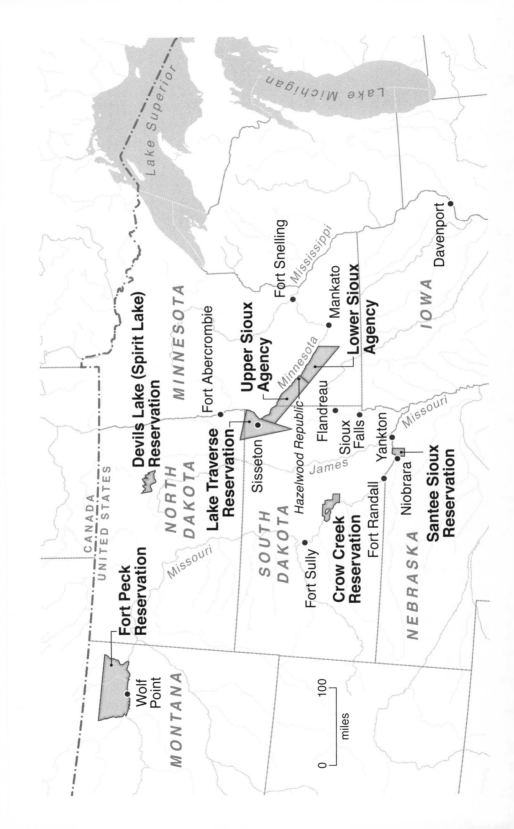

INTRODUCTION

Çaske (First-Born Son) was born in 1830 in southern Minnesota. For the first decade of his life, he grew up as a traditional Dakota. However, by his early teens, he was living near the Lac qui Parle Mission, 150 miles west of St. Paul, where he interacted with Protestant missionaries from the American Board of Commissioners for Foreign Missions (ABCFM). Çaske formed lasting connections with ABCFM missionaries Stephen Riggs and Thomas Williamson and their families. Over the next several years, he attended their church and school, eventually converting to Christianity and learning to read and write in the Dakota language, which the missionaries had translated into an anglicized written form. In the mid-1850s, the missionaries gave Çaske the name Robert Hopkins, after an ABCFM missionary who had drowned in the Minnesota River a few years earlier. In addition to receiving an English name, Robert Hopkins began to dress like the missionaries and to farm. He married Wawiyohiyewin, a Christian Wahpeton woman the missionaries called Sarah, who was the daughter of Catherine Totidutawin (Her Scarlet House Woman), one of the ABCFM's first female converts. In the mid-1850s, he joined the Hazelwood Republic, a Christian community established by Stephen Riggs. By 1860, Robert was living near Thomas Williamson's Pajutazee Mission along the Yellow Medicine River on the Upper Sioux Agency, where he became a ruling elder in Williamson's church.

Like other Christian Dakota, Robert Hopkins faced strong opposition from the majority of Dakota, who rejected both Christianity and American

"civilization." Those Dakota who opposed the missionaries utilized traditional forms of social control—for example, ridicule, intimidation, and ostracism—to shame converts into severing their ties to the ABCFM missionaries.
Hopkins wrote that "most of the young men" faced strong challenges, including aggression (such as cutting their blankets), for attending the Lac qui Parle
school and church meetings. Reportedly, Robert's "own grandfather intimidated him and made it difficult" for him when he converted to Christianity.

Even though Robert's decision to convert put him at odds with the majority of Dakota—including members of his own family—he continued to
associate with the missionaries. In 1862, just before the U.S.-Dakota War
broke out, Stephen Riggs described Hopkins as "a man thirty two or three
years old, quite tall, and good looking." He also noted that Robert possessed
a "great deal of energy." A picture taken by a young photographer named
Adrian Ebell at the Pajutazee Mission on August 17, 1862, confirms Riggs's
description. The image shows a tall Robert Hopkins standing next to his
eight-year-old son, Samuel. In part, this picture would have pleased the missionaries because both father and son wear pantaloons, live in the frame house
shown in the background, and appear to stand next to a farm plot, all of which
the missionaries touted as evidence that Robert had accepted "civilization."
However, the photograph also shows several Dakota men and women, including Robert's wife, Sarah, on his left, wearing traditional Dakota dress (fig. 2).

In March 1869, years after he took the photograph, Ebell sent a copy to
Stephen Riggs. While Riggs thought that the photograph "was a very good
one," he had doubts about the image of Sarah. He contacted the "engraver"
and asked if he could "take Robert away from his wife"—in other words, remove her from the picture. Riggs did not specify why he wanted Sarah erased
from the image. Perhaps he disliked the fact that she did not look "civilized,"
unlike her husband, who resembled the missionaries in his attire. More likely,
he wanted to focus on Hopkins because the missionaries privileged male over
female converts; indeed, Riggs hoped to create a montage of Dakota ministers, all of whom were male. Riggs's desire to remove Sarah from the photograph illustrates a larger problem: the downplaying or outright erasing of
Dakota women's experiences.

Despite Riggs's attempt to remove Sarah from the photograph, she—and
all members of the Hopkins family—intimately experienced all aspects of the
U.S.-Dakota War. They lived through the events that led up to the war, in-

FIGURE 2. Robert and Samuel Hopkins, center, with Sarah Hopkins to the right of Robert, at Thomas Williamson's Pajutazee Mission, August 17, 1862. Photo by Adrian Ebell. Courtesy of the Minnesota Historical Society.

cluding broken treaties, the loss of land, movement to a reservation, and corrupt government officials and policies. On August 18, 1862, the day after Ebell took the family's photograph, the cumulative tensions boiled over and war broke out on the Lower Sioux Agency. Upon hearing of the violence, Robert warned the Williamson family of the danger. Then, risking his own life, he led Thomas Williamson, his family, and several others to safety. After leaving his charges, Hopkins went to Fort Ridgely on the Lower Agency, later recalling that he hoped he would "be able to save some of the white women and children in the settlements." Stephen Riggs offered another explanation for Robert's decision to travel to the area of conflict: he was simply "curious to know the extent of the war." According to his later testimony, Hopkins ended up at New Ulm, Minnesota, and fired a gun at an abandoned house, perhaps killing an ox. It is not clear whether he intended to hit something or someone, or whether he simply fired a warning shot. Despite his protestations of innocence, after the war ended in late September 1862, Robert was arrested, imprisoned, tried, found guilty, and sentenced to be hanged along with 302 other men. In an understatement, Riggs commented that "it seemed unfortunate that he had not remained at home."

After learning of Robert's sentence, several ABCFM missionaries initiated a letter-writing campaign to have him declared innocent and released; these letters ultimately helped to save his life. Thirty-eight other Dakota men, however, did not receive a reprieve. The day after Christmas in 1862, they were hanged in the largest mass execution in United States history.

Although he avoided the gallows that day, Hopkins remained imprisoned in Mankato, Minnesota, while Sarah and their two sons—Samuel and a baby brother—were incarcerated at Fort Snelling, Minnesota. Later in the spring of 1863, the U.S. Congress passed legislation repealing all treaties and removing all Dakota from Minnesota. Government agents transferred Sarah, her sons, and her elderly mother, Catherine Totidutawin, to Crow Creek, an isolated, undeveloped, and drought-plagued reservation in Dakota Territory in what today is central South Dakota. Soldiers, meanwhile, moved Robert to Camp McClellan, a Civil War recruiting and training facility in Davenport, Iowa. In December 1863, government officials decided to build a new prison for the Dakota prisoners. Called Camp Kearney, it was located on the Camp McClellan grounds but fenced off from the Civil War soldiers and training grounds. Both in Davenport and on the reservation, the Dakota suffered from starvation, illness, corrupt and hostile government officials, and high mortality rates. Furthermore, once removed from Minnesota, both Robert and Sarah, like many other Dakota, endured a curious and intrusive public that demanded to see them and treated them as exotic spectacles.

To deal with imprisonment and separation from his family, Robert wrote dozens of letters to the missionaries, asking them to improve the poor living conditions at Camp Kearney and to help him obtain freedom. He also sent letters to Sarah at Crow Creek; similarly, he received letters back relating the terrible conditions his family faced on their reservation more than six hundred miles away, though he could do nothing to help them. During his imprisonment, Robert also continued to work as a surrogate for the ABCFM, serving as its primary religious leader and teacher in the Davenport prison. With his support, hundreds of the Dakota prisoners learned to read and write, which allowed them to contact their relatives and to petition for better treatment and for their release. Robert's close relationship with the missionaries, however, also made him suspect; several of the prisoners questioned his loyalty. Robert did his best to ignore these tensions and continued to work to prove his innocence; he "thought it hard that for no crime he should be condemned and imprisoned, and so long separated from his wife and boys."

With the missionaries' help, Robert finally received his freedom in 1864 and, after six frustrating months of delay, set out to reunite with his family at Crow Creek. The family, however, remained separated even after their promised reunification. When he finally reached Crow Creek, he learned that Sarah had left the reservation to join the families of her two brothers, Lorenzo Lawrence and Joseph Kawanke, who worked as scouts for the U.S. Army on the western frontier of Minnesota and into Dakota Territory. The forced divisions that plagued the Hopkins family became permanent in the late 1860s, when additional treaties divided the Dakota among three separate reservations, all outside Minnesota.

This summary does not do justice to the Hopkinses' story or to the events and divisions that led up to the U.S.-Dakota War. Unfortunately, there is still much that we do not know. Most of the Dakota letters that remain were written by the Davenport prisoners (like Robert) to Protestant missionaries and government officials. Dakota elders have translated and published fifty of these letters; other Dakota scholars, like Gwen Westerman, are currently examining and translating more of them. As of the time of this writing, these additional letters have not been published; once released, they will certainly add new information and nuances to the Dakota's postwar story. Unfortunately, few of the Hopkins family's personal letters were preserved, so we cannot get an intimate look at how Robert and Sarah communicated with each other. Then again, even if these letters were discovered, they would likely have been read and possibly censored by government officials and Protestant missionaries. Despite these limitations, I hope that the following chapters, which elaborate on the Hopkinses' story and the events endured by the Dakota Oyate in general, will add to the dialogue about these understudied years.

Despite the fact that early and contemporary observers, journalists, and historians have written thousands of pages analyzing the causes, battles, and selected events of the U.S.-Dakota War of 1862, few scholars have studied its aftermath in detail. Historian David Martínez notes that historians have failed to "devote much time to the impact of the war trials, the mass execution, and the subsequent exile of the Dakota people." Despite the lack of coverage, the postwar period is extremely important to Dakota because the trauma that followed in the wake of the war continues today. Historian Colette Hyman writes that the outcome of the U.S.-Dakota War "explains a great deal about how loss of land base, economic autonomy, and cultural self-determination affected the Dakota" into the present day. According to Dakota scholar and activist Waziyatawin, "Dakota people remain in the dark shadow of the 1862 war."

Indeed, the U.S.-Dakota War casts a very long shadow. Early historians tended to see the war as a limited event that began on August 18 and ended six weeks later in late September. These historians also tend to portray the war as affecting only the Dakota of Minnesota. A century after the war, beginning in the 1960s, however, historians began to stress the larger significance of the Minnesota war. This book follows those historians who have emphasized the importance of the war to the larger history of the dispossession of the American West. Following the Minnesota war, the United States military launched expeditions into Dakota Territory to punish alleged Dakota warriors. These expeditions drew generally peaceful tribes into the fray and added to the growing tensions on the plains, which intensified over the next three decades. This book builds on the work of historians like Roy Meyer, who argues that the postwar "military campaigns on the prairies lose whatever connection they had with the 1862 outbreak and merge into the long series of wars with the Sioux that ended only with the Wounded Knee massacre in 1890."

In addition to providing context for the larger fight for the plains, the U.S.-Dakota War serves as an all too common example of the problems and violence associated with federal Indian policy in the second half of the nineteenth century. According to Charles Eastman, a nineteenth-century Dakota writer, physician, and philosopher, the causes and consequences of the 1862 war "were practically the same as in many other instances, for in its broad features the history of one Indian tribe is the history of all." Like numerous other Native American nations throughout the nineteenth century, the Dakota Oyate experienced treaty fraud, problems with traders and annuities—cash and goods that the U.S. government paid them for the sale of their lands—and settlers infringing on their lands, among other issues leading up to the war. After the war, they endured the largest mass execution in American history, abrogated treaties, exile from their homeland, and military expeditions designed to punish and kill Dakota warriors. They faced terrible conditions—including starvation, illness, and a lack of medical care—as evidenced by the extremely high death rate at Davenport and Crow Creek. They confronted corrupt government agents and missionaries intent on eradicating their culture and religion. Historian Ned Blackhawk argues that "the narrative of American history . . . has failed to gauge the violence that remade much of the continent before [and during] U.S. expansion." The Dakota's story reinforces Blackhawk's comments by examining one example of the endemic violence against Native Americans during the second half of the nineteenth century. Unfortunately, there were many others.

Finally, the Dakota's postwar experiences illustrate resistance and survival, but always within the context of trauma. In recent years, historians have studied examples of Native American resistance to and survival under many challenging situations, including compulsory boarding schools, missionary Christianization and "civilization" programs, and broken treaties. Members of the Dakota Oyate also resisted and survived as best they could when faced with extreme conditions and trials. For example, prisoners at Camp Kearney found ways to raise money, which they used to purchase material items for themselves and for their distant relatives. Furthermore, Dakota men, women, and children at both Camp Kearney and Crow Creek learned to read and write from the missionaries and from each other so that they could communicate with their separated kin. Although controversial then and now, about three hundred Dakota men agreed to serve as U.S. scouts in the punitive campaign, which both kept them out of prison and provided (at least in theory) rations and salaries. While Dakota people used numerous strategies to survive the postwar period, their efforts could not begin to erase the years of constant hardship. David Martínez writes that while they "deserve praise for surviving the aftermath of an exceptionally bitter conflict . . . we should not fail to acknowledge the grave injustices inflicted against the Dakota."

Dakota in Exile aims to discuss survival and resistance among Dakota in the postwar period by weaving together three intertwined but frequently mutually exclusive narratives: those of Dakota, missionaries, and members of the general public and federal government. Each group had different perspectives and goals; sometimes these converged, but more often than not they clashed. In this book, I seek to examine these multiple perspectives and goals—to begin to untangle and provide insight into the complicated postwar years. As Gwen Westerman notes, the history of Minnesota and the aftermath of the U.S.-Dakota War have "never been and never will be fully or accurately described from a single point of view."

When writing about the U.S.-Dakota War, however, historians have traditionally covered only one point of view—that of the settlers and government officials. Many historians and activists are now challenging this limited interpretation by examining the war from the Dakota's perspective, not only at the time but into the present day. Waziyatawin describes the aftermath of the war as a legacy of "genocide, mass hangings, broken treaties, land theft, concentration camps, and ethnic cleansing" that continues to reverberate in Dakota communities. Dakota scholar John Peacock notes that "Dakota descendants of the war . . . tended to think in terms of how the war has, in fact, never ended. For them, the war's ostensible end was only the beginning of their greater, continuing defeat as a people." Gary Roberts writes that the U.S.-Dakota War, like the tragic Sand Creek Massacre in Colorado two years later, is "an enduring trauma, not history, not even past, certainly not something that can be forgotten."

All Dakota experienced—and continue to confront—the war's legacy, but at the time they did not all respond in the same way. All struggled to survive, but they adopted different strategies to achieve this goal both during and after the war. Some, like Robert Hopkins, rescued settlers and missionaries during the war. Other Dakota men and women tried to remain neutral: they did not rescue settlers, but they did not participate in any battles. Still other warriors attacked settlers and fought U.S. soldiers to get back their lands and to challenge the federal agents who cheated them of annuities and broke treaties. In the postwar period, these varied choices and responses continued. Some Dakota fled to Dakota Territory and Canada to avoid imprisonment and retaliation; some continued alliances or established new alliances with Protestant missionaries; still others served as scouts for the American military.

Although all Dakota fought to survive, Dakota women faced additional challenges during these years. While several historians have written about Dakota women in recent years, according to historian Margaret Jacobs, Native American women and children generally appear "only as the most innocent victims of brutal violence or as footnotes." This pattern of ignoring Dakota women has been long-standing, as graphically illustrated by Stephen

Riggs's desire to physically remove Sarah Hopkins from a prewar photograph. Certainly, Dakota women and children suffered as much as their male counterparts both during and after the war. However, they also needed to subsist on their own at the Crow Creek Reservation, for example, and they adopted many strategies to achieve this goal. Each of the following chapters includes references to Dakota women who struggled to survive at Fort Snelling, Camp Kearney, Crow Creek, and at three separate reservations created in the late 1860s. Dakota women are not subordinate to this history; their stories are central to understanding the Dakota's collective experiences in the postwar years.

Numerous written, oral, and visual sources provide a unique opportunity for historians to examine the varied experiences of Dakota men, women, and children. Thousands of pages of non-Dakota sources—sources traditionally used by scholars writing about Native American history—document and comment on many different aspects of the postwar period. While these sources are useful, they often contain biases and concentrate more on the soldiers, missionaries, and government officials than they do on the Dakota's perspective. Dakota writers, however, also produced a wide array of works detailing their experiences before, during, and after the war. They wrote (or dictated) short articles and memoirs and, most important, composed hundreds of letters in the Dakota language to Protestant missionaries and to each other. Oral histories, recorded and deposited at the Minnesota History Center, document Dakota family stories related to the war and Crow Creek. Finally, photographs and images provide insight into the Dakota's experiences. This book seeks to interpret not only how others portrayed and responded to Dakota in the postwar period but also how Dakota men and women described the war and its aftermath in their own words.

Protestant missionaries also played an integral and controversial role in the aftermath of the U.S.-Dakota War of 1862. Beginning in 1835, the interdenominational (mainly Presbyterian and Congregationalist) ABCFM established two mission stations to convert the Dakota of Minnesota. Over the next three decades, ABCFM-affiliated missionaries opened and closed nine additional stations across southern Minnesota and employed dozens of workers, most prominently members of the Riggs, Williamson, Huggins, and Pond families. In 1860, just before the outbreak of the war, Bishop Henry Whipple established an Episcopal mission called the Mission of St. John, headed by Samuel Hinman, on the Lower Sioux Agency. Despite their best efforts, the ABCFM and Episcopalian missions failed to convert or "civilize" large numbers of Dakota prior to the war. Moreover, those few Dakota who converted or attended a mission school faced strong opposition from the majority, who rejected the missionaries' unyielding message of religious and cultural transformation.

At the time, evangelical publications called missionaries like Riggs, Williamson, Whipple, and Hinman heroes and friends of the Indians for their single-minded devotion to "saving" the Dakota during and after the war. Many present-day scholars and activists, however, strongly challenge this laudatory interpretation and instead see the missionaries' work as part of the larger effort to colonize "Indigenous Peoples, land, and resources." Indeed, Waziyatawin argues that missionaries, government agents, traders, and settlers "all worked to simultaneously assault and attempt to destroy all that made us Dakota people." Missionaries like Bishop Whipple, for example, "believed the Dakota needed saving from their own cultural and spiritual traditions, and was thus an advocate of what may be called ethnocide." Margaret Jacobs notes that these "more subtle and insidious expressions of power and authority over Indian peoples . . . have been just as damaging [as] those outright forms of violence." Acknowledging the missionaries' role in colonialism is but one part of the larger goal of decolonization, defined by Michelle Jacob as healing "the wounds of colonialism" through revitalizing culture, religion, and language and "dismantling oppressive systems that harm [indigenous] people, land, and culture."

Because the Episcopalian and especially the ABCFM missionaries proselytized to Dakota beginning in the 1830s, throughout the postwar period, and even into the twentieth century, this case study of their interactions with Dakota people provides a unique opportunity to study missionary work and ideology over an extended period of time. Indeed, as happened with other missionary children at the time, a second generation (and eventually a third and even a fourth generation) of ABCFM missionaries worked alongside and then succeeded their fathers and mothers. Both generations of missionaries interacted with Dakota at every stage of the war and its aftermath.

In one way, the missionaries were wholly consistent across the decades and generations: they never wavered from their desire to eliminate Dakota culture and religion. Even when faced with the violence of the war and its aftermath, their every action, choice, and decision reflected their unyielding devotion to conversion. For example, they fought for the freedom of Christian Dakota men like Robert Hopkins but often ignored those who had chosen not to convert. They criticized the conditions at Crow Creek and the Davenport prison in large part because they worried that starvation and oppression in these locations impeded the adoption of Christianity. They wanted to teach Dakota men, women, and children to read and write in their own language not to give them tools to help navigate the postwar world but primarily so they could read the Bible, which would lay the foundation for an acceptance of Christianity.

Because of their relentless devotion to eliminating Native American culture and religion, the missionaries certainly should not be considered friends of the Indians. That said, at the time they were perceived as such by government officials and members of the public. Within the context of efforts by settlers and government officials to exterminate all Dakota, the missionaries' even limited support of Christian Dakota, and their calls for better conditions at Crow Creek and Davenport set them apart from most midwesterners. It is also important to note that while the missionaries never collectively abandoned their desire to convert and "civilize" Dakota people, they differed among themselves on several key issues. For example, Thomas Williamson wanted to free all the Davenport prisoners. Henry Whipple, despite his constant denunciations of the corrupt "Indian system," chose not to openly support Williamson's efforts. Stephen Riggs, meanwhile, supported freedom only for Christian Dakota. More so than other missionaries, Riggs formed a close alliance with the government, playing an integral role in the postwar trials and acting as an interpreter during the trials, at the executions, and in the punitive expeditions.

Despite these differences, all the Protestant missionaries shared the same goal of conversion, though they disagreed on how to best achieve it. Similarly, Dakota men and women also pursued a single objective — to survive the postwar years — though they too saw several different paths toward accomplishing this. Under these extreme circumstances, some chose to ally with the missionaries to help them survive. Many used literacy, taught by the missionaries in the Dakota language, not only to study the Bible but also to communicate with their separated kin. Some relied on the missionaries to purchase goods for them; others repeatedly asked the missionaries to fight for their freedom. The Dakota's need to survive temporarily displaced the strong resistance to the missionaries that characterized the prewar years. The opposition of many to Christianity, however, continued underground or even openly with regard to several issues, including polygamy and the practice of their ceremonies and dances.

While the missionaries' main goal was conversion, most federal agents, military officials, and members of the American public wanted to continually punish the Dakota. In the months following the U.S.-Dakota War, the majority of Minnesotans reacted with panic, fear, anger, and outrage. Members of the general public, the Minnesota press, and government officials portrayed all Dakota (and all Sioux in general) as bloodthirsty savages who could not be trusted. This led to harsh reprisals after the war, including calls for extermination, the abrogation of all Dakota treaties and their exile from Minnesota, and punitive summer campaigns in Dakota Territory. Such postwar treatment thus adds to the scholarship surrounding how Euro-American perceptions and stereotypes of Native Americans influenced federal policy. The Dakota's postwar experiences also provide a key early example of the "federal government's capacity to enact, police, and enforce Indian policy," which reached its apex in the late nineteenth and early twentieth centuries.

After the Dakota's removal from Minnesota, however, the public's fear turned to fascination—at least for some. Once the Dakota were removed, they became novelties and objects of interest, a process that anthropologist Renato Rosaldo has called imperialist nostalgia, where people mourn for what they have "intentionally altered or destroyed." Historians have focused on how imperialist nostalgia motivated tourists to view Indians at world's fairs and in Wild West shows during the late nineteenth century, with the Indians performing to fulfill tourists' fantasies of exotic warriors and Indian princesses. While Dakota men and women certainly did not choose to be put on display, hundreds of citizens demanded to see the Indians on their way to the Crow Creek Reservation or, especially, in the Camp Kearney prison in Davenport. Historians have argued that Indians displayed at world's fairs attempted to turn the situation to their advantage, for example, by charging for photographs. The prisoners at Camp Kearney also raised money by making and selling items to the public; they then used this income to purchase material goods for themselves and their kin. They also used the funds to fight for their freedom and to retain kinship ties to their relatives. As such, the tourists' fascination with the Dakota and the Dakota's attempts to use this to their advantage serve as precursors to trends that reached their full fruition decades later in the late nineteenth century.

To examine the changing and often contradictory responses of government officials and the public to Dakota people in the postwar period, I read government documents, reports, and manuscript collections and, most important, newspaper articles. Hundreds of local newspapers published throughout the United States and in midwestern states—especially Minnesota, Iowa, Nebraska, Missouri, and Wisconsin—covered all aspects of the war and its aftermath in exhaustive detail. Recent innovations in digital technology allowed me to search and use these newspapers in ways unavailable to previous generations of researchers. I have not taken the hundreds of newspaper articles I found on the war and its aftermath as fully factual and as evidence of objective truth—indeed, articles on the same topic frequently contradicted each other, offering competing (and frequently inaccurate) statistics, interpretations, and information. Instead, I have used these articles to show how members of the public reacted to, viewed, and interpreted the war and its aftermath, not as objective evidence of how Dakota men, women, and children actually acted in the harsh postwar years.

Many of these newspaper articles were difficult to read; they ranged from horrifying and sickening to absurd and bizarre. The content and tone of the articles depended on their location. In Minnesota, Nebraska, and Dakota Territory, many of the articles demanded extermination and violent retribution against all Dakota even years after the war ended. Newspapers in Iowa and Missouri, however, frequently advertised the prisoners and their families as entertainment—for example, promoting a Fourth of July float with the Davenport prisoners, horse-versus-Indian races in Muscatine, or a séance in St. Louis featuring the just-released prisoners. Whether treating them as violent or as exotic savages, the articles in frontier newspapers dehumanized the Dakota. Thus, Dakota people served as symbols of the public's ever-changing views of Native Americans; in the frontier press, they became "white man's Indians," as historian Robert Berkhofer calls them. These Indians had no relationship to the Dakota's daily lives, personalities, or histories. The articles defined them as caricatures and attempted to silence their voices. However, as will become clear, Dakota men and women used the public's fascination in ways not intended by the dominant culture.

Dakota in Exile considers two sides of the same history: on one side, a history of oppression, death, retribution, stereotypes, and a failed Indian policy; on the other, stories of resilience, resistance, and survival in the face of great hardship. In chapters 1 to 3, I focus on the first side of this equation, tracing what happened historically to Dakota following the U.S.-Dakota War of 1862. These event-centered chapters cover the years 1862 to 1866. Each incorporates multiple voices, including those of Dakota people, government officials, military commanders, members of the public, and Protestant missionaries. They also chronicle Dakota attempts to survive materially during this period. Chapter 1 provides a brief history of the U.S.-Dakota War and its immediate aftermath, including the trials and the hanging of thirty-eight Dakota men in Mankato. It ends with the Dakota's expulsion from Minnesota. Chapter 2 focuses on the Crow Creek Reservation in Dakota Territory, the site of exile for Sarah Hopkins, her mother and children, and hundreds of other Dakota women, children, and elders. Chapter 3 transitions to Davenport, where Robert Hopkins and more than three hundred other Dakota men were incarcerated for their alleged roles in the war.

In chapters 4 to 6, I focus on the same locations and time frame, but I look at three specific themes related to the ways Dakota men, women, and children attempted to survive on the postwar landscape. Chapter 4 concentrates on literacy, arguing that Dakota men, women, and children appropriated missionary-taught literacy for their own purposes in order to communicate with separated family members and to fight for their freedom. Chapter 5 turns to Christianity to examine how some Dakota used religion, as well as the Protestant missionaries associated with the ABCFM and the Episcopal Church, to help them navigate the postwar years. In chapter 6, I study the role that Dakota scouts played in the punitive campaigns that followed the war. Although these three chapters highlight resilience, resistance, and survival, it is important to remember that many Dakota did not survive, many families remained separated, overall government policy did not improve, and the Protestant missionaries, despite their genuine dislike of some government strategies, created additional stress by working to, as Richard Henry Pratt would later state, "kill the Indian in him, and save the man."

Chapter 7 summarizes the years 1866 to 1869 following the prisoners' release from Davenport and the removal of Dakota families from Crow Creek. As the old adage goes, "The more things change, the more they stay the same." Despite the promised reunification, Dakota families instead experienced permanent separation onto three different reservations and various other locations outside Minnesota. In response, many continued to use the same strategies they had developed during their exile after the war to survive their new, but unfortunately similar, situations. In the epilogue, I return to Robert Hopkins and members of his family, briefly tracing their history into the late nineteenth and early twentieth centuries. Their postwar odyssey included imprisonment, separation, illness, and starvation. However, their story also illustrates survival and perseverance. The two sides of this bitter history continued long after the war ended, not just for the Hopkins family but for all Dakota.

1 ✳ WAR, TRIALS, EXECUTION, AND EXILE, 1862-1863

In October 1862, Robert Hopkins Çaske, recorded as Prisoner 163, went before a five-man military commission tasked with trying Dakota men for their alleged roles in the U.S.-Dakota War. His trial took place on the Lower Sioux Agency in a trader's small summer kitchen, one of the few buildings left standing after the war (fig. 3). According to notes taken at the trial by Isaac Heard, the commission's recorder, Prisoner 163 supposedly "did join with and participate in the various Murders and Robberies and outrages committed by the Sioux Tribe of Indians on the Minnesota Frontier . . . particularly in the battles at the Fort, New Ulm, Birch Coulee and Wood Lake." After hearing these charges against him, Robert spoke for a few short minutes. According to the written testimony, he admitted to being present at the battles of Wood Lake and Birch Coulee and stated that he fired a shot but was unsure "whether I hit a horse or not." A witness named David Faribault—a mixed-blood trader married to a Dakota woman—testified that he had heard the accused say that he had shot a white man at New Ulm. Following Faribault's testimony, Robert did not (or was not allowed to) offer any rebuttal. The courtroom then cleared, and the members of the commission began their deliberations. After only a short time, they declared the prisoner "guilty of the charge" and sentenced him "to be hanged by the neck until he

FIGURE 3. The trials of the captured Dakota men took place in a trader's small summer kitchen. Courtesy of the Minnesota Historical Society.

is dead." A summary of the entire trial consisted of only a few handwritten pages, and the trial was probably concluded in a matter of minutes.

Unlike the majority of the other 302 prisoners sentenced to death, Robert Hopkins had prominent missionary supporters who fought against his execution. Even during the trial itself, ABCFM missionary Stephen Riggs spoke briefly in his defense. Although Riggs did not specifically address the charge of firing a gun, he informed the commission that Robert had saved "the lives of Dr. Williamson and his family." Riggs also noted that Robert had rescued Sophia Huggins, another missionary worker, who had been captured by Dakota warriors during the war. After the trial, Riggs wrote a letter urging President Lincoln to commute Robert's sentence based on new testimony that he had killed an ox, not a person. Other ABCFM missionaries, especially Thomas Williamson and his sister Jane Williamson, also protested the conviction and sentence. Thomas Williamson requested all papers related to the trial. Looking over the transcripts convinced him that the "strong excitement" caused by the war led the judges "to think the testimony stronger than it really was." He wrote to Lincoln and the commissioner of Indian affairs, William Dole, asking them to look into the case. Jane Williamson, who worked as a teacher at her brother's mission, also penned "a very strong appeal" to Lincoln. She claimed that Robert was a victim of circumstances and had played no role in the war, except to save settlers. While these letters ultimately saved him from hanging, Hopkins remained incarcerated for an additional three years, first in Mankato and later in Davenport. During these years, he did not see his wife or his sons.

Unlike Robert Hopkins and his family, only a handful of Dakota prisoners had such prominent advocates. However, even those with outside support were swept up in the postwar hysteria that led to controversial trials, executions, and exile from Minnesota. As Stephen Riggs commented, in the panicked months that followed the war, it was impossible for the "innocent to make their innocency appear." Thomas Williamson underscored this same point: "innocence [was] no guarantee of safety."

In very different ways, the war also affected Minnesota settlers, government officials, and Protestant missionaries. Each of these groups expressed their opinions at length in newspapers, letters, and speeches. In the postwar months, most members of the public demanded extermination or, at the very least, retribution for all Dakota. Even those who purported to support the Dakota, such as the Protestant missionaries, had their own goals, which kept them from understanding the Dakota's perspective. Nor could the missionaries influence the tide of public opinion that led to the series of traumatic events that followed the war.

Beginning in 1851, about a decade before the U.S.-Dakota War, the Dakota of Minnesota inhabited a temporary, narrow, diagonal-shaped reservation in southwestern Minnesota. Approximately 2,300 Dakota resided on the Lower Sioux Agency near the Minnesota River, while 4,000 lived on the Upper Sioux Agency near the Yellow Medicine River. The Mdewakanton and Wahpekute were located on the Lower Agency, while the Sisseton and Wahpeton lived on the Upper Agency; together, they comprised the Eastern, Isanyati, or Santee Dakota. From their small reservation, the Eastern Dakota struggled to survive in the years leading up to the war.

Most prominently, decades of continuous land loss had created hardships for Dakota families. By 1862, they had lost 90 percent of their traditional homeland, following a series of problematic treaties ratified in 1837, 1851, and 1858. The treaties of 1851 and 1858 alone included land cessions totaling approximately 22 to 35 million acres and confined the Dakota to a 140-mile-long, 10-mile-wide reservation of about 900,000 acres. Settlers eager for more farmland, however, threatened even the remaining reservation lands. The number of farms established in just one short decade illustrates the loss of Indian lands to non-Indian farmers. In 1850, Minnesota had only 157 recorded farms; by 1860, that number had jumped to 18,081.

Land loss and confinement to a small reservation made it difficult for Dakota men and women to continue their traditional subsistence practices of farming, hunting, and gathering, which led to food shortages. When telling her family about the war, Dakota Hannah Frazier always began her story with "they were starving in Minnesota." The lack of food made families like the Fraziers dependent on government officials and traders for rations and other supplies. However, traders notoriously took advantage of the Dakota by demanding all their annuity funds in exchange for relatively few goods. Episcopal missionary Bishop Henry Whipple charged that traders appropriated the majority of Dakota annuities, leaving not "one cent" for the Dakota. In the summer of 1862, just before the outbreak of the war, government annuities were delayed and traders threatened to cut off Dakota purchases. According to ABCFM missionary John Williamson, Thomas Williamson's son, the government "had no rations for them. There were four stores at the agency . . . but they would not give credit to the Indians."

Corrupt officials also contributed to the lack of food and supplies. In January 1862, eight months before the outbreak of the war, George E. H. Day, who had been appointed special commissioner to investigate Indian affairs in Minnesota, sent a scathing letter to Lincoln reporting his findings. He informed the president that he had "discovered numerous violations of law and many frauds committed by past Agents and a superintendent." These violations included defrauding the Dakota (and the Ojibwe) of thousands of dollars; this stolen money made the local superintendent and agents rich. Day predicted that if this system was not reformed, "the vengeance of heaven" would be "poured out and visited upon this nation for its abuses and cruelty to the Indian." Unfortunately, Lincoln and other government officials ignored this prescient warning. In his letter, Day himself realized that Lincoln was "overwhelmed with cares" at the time—chief among them the events surrounding the Civil War—which made it difficult for him to focus on Indian affairs. Moreover, by 1862 warnings like Day's—not just from Minnesota but from around the country—were so common that they were routinely ignored.

In addition to dealing with unscrupulous officials, Dakota men, women, and children faced increasingly aggressive "civilization" and Christianization programs promoted by government agents and ABCFM and Episcopalian missionaries. "Civilized" Dakota needed to be literate, eventually speak and read English, abide by Euro-American gender roles, and dress like their white counterparts, among many other things. A Dakota man named Paul Mazakutemani summarized succinctly what "civilization" meant: they must "follow the white man's customs alone." Attempts to eliminate Dakota culture and religion, especially by government agents, intensified in the early 1860s.

Ironically, at the same time that government officials and missionaries demanded that Dakota men and women adopt "civilization," an enterprising steamer company enticed tourists to sign up for an excursion to view the "uncivilized" Dakota for entertainment. In June 1861, Davidson's Steamer Line ran an advertisement in the St. Paul *Pioneer and Democrat* announcing a "grand pleasure excursion" to the Lower Sioux Agency. In addition to visiting this "splendid region of country," the company promised that tourists would witness "the ceremonies of the [annuity] payments of nearly FIVE THOUSAND INDIANS." The advertisement urged interested sightseers to book their staterooms on one of two steamers, including the *Favorite* (fig. 4). The advertisement worked, even convincing an English tourist named Arthur Sterry to purchase a ticket. During his year-long tour of the United States, Sterry stopped in Minnesota and was immediately intrigued by an "advertisement in a St. Paul newspaper" promoting a trip to "see the Indians." He purchased a ticket, feeling that "the excursion would be to me a novel one." However, he was disappointed when he learned that the captain "had no intention of fulfilling the implied terms of the advertisement by remaining at the [Indian] Agency for a couple of days." Instead, the steamer stayed only a few hours.

This increasingly tense relationship among Dakota, government officials, Protestant missionaries, settlers, and even tourists set the stage for war. On August 17, 1862, four young Dakota men killed five settlers near Acton, Minnesota, on the Lower Agency. That night, Taoyateduta (Little Crow) reluctantly agreed to help lead the fight to regain lost lands and redress other longstanding issues. The following morning, Dakota warriors attacked the Lower Agency, killing government officials, traders, and settlers. News of the war did not reach the Upper Agency for several days; when it did, many Sisse-

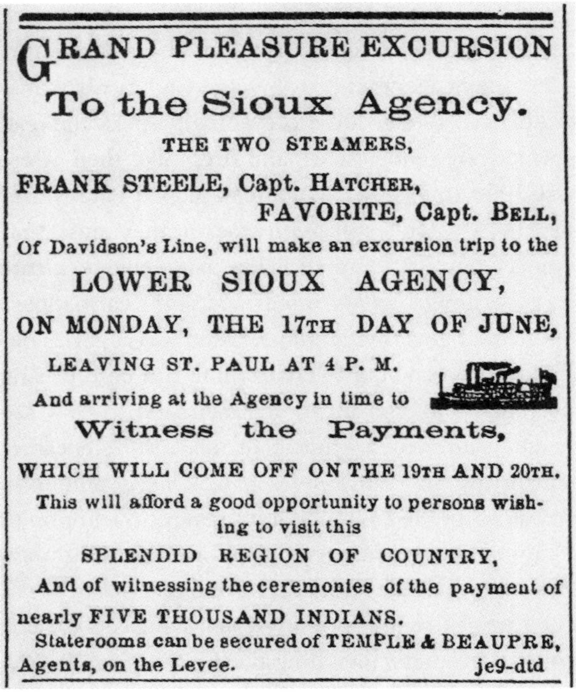

GRAND PLEASURE EXCURSION

To the Sioux Agency.

THE TWO STEAMERS,

FRANK STEELE, Capt. HATCHER,

FAVORITE, Capt. BELL,

Of Davidson's Line, will make an excursion trip to the

LOWER SIOUX AGENCY,

ON MONDAY, THE 17TH DAY OF JUNE,

LEAVING ST. PAUL AT 4 P. M.

And arriving at the Agency in time to

Witness the Payments,

WHICH WILL COME OFF ON THE 19TH AND 20TH.

This will afford a good opportunity to persons wishing to visit this

SPLENDID REGION OF COUNTRY,

And of witnessing the ceremonies of the payment of nearly FIVE THOUSAND INDIANS.

Staterooms can be secured of TEMPLE & BEAUPRE, Agents, on the Levee.   je9-dtd

FIGURE 4.
Davidson's Steamer Line's June 1861 advertisement for a "grand pleasure excursion" to the Lower Sioux Agency, St. Paul *Pioneer and Democrat.*

ton and Wahpeton debated whether to join the war or not. Although many Dakota ultimately chose not to participate in the war, over the next several weeks violence spread to settlements throughout the Minnesota River valley.

Faced with the growing war across southwest Minnesota, Governor Alexander Ramsey appointed Colonel Henry Hastings Sibley—a Minnesota fur trader, settler, and politician—to lead a volunteer army against the Dakota. The following month, Lincoln sent Major General John Pope to join Sibley after the general's defeat at the Second Battle of Bull Run. Pope would lead the newly created Department of the Northwest, headquartered in St. Paul and established to defeat the Dakota. Under the leadership of Sibley and Pope, battles occurred at Fort Ridgely, New Ulm, Birch Coulee, and other locations. On September 23, Pope and Sibley's forces defeated the Dakota at the Battle of Wood Lake, effectively ending the military side of the war thirty-seven days after it began.

Scholar John Peacock calls the military events of the war "asymmetrical

. . . with a foregone conclusion: just a matter of time before the U.S. forces prevailed with their overwhelming numbers and firepower." Although the war ended fairly quickly, approximately four hundred to six hundred white settlers, traders, and soldiers died; around sixty Dakota also perished in the fighting, although fatalities among the Dakota increased substantially following the war. In the first two weeks of the war, fifteen to twenty frontier communities were almost depopulated; by the end of the war, settlers had abandoned their homes and fields in more than twenty-three southwestern Minnesota counties and even in northern Iowa.

In the chaotic aftermath of the Battle of Wood Lake, so-called friendly Dakota—those who had not participated in the war, especially men like Robert Hopkins who had converted to Christianity—turned over just under 300 white captives to Brigadier General Sibley (promoted from colonel on September 29) at a location dubbed Camp Release on the Upper Agency. Taopi, one of Bishop Whipple's converts, reportedly saved 255 captives. Lorenzo Lawrence, Robert Hopkins's brother-in-law, rescued 10 captives, making sure to note that "there was a great company of men 'who saw me bring them in,' including General Sibley and three missionaries." Joseph La-Framboise, another ABCFM convert, saved the lives of 22 men and 40 women and children when he warned them to leave Pajutazee and Hazelwood. Similarly, John Other Day, also affiliated with the ABCFM, saved 62 settlers. Other Day "advised the whites to make their escape, and offered to pilot them out of danger."

Although originally created as a place for the freed captives and the "friendly Dakota" who rescued them, Camp Release soon held more than 1,200 Dakota, including some of the defeated warriors, plus a large contingent of men, women, and children who had not participated in the war. Over the next several weeks, more Dakota families arrived at the camp, swelling the number to more than 2,000 by October. Sibley informed those who surrendered that they would be treated fairly and humanely. He promised that he had "not come into this country to injure any innocent person, but to punish those who have committed cruel murders upon innocent men, women, and children." He assured those who "hoist[ed] a flag of peace" that they would receive protection. He did not want "to make war upon those who are innocent, but upon the guilty." Those who surrendered would be "counted good Indians, friends of the whites."

Many Dakota men took Sibley at his word and surrendered with the assumption that they would be treated fairly. For example, Sibley promised Ta-tanka-nazin (Standing Buffalo) protection if he surrendered. Sibley informed Ta-tanka-nazin that if he was a "friend of the Great American Father you are my friend also. I have not come to make war upon any bands who have not been concerned with the horrible murders upon white people." Ta-tanka-nazin must have questioned Sibley's sincerity, because he joined a group of Dakota who fled to Canada immediately following the war. Several years later, he returned to settle in Montana—he never went back to Minnesota—where he passed away in 1871. Wakandayamani (George Quinn), however, took Sibley at his word. In an 1898 interview, he stated that he surrendered and was put under guard but was promised that he "would not be a prisoner very long." His incarceration lasted four years.

Wakandayamani's experience was common. Indeed, Sibley's public words of peace were belied by his actions inside and outside Camp Release. Sibley informed Charles Flandreau—a Minnesota judge and honorary colonel in the war—that he increasingly questioned the "friendly" status of those at Camp Release and needed "to purge" the camp "of suspected characters." He justified going against his assurances of protection by stating that "new developments take place daily incriminating parties in the friendly camp." Sibley set up an elaborate ruse to arrest Dakota men. He informed Dakota families at Camp Release that the government needed to count them in order to distribute their long-awaited annuities. Early one morning, families arrived at a warehouse where the Dakota's agent, Thomas J. Galbraith, and several men posing as clerks made a production of counting them. After this fictional count, they sent the women and children out one door and told the men to step aside because they needed to be counted again so they could receive extra annuities. Soldiers then confiscated all the men's guns and knives and put them in irons.

Similar retribution occurred outside Camp Release. Sibley ordered his soldiers to burn all Dakota crops and to destroy their homes, even of those who had not participated in the war. This order had caveats, however. Sibley noted that "there are many pretty good houses on the Indian reservation near the lower agency which add value to the land, and can be of no future service to the Indians. . . . These I shall not destroy." He also spared some Dakota crops for military consumption. The Ho-Chunk, the Dakota's neighbors to the south, had not participated in the war but had their crops burned or con-fiscated nonetheless.

While many Dakota surrendered and sought protection at Camp Release, those who fled from Minnesota began a diaspora that continues into the pres-ent day. In the weeks following the war's end, Taoyateduta and at least 150 Dakota escaped to the western prairies. Other Dakota families, especially Sisseton and Wahpeton who had not participated in the war, also fled from Minnesota, eventually settling in Montana, Nebraska, Dakota Territory, and Canada.

As Dakota warriors and families decided whether to surrender or flee, Minnesotans reacted to the war. The Minnesota press played a large role in both reflecting and molding the public's perception of the postwar era. By 1860, more than a hundred newspapers were published across the state; each covered the events of the war and its aftermath in graphic detail. These newspapers, according to scholar Charles Lewis, helped create "a climate of fear and hatred through their coverage of Indian-related events in southern Minnesota." In addition to the press, local and national government officials and military commanders also commented on the war. Protestant missionar-ies who worked with Dakota added to the multiple voices that discussed and evaluated the conflict as well. Conspicuously absent in all the public com-mentary, however, were the voices of the Dakota themselves. Although it is difficult to read the extreme rhetoric used in newspapers, public records, speeches, and private correspondence, it is essential to review some of these vitriolic comments in order to understand the postwar hysteria in Minnesota, which would eventually lead to the Dakota's trials, executions, and exile from their homeland.

Following the war, any prewar fascination with the Dakota ended and was replaced with strong negative emotions based on the belief that the Dakota were solely responsible for the war and that Minnesotans had done nothing to warrant attacks on their lives and property. Postwar rhetoric portrayed settlers as innocent, blameless, and peaceful. Commissioner William Dole described them as "quiet, inoffensive, and unarmed" citizens who "fell vic-tim to savage fury." U.S. Indian Agent Thomas Galbraith called the settlers in Minnesota "peaceful and industrious . . . unarmed and engaged in their peaceful avocations."

If the settlers viewed themselves as wholly innocent, most saw all Dakota as guilty with little justification for going to war. Newspapers and books published in the immediate postwar period placed the blame for the war squarely on the Dakota's shoulders. Many commentators stated that the war began not because of legitimate grievances (although some did mention problems only to dismiss or downplay them), but because Dakota had a defective character. An article in the *Dakotian* argued that the uprising occurred because of the Dakota's "cruelty, blood-thirstiness and general bad character." The first published histories of the war blamed the Dakota's poor temperament, describing them as "backward, evil, pagan savages who committed atrocious acts." Isaac Heard, who in 1863 published his *History of the Sioux War and Massacres of 1862 and 1863*, opened "The Causes of the Outbreak" chapter with the stark statement that the war occurred because the "Indians were predisposed against the whites." Harriet Bishop McConkey, in *Dakota War Whoop: or, Indian Massacres and War in Minnesota of 1862–'3*, argued that the war arose because when Dakota "feel they have been wronged, they proceed (actuated solely by a desire for revenge) to wreak their vengeance upon defenseless, helpless women and children."

Many of early histories went one step further and attributed the war to the Dakota's supposed racial inferiority; indeed, they often described Dakota as akin to animals. *Dakota War Whoop* lectured its readers that "in the great chain of nature, the Indian is a connecting link between the wild beast and the human species. . . . In almost all his actions, he seems to be guided by instinct, rather than reason." Newspapers echoed this racialized rhetoric. On September 4, 1862, the front page of the *St. Cloud Democrat*, edited by Jane Grey Swisshelm, one of the few female newspaper editors of the era, urged "every man or woman with an ounce of Anglo Saxon blood in his or her veins" to defend themselves "against those biped tigers." Time did not temper Swisshelm's rhetoric. In a November article, she referred to Dakota as "Red Fiends," "wild beasts," "hyenas," and "red-jawed tigers whose fangs are dripping with the blood of innocents!" In various other articles, she called them "lazy vermin," "savage assassins," and "Hell Hounds." Ironically, prior to the war Swisshelm was a committed reformer, championing the cause of women, slaves, convicted criminals, and even Native Americans, albeit advocating for their assimilation. As with many other erstwhile middle- and upper-class reformers, however, the war completely changed Swisshelm's opinion, leading her to view Dakota "as little better than beasts of prey."

Swisshelm's racialized and vitriolic rhetoric included demands that citizens "exterminate the wild beasts." In March, she called for Minnesotans to "hunt them, shoot them, set traps for them, put out poisoned bait for them, kill them by any means we would use to exterminate wild panthers. We cannot breathe the same air with those demon violators of women and crucifiers of infants." She was not alone; other newspapers also called for extermination. On September 12, the *Weekly Pioneer and Democrat* printed an article entitled "Let the Sioux Race Be Annihilated." The author praised soldiers for pledging to "persecute a war of utter extermination of the entire Sioux race": "The race must be annihilated—every vestige of it blotted from the face of God's green earth. Otherwise our State will be ruined and white men slaughtered or driven from our noble young state. ANNIHILATION;—that is the word."

Many government and military officials echoed the newspapers' demands for retribution and extermination. Governor Alexander Ramsey called all Dakota "ruthless assassins," ravishers of "wives and sisters and daughters," and "destroyers of . . . homes and property." Because of these crimes, Ramsey demanded, "the Sioux Indians of Minnesota must be exterminated or driven forever beyond the borders of the state." Major General John Pope echoed that sentiment, stating that "the horrible massacres of women and children and the outrageous abuse of female prisoners . . . call for punishment beyond the human power to inflict. . . . It is my purpose utterly to exterminate the Sioux if I have the power to do so. . . . They are to be treated as maniacs or wild beasts." In his report to the commissioner of Indian affairs, the Dakota's agent, Thomas Galbraith, summarized the deadly proposals suggested to deal with them, which included "extermination, massacre, banishment, torture . . . killing with small-pox, and poison." A letter addressed to Governor Ramsey likewise proposed killing "all of them off by inoculating them with the small-pox."

The calls for extermination were not mere rhetoric. Across Minnesota, bounties were offered for the scalps of every Dakota man killed. I. C. George, E. B. Ames, and William Caine, agents for the railroad and steamship lines, offered to pay $25 for every five Dakota scalps they received. Jane Grey Swisshelm demanded that the Minnesota legislature "offer a bounty of $10 for every Sioux scalp. . . . It will cost five times that much to exterminate them by regular modes of warfare and they should be got rid of in the cheapest and quickest manner." Even manufacturers attempted to capitalize on the public's cries for vengeance. A company called "Costar's" Vermin Exterminators placed an advertisement in the *Mankato Weekly Record* that suggested "Col. Sibley" purchase "Dr. Costar's remedies in his war of extermination" because Dakota were classed as "vermin" (fig. 5).

As calls for the extermination of all Dakota reverberated across Minnesota, others demanded that all Dakota—and all Ojibwe and Ho-Chunk as well—be completely removed from the state. Agent Galbraith articulated this viewpoint: "the recent atrocities of the Sioux have so exasperated the people of the State, as a body politic, that these people and the Sioux Indians can never again exist together with safety or benefit to either in the same State limits." Thus, he reasoned, the "Indians must be sent out and kept out of the State." Most Minnesota newspapers strongly supported Galbraith's recommendation. An article in the *Goodhue Volunteer* demanded that all Dakota be "removed by the Government to some isolated place, where they can live by their industry or starve, as they choose." Advocates of removal suggested that Isle Royale, in Lake Superior near Ontario, be established as an "Indian penal colony," where all Dakota (and Native Americans from Michigan, Wisconsin, Minnesota, and Dakota Territory as well) would be forced to relocate. Guards would be stationed at all entrances and exits to the colony. The prisoners would be completely isolated from white society, except for limited contact with missionaries and government officials. They also would be disarmed, except for fishhooks. The idea of sending Dakota families (and other Native American families totaling almost 47,000) to Isle Royale gained immense popularity among the general public, as well as many government policy makers. Even if Isle Royale was not chosen, Governor Ramsey recommended to President Lincoln "their removal to some distant locality 'far beyond our borders.'"

Certainly, not all Minnesotans advocated the extermination or exile of all Dakota. Most prominently, missionaries affiliated with the ABCFM and the Episcopal Church spoke out against the wholesale extermination of innocent (mainly Christian) Dakota. ABCFM missionary Thomas Williamson worried that innocent Dakota "may be murdered by equally wicked white men." Likewise, John Williamson "detested the avowed determination of perhaps a majority of the citizens of this State that they will never rest till the race is exterminated by war or sent to a hangman . . . grave." Martha Riggs, Stephen Riggs's daughter, lectured that cries to "exterminate the fiends" would "bring

FIGURE 5. "Costar's" Vermin Exterminators suggested for Sibley's "war of extermination," September 12, 1862, *Mankato Weekly Record.*

a curse upon ourselves and on our future generations." Episcopalian Bishop Henry Whipple decried calls in "our papers . . . to exterminate every one who had a red skin."

Some of the missionaries also spoke out against the removal of all Dakota from Minnesota. Thomas Williamson hoped that they "may yet be permitted again to occupy most of their late reservation." He felt it was unfair that a population of 6,000 lost their lands and annuities because of "the murders committed by about 300 wicked men." In an article entitled "The Indian Question," he made the same point. He realized that "some of our people believe" that the Indians must "leave the land in which they were born and the graves of their fathers, and go and reside in a country which is to them unsalubrious and unpleasant." The United States, however, had no "right to enforce our opinion . . . against the Indian." Stephen Riggs called removing all Dakota from Minnesota "altogether unnecessary and bad policy."

The missionaries, however, did not protest against removal based on the Dakota's treaty rights or sovereignty. Rather, remaining in Minnesota would promote their "civilization" and Christianization. Bishop Whipple, for example, wrote the secretary of the interior that separating "wives, children, and friends" outside Minnesota would make them "outlaws" and work against their eventual assimilation into American society. In lieu of exile, Whipple suggested that the government should "organize for them a prison on the plan of a reform school. They should be taught trades and educated so as to be leaders of their people whenever they are discharged." The war and imprisonment "will make them docile pupils."

While missionaries like Whipple defended their Dakota converts and argued against extermination and exile, they also believed that the guilty should be punished and even executed. Thomas Williamson encapsulates this sentiment, writing that "those who [were] fairly convicted of murder should be sentenced to death." Bishop Whipple agreed. "There is no man who does not feel that the savages who have committed these deeds of violence must meet their doom," he commented. "The law of God and man alike require the stern necessities of self-protection demand it." Whipple's only wish was "that the trial of all shall be such as to carefully scrutinize between the guilty and the innocent."

Although Stephen and Martha Riggs, Thomas and John Williamson, and Henry Whipple spoke out against the extermination and removal of all

Dakota and demanded fair trials, their support was tempered by their own religious beliefs, which placed so-called friends of the white man—or, in Whipple's words, "our beloved Christian Indians"—above others and thus worthy of salvation. In the context of public demands for vengeance, however, even this limited support placed the missionaries in opposition to most Minnesotans and government and military officials. Contemporary author Diane Wilson notes the irony of missionaries who were "considered a friend of the Native people by virtue of not supporting extermination."

General Sibley, however, ignored the missionaries' calls for restraint and created a five-man commission to try the Dakota men held at Camp Release. These five commissioners were military officers who had each fought against the Dakota just days earlier, which presented a clear conflict of interest. On September 28, 1862, when the trials began, Sibley gave the commissioners a short set of instructions. They were to "summarily try" the Dakota men and pass judgment on those found guilty of "murder and other outrages." Those found guilty would be executed without delay. While Sibley conceded that immediate executions might "perhaps . . . be a stretch of my authority," he argued that "necessity must be my justification."

When the trials ended on November 3, 1862, a little over a month after they began, the military had brought 392 Dakota men before the commission and convicted 323. Of those convicted, 303 were sentenced to death, 20 received prison sentences, and 69 were acquitted. If Sibley had executed all those found guilty as he planned, it would have meant the immediate elimination of approximately 10 percent of the total male Dakota population in Minnesota at the time of the war.

Both at the time and since, the trials have been sharply criticized and are highly controversial. At the time, Protestant missionaries, especially Thomas, John, and Jane Williamson and Henry Whipple, were some of the harshest critics. Thomas Williamson called the court "incompetent to try Indians for their lives." Bishop Whipple allegedly "wept" when "all those who came in under a flag of truce (especially those Christian Indians who delivered the white captives) were tried by a military commission." Whipple wrote several articles in Minnesota newspapers defending the Dakota and traveled to Washington, D.C., to appeal for clemency for the condemned prisoners. Likewise, the Williamsons publicized the injustices of the trials, which they hoped would lead to new hearings for the hundreds of convicted men.

Stating that "even a murderer deserves a fair trial," John Williamson and his fellow missionaries listed numerous abuses that discredited the trials. Contemporary historians have largely agreed with their criticisms. Most fundamentally, the commissioners did not give the defendants basic judicial rights. John Williamson accused them of assuming that a man was guilty until proven innocent. The defendants also did not have counsel and lacked due process protections. The prisoners were not informed about their legal right against self-incrimination; indeed, many believed that honest answers would lead to fair treatment. This meant that some defendants admitted to firing a weapon (like Robert Hopkins), but this admission was then used against them. The commission also accepted hearsay evidence. The proceedings were conducted in English, generally without adequate translation.

Moreover, many commentators, at the time and since, criticized the speed of the trials. Bishop Whipple complained that they were "conducted with such haste as to forbid all justice." From October 5 to November 5, the court tried 363 cases. According to John Williamson, the commission tried almost 400 cases in the same time that it generally took to try one white man for murder. On November 2 alone, the court resolved more than 40 cases, with some trials lasting only a few minutes. The commission also applied different standards to mixed- and full-blood Dakota. While it ruled that a mixed-blood Dakota person could have been forced to participate in a battle against his will, a full-blood Dakota could not use this defense. Finally, in effect the trials had only two possible results: innocence or execution. The punishment of execution was given whether a Dakota man had killed a white settler or fired a gun at an empty house or an animal. In sum, Thomas Williamson declared the trials so unfair and prejudicial that they were insufficient to convict someone of "killing a dog worth five dollars."

Despite the biases of the trials, Henry Sibley and John Pope rushed to carry out all the executions. Federal law, however, required that the president approve the death sentences. As such, Pope reluctantly forwarded the names of the condemned men to President Lincoln in early November; a few days later, at Lincoln's request, he also sent all the trial records. Lincoln appointed two men to review the sentences, first instructing them to identify all defendants who were guilty of rape. When the reviewers determined that only two defendants fell into this category, Lincoln expanded his criteria for execution to include rape and murder. He ordered the reviewers to attempt to distinguish those who had participated in "massacres" from those who had participated in "battles."

As Lincoln waited for the reviewers' recommendations, he was flooded with letters, petitions, and visits from those supporting (the majority) or opposing (the minority) the executions. Most Minnesotans demanded the immediate execution of all 303. Governor Ramsey wrote to Lincoln calling for "the execution of every Sioux Indian condemned by the military court." Likewise, Major General John Pope demanded that "the criminals condemned ought in every view to be at once executed without exception." Minnesota Senator Morton Wilkinson and Representatives Cyrus Aldrich and William Windom also gave speeches in Congress and wrote lengthy letters and articles railing against pardoning any Dakota.

The Protestant missionaries, however, waged their own campaign to convince Lincoln to reduce the number of executions. Again, they mainly defended their church members and those who had rescued settlers, such as Robert Hopkins. In addition to defending Hopkins, Jane Williamson wrote to Lincoln seeking to overturn Tapaytatanka's conviction. She told him that "Tapaytatanka with his father . . . both used all their influence to prevent an attack upon the people of the Agency." Like his fellow missionaries, Stephen Riggs urged Lincoln to consider clemency for the "few men who in the great uprising proved themselves loyal to our government and people." Bishop Whipple pleaded the cases of Taopi, Good Thunder, Anawangmani, and Wabasha, informing Lincoln that they had refused to fight in the outbreak and had rescued white captives.

General Sibley attempted to counter the barrage of missionary letters. He wrote Lincoln that he was "aware that representations have been made to you by Missionaries and others long resident in the Country, who had natural and pardonable attachments for particular Indians." However, he argued, "the great majority of the prisoners are deeply guilty, and deserve hanging." Sibley also wrote Bishop Whipple, admonishing him for his support of the Dakota, which "can do no good in the present excited state of the public mind in this state, and may really do very much evil." He even warned Whipple that his condemnation of the trials could ignite a "war of races." Senator Wilkinson also complained about missionaries who sympathized with the Dakota, "insisting that nothing but hanging the leaders will give any security for the good conduct of the Indians in future."

As the war of words flew between Minnesota and the nation's capital, Sibley and Pope decided to relocate the 303 condemned Dakota prisoners, including Robert Hopkins, to Mankato, about eighty-five miles southwest of Minneapolis–St. Paul. As the manacled prisoners moved through the largely German settlement of New Ulm, angry citizens pelted them with bricks, seriously injuring some of the prisoners and their guards. Stephen Riggs, who accompanied the prisoners, characterized this attack as "insane." Once the men arrived at their new prison, called Camp Lincoln, the mob violence continued. On December 4, 1862, an "army of 150 citizens" attacked the prison camp armed "with hatchets, knives, and other weapons." They "forced their way through the guard . . . with the avowed intention of murdering the Indian prisoners." Guards arrested the citizens, but they were immediately "released on parole." Following the attack, guards relocated the prisoners to a small structure in the center of Mankato to await Lincoln's decision. According to Stephen Riggs, this temporary prison was so cramped that "there was only room for all the prisoners to lie down."

While Robert and the other men suffered in Mankato, their family members also experienced great distress. Soldiers marched 1,600 or 1,700 women, children, elders, and so-called friendly men to Fort Snelling, south of present-day St. Paul. "It was a sad sight," wrote John Williamson, "to see so many women and children marching off, not knowing whether they shall ever see their husbands and fathers again." Although the military escorted the families, they nonetheless encountered violence. John Williamson, who accompanied the families to Fort Snelling, said that crowds pelted them with "stones and sticks, to say nothing of the curses which were heaped upon them from the doorways and hillsides." Samuel Brown, a mixed-blood Dakota, also reported violence. At Henderson, he witnessed "the streets crowded with an angry and excited populace, cursing, shouting, and crying. Men, women, and children, armed with guns, knives, clubs, and stones, rushed upon the Indians." The crowd indiscriminately pulled elderly men, women, and children from the wagons by "the hair of the head and [started] beating them." As she walked to Fort Snelling with her children, Mary Renville was especially "afraid of the Germans [at New Ulm]; they are so furious."

By winter 1862, only those Dakota who fled west in the immediate aftermath of the war and a very small number of Indians considered to be friendly had escaped imprisonment. Indeed, such a large number of Dakota were imprisoned that purportedly even the environment around southern Minnesota changed. One newspaper article claimed that for the first time in years, settlers had "shot buffalo within sixty miles of St. Paul, Minnesota." Another article noted more deer "than during any previous season." Both articles attributed the increase in animals to the Dakota's imprisonment, which "rendered the region so uninhabited, that bisons, wolves, & c., roam freely where they have not been seen for years."

Isolated from their traditional villages and hunting grounds, separated from their families and other kin, living in poor conditions, and without their freedom, Dakota men, women, and children nervously waited for President Lincoln's decision. Finally, on December 6, 1862, Lincoln issued an executive order reducing the number of Dakota to be hanged from 303 to 39. Overall, the missionaries and other "East Coast Indian reformers" (as some Minnesotans derisively called them at the time) were pleased with the reduction. However, in Minnesota, an immediate outcry arose over Lincoln's decision. Newspapers across the state published angry articles condemning his leniency. An article in the *Goodhue Volunteer*, for example, reported that Minnesota citizens were "indignant and disgusted" with the president's ruling. The article blamed "sniveling and whining . . . philanthropists," such as Whipple, the Riggses, and the Williamsons, as well as eastern Quakers, for influencing Lincoln. It exhorted citizens to take matters into their own hands, as the "President of the United States does not have power enough to shield these murderers from justice."

Over the next century, Lincoln's decision to decrease the number of those executed continued to incite both praise and condemnation. Just as Minnesota missionaries and eastern philanthropists lauded his decision, so too have some modern historians praised the president for his "humane" decision. Legal historian Paul Finkelman, for example, focuses not on those executed but on those Lincoln saved; he highlights clemency rather than condemnation. While Finkelman does note that the hangings were the largest mass execution in U.S. history, he praises Lincoln for saving seven out of every eight who were condemned—87 percent by his calculations—making Lincoln's decision the "largest mass clemency of people sentenced to death in American history." Other historians, however, have soundly condemned Lincoln's decision, noting that the president condemned thirty-nine men based on trials he knew were unfair. Historian David Martínez, for instance, harshly challenges what he terms the "myth of [Lincoln's] magnanimity," instead calling the president "a cold and insensitive politician who deliberately ordered a mass execution of thirty-eight men illegitimately tried in kangaroo courts." A list of the condemned men and their sentence of death, without further commentary, published in 2004 in the *American Indian Quarterly* powerfully illustrates Martínez's point that hundreds of fathers, husbands, sons, and brothers were condemned after arbitrary trials.

Other historians have attempted to walk a middle ground, citing numerous mitigating factors that made Lincoln's decision very difficult. Of course, Lincoln was presiding over the Civil War at the time, which was not going well militarily or politically. Ironically, he was also working on the Emancipation Proclamation (issued January 1, 1863), which granted freedom to slaves in areas under Confederate control, at the same time that he was forced to deal with those Dakota who had lost their own freedom. And he was distracted with grief over the death of his young son several months previously. In addition to these numerous political, military, and personal issues, historians have noted that as in all aspects of Lincoln's political career, the president tended to be politically moderate and desired compromise. Indeed, in one of the very few public comments Lincoln made about the Dakota executions, he articulated a desire to find a middle ground. He was "anxious to not act with so much clemency as to encourage another outbreak on the one hand, nor with so much severity as to be real cruelty on the other."

Ultimately, this middle ground was impossible to obtain, especially in the context of how Sibley and Pope carried out Lincoln's orders and the way members of the public who witnessed the executions responded. After receiving Lincoln's order, Sibley and Pope immediately decided to publicly execute the 39 men. On December 26, 1862, 38 Dakota men (one man received a last-minute reprieve from Lincoln) were simultaneously hanged on a specially constructed wooden gallows in Mankato. Approximately 1,400 soldiers—both standing and mounted on horses—and a crowd of more than 4,000 spectators who had traveled from neighboring towns of New Ulm, St. Peter, and Le Sueur witnessed the deaths of the condemned prisoners. The *New York Times* reported that following the hangings a "prolonged cheer [arose] from the soldiery and citizens who were spectators" (fig. 6).

After the hangings, most of the crowd dispersed, but some remained behind clamoring for souvenirs from the bodies, including ornaments, locks of

FIGURE 6. December 26, 1862, the largest mass execution in U.S. history. From *Frank Leslie's Illustrated Newspaper*, January 24, 1863.

hair, and pieces of clothing, before their burial. Spectators could also purchase portions of the wooden gallows as souvenirs. The thirty-eight men were then buried in a shallow grave, but local physicians quickly exhumed the bodies for so-called scientific study. In the months and years after the hangings and burials, the public's macabre fascination with the executed men continued. In June 1863, a local post office boasted of displaying one of the ropes that "had the honor of squeezing the neck of an Indian at Mankato." Later spoons, coins, and even a beer tray were engraved with the hanging scene and sold as mementos. John Wise, the editor of the *Mankato Weekly Record*, raised extra income selling lithographs of the mass execution.

The popularity of these souvenirs illustrated, according to the *St. Cloud Democrat*, the public's "morbid curiosity" and "deep interest" in seeing the "doomed ones." Even at the time, *Harper's Weekly* described the citizens' desire to observe and then commemorate the executions as an "awful interest." The exhumation of the Dakota men's skeletons serves as an especially macabre example of this "awful interest." Throughout the nineteenth century, self-described scientists disinterred Indian remains to study the "physical and cultural differences between peoples." Their findings would inevitably "validate theories of white supremacy." Tragically, as I discuss throughout the following chapters, the exhumation and desecration of Dakota bodies continued in the years after the Mankato hangings at Camp Kearney, following Little Crow's death, and during the government's punitive expeditions into Dakota Territory. On these expeditions and in other locations, military officials and members of the public also seized Dakota tipis, clothing, and other items.

Today, tribal activists are working to repatriate these stolen skeletons, skulls, and artifacts. However, with regard to the executed men, only three of the original thirty-eight have currently been repatriated to the Dakota Oyate. In 2000, the remains of leader Marpiya Okinajin, He Who Stands in the Clouds, were repatriated to the Lower Sioux Indian Community in Morton, Minnesota, for reburial in the Mdewakanton Ehdakupi Wanagi Makoce (Mdewakanton Repatriation Burial Site), 138 years after his execution. In 2018, a sacred pipe from White Dog, a Mdewakanton Dakota executed at Mankato, was also returned to the Lower Sioux Indian Community (see fig. 1). However, the majority of artifacts taken after the hangings and in the years following the war have not been repatriated.

After the executions and their chilling aftermath, Robert Hopkins and the other convicted Dakota continued to be held as prisoners in Mankato. Sarah, their children, and the other Dakota families, meanwhile, remained imprisoned at Fort Snelling and could not visit their relatives. This isolation led to rampant speculation in both prisons. One week, rumors flew back and forth that "the thirty eight hung at Mankato was the first installment, and the women and children scattered and made slaves." Another week, they feared that "they were all to be taken to a rocky, barren island, somewhere, and left with nothing but fish for support, and again they were to be taken away down south, where it was so hot they would all die of fever and ague." Of course, all these rumors were suggestions prominently featured in Minnesota newspapers.

The conditions at both prisons served to heighten their fears. At both Mankato and Fort Snelling, families faced illness, starvation, and high death rates. Mahpiyatowin (Esther Wakeman), who fled to Canada during the war and returned to Minnesota only to be imprisoned at Fort Snelling, characterized the conditions in the camp as "terrible." In their weakened condition, three of Mahpiyatowin's brothers died of smallpox at Fort Snelling. A woman whose brother had been hanged in Mankato died from starvation; reportedly, she had been so affected by her brother's death that "she refused to partake of any kind of food." These deaths were not the only ones that occurred at the fort. A military census taken in December 1862 reported 1,601 Dakota prisoners at Fort Snelling; another census in May 1863 counted only 1,318. The illness and death rate was also high at Mankato. The prisoners suffered from various illnesses, especially pulmonary consumption (tuberculosis) caused by the drafty and damp conditions. In the months of March and April, four prisoners died; the death rate was higher in the winter months.

In the midst of sickness and death, Dakota families learned in spring 1863 that they could not remain in Minnesota. On February 16, 1863, the U.S. Congress enacted legislation that "abrogated and annulled" all previous treaties with the four bands of Dakota, took away their "lands and rights of occupancy in the State of Minnesota," and stripped them of their annuities. Congress also established a Sioux Claims Commission to determine compensation for Minnesotans' war-incurred losses; these claims would be paid with Dakota money. The act explicitly blamed all Dakota for their pending exile from Minnesota and loss of annuities, stating that they had "made an unprovoked, aggressive, and most savage war upon the United States." On February 21, 1863, Congress also voted to remove the Ho-Chunk from Minnesota, even though they had not participated in the 1862 war. This would be another in a series of land cessions and removals for the Ho-Chunk; they had been relocated just a few years earlier to a reservation southwest of Mankato after losing lands in Wisconsin and Iowa.

On March 3, 1863, Congress passed another act that authorized the president to remove Dakota and Ho-Chunk to an unspecified "tract of unoccupied land outside of the limits of any state." According to historian William Lass, the location of the new reservation was "very generally worded in order to give the Indian office maximum leeway in selection of the new location." Legal scholar Howard Vogel harshly condemns the legal and moral justification for all these acts. Arguing that this legislation used the war as a pretext to steal Dakota and Ho-Chunk lands and enact "a program of ethnic cleansing of genocidal proportion," he calls the acts "without legal foundation under both international and domestic law."

In April 1863, shortly after Congress passed the abrogation and removal acts, the head of the Northern Superintendency, Clark Thompson, left for

Dakota Territory to select a reservation for both the Dakota and the Ho-Chunk. The Dakota's agent, Thomas Galbraith, directed Thompson to choose a location as far as possible from white settlements. "The place to which the Sioux ought to be sent should then be, as nearly as possible an isolated one," he lectured, "not only isolated now, but one which would promise to be easily kept isolated for as long time as possible."

As the prisoners and their families waited to learn the location of their new reservation, as well as if and when they could reunite with their kin, they experienced "a good deal of anxiety about their future." Dakota prisoner Paul Mazakutemani expressed this anxiety, predicting great "difficulty . . . [in] the spring." Unfortunately, his fears about their impending exile proved to be prescient. Over the next years, Dakota suffered continued separation from their kin, illness, starvation, and death at Crow Creek, the site Thompson eventually selected for Sarah, her children, and other Dakota families, and Camp McClellan in Davenport, where Robert and many of the men were incarcerated. As Thomas Williamson commented, "the war instead of being ended [was] but just beginning."

2 ✳ CROW CREEK, DAKOTA TERRITORY, 1863–1866

In May 1863, Sarah Hopkins, her two boys, Samuel and his baby brother, and her seventy-two-year-old mother, Catherine Totidutawin, left Fort Snelling and boarded a steamer that would remove them from Minnesota. Sarah had no idea where the steamer would transport her and her family; then again, neither did Superintendent Clark Thompson, who had still not chosen the site of their new reservation in Dakota Territory when the families left Minnesota. Given this clear lack of planning, Thompson ultimately selected a poor location. The reservation, eventually named Crow Creek, suffered from drought, contaminated drinking water, poor farmland, inadequate wood, little infrastructure and few buildings because of its last-minute selection, and angry Ho-Chunk neighbors. The Dakota families also endured corrupt agents, nonexistent medical care, and missing and poor-quality rations. All these problems led to more than three years of illness, starvation, death, and the rape of vulnerable women. At Crow Creek, Sarah contracted consumption; her baby boy also became gravely ill. While Sarah survived her time at Crow Creek, her battle with tuberculosis consumed her for the rest of her life. Tragically, her little boy died. Like Sarah and her baby son, hundreds of other Dakota, especially children, became sick and passed away while living in exile. Sarah sadly reported that during her time at Crow Creek her family was "living in difficulty" and "having a hard time."

While Sarah struggled to survive at Crow Creek, Robert was imprisoned more than six hundred miles away in Davenport. Most of the families were forced to survive on the undeveloped reservation without male kin to help with farming and hunting. Even if the women attempted to hunt, they did not have guns, ammunition, or horses, which had been confiscated after the war. Stephen Riggs summarized Sarah Hopkins's hardships at Crow Creek. "The years of her husband's imprisonment were hard years for her," he wrote. "She had her two boys to care for and already had consumption fastened itself upon her." Mary Riggs, Stephen's wife, also worried about the Hopkins family, writing that she was "very sorry on [Robert's] account and for Sarah also."

In historical memory, Crow Creek looms large for many Dakota because of the separation from their kin, the inhumane conditions, and the large number of deaths that occurred during their years on the reservation. Even at the time, ABCFM missionary John Williamson foresaw the historical significance of Crow Creek. In 1873, a decade after the Dakota's exile from Minnesota, he wrote that the hills around the reservation were "soon covered with graves. The very memory of Crow Creek became horrible to the Santees who still hush their voices at the mention of the name." Into the present day, the conditions at Crow Creek continue to spark anger and sadness. Hannah Frazier, the great-grandmother of contemporary Dakota author Virginia Driving Hawk Sneve, "uttered the name [Crow Creek] in low, mournful tones as she recalled almost one hundred years later what survivors had told of the place. It was bad. Horrible. . . . All around the hills were graves."

In early spring 1863, Dakota women, children, and their elderly relatives held at Fort Snelling had no idea of the terrible conditions they would face at Crow Creek. But even without specific knowledge of what was to come, they emphatically did not want to leave their homeland in Minnesota. John Williamson reported that thoughts of leaving Minnesota created "a dark cloud . . . crushing their hearts." Ta-tanka-nazin (Standing Buffalo) recalled his desire to remain in Minnesota: "I loved my lands, it was on them that I had been raised and fed, it was the land of my fathers. I therefore had reason to love it." Contemporary author Diane Wilson summarized the trauma caused by the government's decision: Dakota families were leaving "the graves of their ancestors as well as their sacred places at a time when they were forbidden to use their own spiritual practices."

Government officials ignored their desire to remain in Minnesota and proceeded with their removal. In the early morning hours of May 4, 1863, soldiers loaded 1,310 Dakota who had been imprisoned at Fort Snelling onto two steamboats; 770 left on one steamer accompanied by Episcopalian missionary Samuel Hinman, while the other 540 sailed with ABCFM missionary John Williamson. Thus, the two missionary groups who had labored to convert the Dakota to Christianity before the war would continue their proselytizing outside Minnesota. Benjamin Thompson, the brother of Superintendent Clark Thompson, oversaw the removal. According to John Williamson, Thompson did not speak Dakota, nor did he have an official interpreter. Instead, Williamson and Lorenzo Lawrence, Sarah Hopkins's brother, a missionary-educated Dakota, acted as unofficial translators throughout the trip. About forty soldiers guarded the families. More than 85 percent of the passengers were women and children, many of whose husbands, fathers, sons, and brothers had been executed at Mankato or were being transferred to the prison in Davenport. When they boarded the steamers, John Williamson complained that they had "not yet heard anything more about where we are going."

After departing Minnesota, the two steamboats took different but equally circuitous routes from Fort Snelling to Dakota Territory, eventually covering about two thousand miles. The steamers initially traveled south down the Mississippi River together but then parted ways. One boat stopped at Hannibal, Missouri, where guards transferred the families to crowded railway freight cars for their next leg to St. Joseph, Missouri. The other steamer stopped at St. Louis, where Dakota families were moved to another steamer to continue their journey west and north. The two groups came together at St. Joseph, transferred to one boat, and made their way up the Missouri River into Dakota Territory. John Williamson postulated that officials designed the lengthy routes so that "the Indians . . . can never find their way back."

The boats were extremely crowded, especially after the two groups reunited in St. Joseph. Williamson called the overcrowding "nearly as bad as the Middle Passage for slaves. . . . But these folks say they are only Indians." Guards confined the Dakota to the lower decks and excluded them from the cabins. This meant that at night they were "so crowded that there was not room enough for all of them to lie down at the same time." Williamson claimed that he protested to the commander and guards against the "inhumanity of such crowding," but his complaints were "in vain."

The prisoners also faced emotional and physical abuse. On the first leg of their journey, the Dakota were literally treated as freight and not passengers; the manifest of the cargo carried on Williamson's boat listed "*30 horses, 540 Indians.*" According to Williamson, the guards spent "all the time picking on the Indians." In addition to emotional abuse, the Dakota lacked sufficient and edible food. The food was "not more than about one-half of soldier's rations" and mostly consisted of "musty hardtack and briny pork which they had not half a chance to cook." They drank the contaminated river water, which caused sickness, but the ship did not provide a doctor or adequate medical supplies. Several deaths occurred because of the overcrowding; the lack of food, water, and medical care; and general weakness from their imprisonment at Fort Snelling. By the end of their journey, Williamson had written several letters documenting Dakota deaths; by his account, thirteen Dakota had died during the first portion of the trip—one man, three women, and nine children. By the time the steamer arrived at its destination at the end of May, twenty-four people had died. The guards did not allow relatives to properly bury their kin. In one tragic instance, a small child who passed away was buried in "a wood yard a little below Burlington, Iowa."

Alongside physical deprivation, illness, and death, families faced hostility from Minnesota citizens. As Dakota women and children boarded the steamers and left Minnesota, some citizens reacted with the same aggression that had characterized the months immediately following the war. For example, after leaving Fort Snelling, one of the steamers stopped briefly in St. Paul to take on cargo. A crowd gathered and started throwing rocks, which injured several women. The mob dispersed only after the captain of the steamer threatened to charge the crowd.

Ironically, at the same time that the families faced violence and hostility, some members of the public expressed a nascent fascination with the prisoners. When newspapers published the news of the Dakota's impending departure, tourists traveled to Fort Snelling to see the Indians before they left. Small groups walked around the prison, gawking at the families and asking the women to sell their personal items. An article in the *Semi-Weekly Wisconsin* reported, "Strings of beads sold from a dollar to two and a half, according to their beauty and the cupidity of the owner. Small bark sacks brought three dollars, and neatly braided matting was sold at a dollar a yard." Some women sold items to raise money, but "the majority would refuse to sell anything." The article included a textbook definition of this phenomenon of imperialist nostalgia, the act of remembering and commemorating what has been intentionally destroyed: visitors wanted to purchase these souvenirs "lest they forget that Indians had inhabited this State." Of course, the article neglected to acknowledge that these tourists were undoubtedly the same ones who adamantly demanded the Dakota families' removal from Minnesota and the execution of their husbands, sons, fathers, and brothers. As historian Jean O'Brien notes, the acts of "relic collecting place Indians in the past [and] commemorate Indian peoples and practices that are asserted as extinct."

Once the steamers left Minnesota, the public's fascination with the Dakota grew even stronger. John Williamson reported that during stops the passengers faced "many visitors thronging around them all day." As the steamers passed towns, "the Whites gather around so thick that [it] is really very unpleasant." Members of the public became even more intrusive in St. Joseph, Missouri. The Dakota on Williamson's steamer arrived first and set up camp to wait for the second ship, staying almost a week.

During this time, St. Joseph's *Morning Herald* invited members of the public who wished "to see Nature in her wildest" to "go down and take a peep at the Sioux tribe of Copperheads." People traveled from far and wide to witness the "tough looking customers" and "fine looking specimens"; "hundreds of our citizens have been visiting these red skins, and are probably well-posted by this time in the science of Indianery." The article, however, may have worked too well at enticing the public to visit the Dakota's camp. In a followup, the paper told the public that "it is very annoying to the Indians and those who have them in charge, to have visitors at the camp after 6 o'clock, P.M. . . . Will our citizens bear this in mind? There is plenty of time before that late hour in the day for visiting the tribe and seeing all that is worth of observation." The St. Joseph residents visited the camp out of interest and for amusement; they did not fear the Dakota. The audience saw the families as entertainment and defined them by stereotypes; they did not seem to view them as traumatized people with uncertain futures.

On May 30, 1863, after enduring a voyage of two thousand miles and an intrusive public along the way, the Dakota arrived at their new reservation. Almost a month later, on June 24, the Ho-Chunk also reached Crow Creek. Superintendent Clark Thompson had selected the reservation's location mainly for its isolation, according to his official charge. Crow Creek was situated far from any white settlements "near the mouth of Crow Creek, about

150 miles above Fort Randall," in present-day central South Dakota. As an added bonus, Thompson noted that "white people will never desire this country, and, therefore, it is just the place for Indians." William Jayne, the former governor of Dakota Territory, agreed with Thompson's choice, noting that the area around Crow Creek "never will have a sufficient number of inhabitants for a State. If this is the case, it is just the place for refractory Indians, and we congratulate the Government upon their location."

Thompson promised the commissioner of Indian affairs, William Dole, that the new reservation, despite its isolation, had "good soil, good timber, and plenty of water." While Thompson extolled the virtues of his choice, John Williamson was wary of the location as soon as he stepped off the steamer. He charged Thompson with choosing the new reservation solely because it was a "land not desired by white immigrants at that time," not because it was suitable for inhabitation or economic development. While Thompson saw potential for agriculture, Williamson believed that the poor soil would never produce enough crops for the Dakota to survive. The area also resembled a "ghost land" due to an extreme drought. The Dakota "looked in vain for the fresh greenness to which they had been accustomed at that season of the year," but the drought had "burned out even the grass roots." Because of the poor location and soil and the severe drought, Williamson predicted that the "Indians can never remain here without a great expense to the Government, and such an expense as the Government will never go to." His final sentence in a letter to his father summarized his evaluation of Crow Creek: "This reservation is a barren waste. Pray for me."

Despite the poor prospects for agriculture, Thompson optimistically hired white laborers to establish farms for the Indians. The superintendent had such faith in his crops that he did not import other rations to sustain the Dakota and Ho-Chunk peoples. He also set his laborers to work laying out the shared reservation. He first ordered them to build a wooden stockade to divide the reservation into Dakota and Ho-Chunk sides; more important to Thompson, this stockade would also protect "government employees and property." Once constructed, the stockade contained soldiers' barracks, a warehouse, a blacksmith's workshop, and homes for the agent and other reservation employees. Thompson ordered that "no Indian is to be allowed inside [the stockade], except on a pass, for important business, and only one at a time." This stockade took up whatever timber existed on the reservation.

FIGURE 7. Crow Creek Reservation, Dakota Territory, 1865. Courtesy of the Minnesota Historical Society.

Given the focus on the stockade and agency buildings, the laborers did not build any homes for the Dakota, forcing them to live in "some slab shanties covered with earth, which [they] have made for themselves." After a creek overflowed, many of these structures were destroyed, leaving the families to live in "poor ragged tents" where the unrelenting wind made "sad havoc of them" (fig. 7).

When he initially arrived at Crow Creek, John Williamson had questioned whether the area would support agriculture, and his first weeks on the reservation did little to change his mind. He talked to a settler who had lived in the area for forty-five years. The settler recounted that he had repeatedly attempted to farm near Crow Creek. He spent more than "$400 trying to start a farm just above Fort Randall and did not grow a potatoe as large as the end of his thumb, or enough nubbins for his corn—so he gave it up." After talking with settlers and making his own observations, Williamson informed his father that "the Superintendent . . . is making large calculations on opening farms for the Indians, but I don't think they can make a comfortable living here. . . . I think the land is too barren—not so much from the nature of the soil—as for the want of rain." Williamson was "quite confident that the Indi-

FIGURE 8. In this 1862 photograph from Minnesota, women and children like Sarah and Samuel Hopkins (front) cultivated corn. The drought and poor soil of Crow Creek did not produce such bounty. Photo by Adrian Ebell. Courtesy of the Minnesota Historical Society.

ans can never earn or raise anything of a living there." Unfortunately, he was correct. By summer 1863, Thompson's initial crops had completely failed.

After the crops died, Dakota women had few other options for food. In Minnesota, they had subsisted on what one government agent termed "the very garden of Minnesota" (fig. 8). The area around Crow Creek, however, had a semiarid environment, which "was ill-suited to the subsistence skills and strategies that had sustained the Dakota along the Mississippi and its tributaries." Even if they wanted to attempt to hunt and gather, the government considered the Dakota at Crow Creek to be prisoners of war, which meant they were not supposed to leave the reservation to gather the "berries and roots that would have helped them through the summer." Furthermore, families did not have guns or horses to hunt with—both had been confiscated following the 1862 war.

To no one's surprise, Superintendent Thompson did not have enough provisions to sustain the Dakota and Ho-Chunk throughout the summer.

Starvation became an ever-present worry. Williamson noted that "the nation was in the throes of the Civil War at this time, and the matter of a band of Indians starving at Crow Creek did not receive prompt attention from the Government." In addition, deadly illnesses swept through the reservation— Williamson recorded the presence of diarrhea, dysentery, sore throats, scrofula (a form of tuberculosis), and whooping cough. In the midst of the sickness and starvation, Ite-wakan-hdi-win (Lightning-Face Woman) lost her elderly father and then, a few weeks later, her little boy. Her tragic story was just one of many. For six weeks after they arrived at Crow Creek, Dakota men, women, and especially children died at the average rate of two, three, or more a day. By July, just over a month after arriving at Crow Creek, 70 had died from illness and starvation. By September, Williamson reported that about 150 had died, noting that "there are hardly any babies and small children left." By 1864, Samuel Hinman reported that more than six hundred children had died from starvation and illness. By 1865, the Dakota also suffered from scurvy and inflammatory rheumatism.

Faced with this high death rate, Superintendent Thompson finally grasped the fact that he needed to order provisions for the reservation. However, he continued to deliberately make poor choices, which ultimately led to a deterioration in the already poor living conditions at Crow Creek. Instead of ordering supplies from the closer settlement of Sioux Falls, Dakota Territory, he contracted to receive them from Mankato. Historian William Lass argues that Thompson based this decision on political considerations—he wanted to reward his political ally James Hubbell, a trader in Mankato. As a result, the supplies traveled three hundred miles overland and were delayed, depleted, and spoiled on the way.

As winter approached, St. Andre Durand Balcombe, the Ho-Chunk's agent, took unofficial charge of the Dakota side of Crow Creek after Thompson returned to Minnesota and their assigned agent failed to arrive. "Agent Balcombe," John Williamson bluntly stated, "hates the Sioux and has said that they all deserved to starve to death." Balcombe's animosity toward the Dakota was palpable. He refused to hire an interpreter, because "he likes it better—they can't trouble him too much." He also allotted the poorest cattle to the Dakota, reserving the better animals for his family. This meant that Dakota families often received "nothing but heads, and sometimes nothing but entrails and feet." After Balcombe distributed a few sickly cattle to the

Dakota, he ordered agency employees to slaughter the rest and spread out the carcasses to freeze over the winter. Agency workers stacked the dead animals inside and outside the agency warehouse and covered them with sawdust. According to Edward Pond, an ABCFM teacher, by spring the meat was "spoiled and tainted and produced an offensive odor" and was swarming with maggots. Balcombe, however, issued the spoiled meat to the families until the following June.

Dakota families also continued to lack adequate clothing and shelter. Both Williamson and Pond noted that families did not receive clothing or blankets for many months, which caused the "Indians [to] suffer a good deal in cold weather and they are afraid to venture out on the prairies [to find food] in their thin clothing." When Agent Balcombe finally issued clothing and blankets, he did so in a way that humiliated and dehumanized the women. He allegedly stood at the top window of the warehouse and threw out a dress and a blanket for each family. He had the women stand below to catch the supplies. Unfortunately, strong winds blew many of the dresses and blankets away, forcing the women to chase them across the prairies. Later, the women found out that much of the clothing had not been distributed and was being used by the reservation staff. Wicahpewastewin (Good Star Woman) recalled that "the Indians were almost naked. They wound burlap around their legs to keep warm. Many of the women had to wear burlap gotten from the soldiers, and nobody had any sleeves in their garments." Wasuhiya-ye-dom (Passing Hail), one of the few men on the reservation, stated that the lack of clothing led to the women and children "crying with cold."

The Dakota's treatment by Balcombe, the Ho-Chunk's agent, reflected a larger tension between the two tribes on the shared reservation. Even before their arrival at Crow Creek, many of the Ho-Chunk resented the Dakota, blaming them for their removal from Minnesota. Ho-Chunk leader Little Hill articulated this anger over having his tribe "compelled to leave Minnesota" and abandon their farms, homes, and livestock, all because "another tribe of Indians committed depredations against the whites." In Dakota Territory, these tensions only increased, as the two tribes lived separated by an invisible line and competed for scarce or nonexistent resources. Moreover, Balcombe clearly favored the Ho-Chunk and provided them with more (although still deficient) supplies and blankets. Each side also feared attacks from the other.

As winter approached, both the Dakota and Ho-Chunk felt enormous strain from a continued lack of provisions. In November, Samuel Brown, a young interpreter, worried that "the Indians will starve to death [because] they only have half rations." David Faribault, a mixed-blood Dakota trader, also reported starvation at Crow Creek: "At times they have been two days without anything to eat, especially the women who had no men to provide for them." The food they received was often spoiled or of poor quality. They ate flour that was "very coarse, black, and sticky, and so poor that it was almost impossible to make bread out of it."

To combat the widespread starvation, Superintendent Thompson prepared and distributed "cottonwood soup." Workers constructed a large tank of cottonwood boards, which they filled with water, flour, and a small piece of pork and heated overnight. Dakota families received one ladle of this "thin gruel" every other day. By all accounts, the soup was inedible and "had a very offensive odor." The reservation's physician noted that the vat "smelt like carrion—like decomposed meat." The Dakota asked John Williamson to sample the soup, but he "could not eat it; that is, it was very unpalatable." The soup played a prominent role in a short letter Catherine Totidutawin wrote to Stephen Riggs. "They give us soup. They throw away the bone," she noted. "That is what we live on. . . . I am in trouble." Several years later, Wasuhiya-ye-dom testified at a congressional hearing that cottonwood soup "is the reason these hills . . . are filled with children's graves."

If they wanted anything other than this horrible soup, the women had to scavenge for food on or near the reservation, and each option was worse than the next. Some ate wolves that the soldiers had poisoned with strychnine. Others visited abandoned military camps and picked up "the scattered corn that had been left by the horses and mules when fed, for the purpose of eating it." Those who attempted to kill agency cattle received severe punishments if caught. Edward Pond reported that a Dakota woman and her young son, "being very hungry," killed one of the agency cattle. Agent Balcombe found out and "put them in a very cold house in very cold weather and kept them there nearly a week without fire . . . and fed them on bread and water." Another woman attempted to collect some blood from the slaughtered cattle to feed her family. Balcombe also put her in a "cold house" and did not even allow her to leave so she could feed her week-old infant.

The reservation's extreme gender imbalance compounded the problems.

On June 9, 1863, Superintendent Thompson recorded a census. Of about 1,300 total Dakota, males over the age of fifteen totaled 116; the rest were women and children. By 1865, of 1,043 Dakota counted at Crow Creek, only about 100 were men. The 1865 number highlights not only the continued gender imbalance but the high death rate as well. Historian Colette Hyman notes that Dakota culture traditionally "emphasized complementary contributions of women and men to community subsistence." At Crow Creek, however, women "were forced to sustain themselves, their children, and their elders without the benefit of the labor or companionship of fathers, brothers, husbands, or adult sons." Although the women did all they could, Waziyatawin writes that "the forced gender segregation combined with the death, disease, and starvation that characterized life in exile all served to severely and effectively diminish the Dakota population."

Needless to say, the women also missed their relatives. According to letters written by interpreter Samuel Brown, every evening, after the sun set, the reservation became even more "dismal" as women cried for their relatives at Davenport. Their suffering aged them prematurely. Joseph Brown, Samuel's father, commented that after only eight months at Crow Creek "Mazetouwin . . . looks ten years older than when I last saw her. She is very poor and destitute . . . she too is badly clad . . . in fact the whole camp are ragged and dirty."

Despite these extreme hardships, Dakota women did what they could to care for their families at Crow Creek. Some women challenged traditional gender roles—and the agent's orders—by attempting to hunt away from the reservation. Sarah Hopkins wrote that she left the reservation to hunt buffalo; she appeared to be successful because she "wore [carried] Buffalo meat" back to Crow Creek. One of the Camp Kearney prisoners wrote Stephen Riggs that his mother and grandmother also attempted to survive by hunting at Crow Creek. In summer 1864, John Williamson recounted that "a great many families of women and children went off [hunting] on the prairies, without a man or a gun." While searching for animals, the women also tried to gather wild berries. While not very "plentiful or good," these berries "compose[d] their principal food." This food source, however, was short-lived. In summer 1864, grasshoppers ate almost all the berries, leaving "only seeds hanging from the trees."

By early 1864, the efforts of individual women to hunt and gather enough food had failed. As a result, the entire community approached Superintendent Thompson and insisted that he allow them to leave the reservation to hunt buffalo. When he ignored their plea, the women enlisted the support of John Williamson. Williamson agreed to help, adding "his entreaties to theirs, showing the inhumanity of allowing innocent, helpless women and children to starve to death when food could be had near at hand." Still, for several weeks, Thompson refused their request. Finally, he authorized one buffalo hunt, as long as Williamson accompanied them to make sure that they did not "desert to the hostiles."

In early February, a group of about five hundred Dakota left to hunt buffalo. No more than eighty were men; the rest were hungry women and children. The group faced numerous obstacles. They did not have any horses (except for Williamson's) to aid in the hunt. In an understatement, Williamson noted that "hunting buffaloes on level prairie without horses is hard work." The women also had to carry their belongings on their backs instead of using their traditional travois pulled by horses. The agent had supplied the entire hunting party with only half a dozen guns and little ammunition. Despite these limitations, the group walked approximately a hundred miles searching for buffalo. Finally, they found and killed several. Williamson reported that after this successful hunt, "hollow eyes and emaciated forms became round and sleek. Their faces took on a happy and contented expression."

The mission press lauded Williamson's role in the hunt. Williamson's biographer states that without his intervention, Dakota families "would all have died of starvation at Crow Creek and they never forgot the debt of gratitude they owed him for accompanying them on the life-saving buffalo hunt." The *Annual Report of the American Board of Commissioners for Foreign Missions* lavished even more praise, calling Williamson "a *moral hero*, such as one does not often meet with." Some of this praise is warranted. Although the hunt was entirely at the women's initiative, they were unsuccessful with the superintendent until Williamson agreed to accompany them. Williamson, however, had his own agenda. While he certainly wanted to alleviate starvation, he also hoped to achieve religious goals, including having families attend morning and evening prayers and making sure they rested on Sundays. Williamson supported what he had often called "uncivilized hunts" in the service of humanitarianism as well as the opportunity to proselytize to a captive audience. He rejoiced that "he had shown them that they could traverse the prairies and keep the Sabbath; kill buffaloes, without resorting to charms"; in other words, they could hunt "and yet serve the Lord." Indeed, Edward Pond linked the hunt with increased interest in the missionaries' work, noting that his school "has increased since John went on the buffalo hunt." Williamson also hoped to scout locations where the Dakota might be settled away from Crow Creek.

However, not everyone saw the hunt in such a positive light. Wasuhiya-ye-dom offered another, more reprehensible interpretation of why the superintendent finally allowed it that has nothing to do with Williamson. He charged that Thompson and the other reservation officials wanted them away so they could steal the Dakota's goods when a new shipment of supplies arrived. He testified that "the agent told us to go out on a hunt, and while they were out on the hunt the goods came, and we suppose the reason he wanted us to go on the hunt was, he did not want us to see what was done with the goods." Issuing another shameful charge, Samuel Hinman accused groups of "eight or ten soldiers" of following the "hundred Indians" to "retake their plunder" during the buffalo hunt.

Because government agents and soldiers countered Dakota efforts to obtain sustenance at every turn, both young and elderly women and children as young as ten years old were forced to work at jobs on and off the reservation. On the reservation, they mainly cut and carried heavy wood long distances for the agents. They did not receive cash for their efforts but were paid for their labor in flour. Women also sought work just outside the reservation among the few local settlers. They "cut and hauled wood to the saw mills, to the boatyard to feed the boilers of the steamships, and to the stoves of the white settlers in the area." Stephen Riggs reported that women and children carried "water for all the white settlers for the territory." Sometimes the settlers paid with cash; other times, with food.

Despite their best efforts, most women could not find enough work on or near Crow Creek. This led some to defy the agent's orders and leave the reservation to travel hundreds of miles to multiple locations in search of food and work. Sarah, Catherine, and Samuel walked to Fort Abercrombie—a military installation in present-day North Dakota—and the Yankton Agency—on the border of present-day South Dakota and Nebraska—in search of food and supplies. Others undertook lengthy travels as well. In February 1864, "between two and three hundred went below to the Yankton Agency, in search of food." Even though the Yankton also lacked food and supplies, they took care of their Dakota cousins, providing enough to "keep them alive." Other women also traveled to Forts Sully, Randall, and Abercrombie. In 1864, more than a hundred Dakota women walked over two hundred miles to Fort Abercrombie to find work and provisions for their families. At the fort, the women labored as servants, laundry workers, and cooks and even dug trenches for the army. Even those who did not immediately find work appeared to receive provisions, at least for a time. For instance, Mazetouwin and her children traveled to Fort Abercrombie and received daily supplies from the fort. In February 1864, during the height of winter starvation, Joseph Brown, from his military position in Dakota Territory, reported that there are "nearly one hundred (mostly women and children) here now. They are fed from the commissary store and are as comfortable as they could be in their ragged condition."

While at Fort Abercrombie, Brown reported that some mothers "sold" their daughters to local families to work as servants. Mazetouwin "gave her youngest daughter Augusta to an English family"; in return, her mother and other siblings received money that they used to purchase food. Brown noted that "some twenty or more children have been sold at the settlement to save the parents from starvation." However, the Dakota women and the white settlers had very different ideas about the girls' service. "Mazetouwin says she did not sell Augusta but left her with the family under the understanding that she could take her again when she pleased." The white settlers, however, saw the transaction as more permanent, and her mother was "not likely to see Augusta again at least for a long time."

What began as working as a servant, however, could easily turn into rape and prostitution. Reports circulated about women who were raped and forced into prostitution at the forts and on the Crow Creek Reservation. John Williamson testified that "many of the women [were] compelled to prostitute themselves in order to enable themselves to get something to eat." David Faribault also reported similar tragedies. "I know of many such cases—women who were virtuous before they came here" were forced through starvation "to sell them[selves] for something to eat." Williamson angrily blamed U.S. soldiers and agency workers for exploiting these vulnerable women. He called the soldiers' actions reprehensible and un-Christian, saying that they "shamed themselves and the American race by their foul licentiousness." ABCFM teacher Mary Pond also charged that "the influence of the soldiers over the Indians is very bad. They . . . all went to both the Sioux and Winnebago camps for all the women and girls they could get." Of course, the soldiers had guns and power; the often starving and unarmed women had few ways to protect themselves and their daughters. Samuel Hinman summarized the women's situation at the hands of soldiers and government workers: "all is blasphemy, robbery, and wrong."

Despite this abuse, exploitation, and starvation, many of the women scraped together what little they had to help their relatives being held in Davenport. During their years of separation, women sent moccasins, clothing, blankets, and money from Crow Creek to Camp Kearney. For example, in 1864, several women sent money to their kin in Davenport. In January 1865, Crow Creek women also mailed "a supply of clothing" to their relatives there. The Protestant missionaries frequently served as their intermediaries to send and deliver money and goods. In 1865, John Williamson mailed moccasins from Crow Creek to the Davenport prisoners labeled "miscellaneous packages." This perhaps allowed the goods to skirt restrictions that barred prisoners from receiving "presents of food or clothing of any kind."

The Dakota women's devotion to caring for their kin indicates the continuation of one of their central cultural practices. "Kinship," according to anthropologist Patricia Albers, "was the primary idiom through which the Sioux . . . ordered their social relations of production, trade, war, ceremony, and recreation." No matter how distant, "people who recognize each other as kin are expected to provide assistance." Ella Deloria, a Dakota anthropologist, summarizes the importance of kinship: "The ultimate aim of Dakota life, stripped of accessories, was quite simple: one must obey kinship rules; one must be a good relative. . . . In the last analysis every other consideration was secondary — property, personal ambition, glory, good times, life itself." Their male relatives in Davenport also sought to take care of their families, as I discuss in the next chapter.

Scholar Christopher Pexa argues that continuing kinship relations in this colonial context served as a subtle but profound act of resistance. The Dakota prisoners and their families "were able to maintain, and even to extend, kinship epistemologies and so reclaimed an important basis for remembering, decolonizing, and remaking a wounded Dakota peoplehood." Patricia Albers also characterizes the continued focus on kinship as a form of resistance: "de-

spite federal attempts to undermine its role in organizing Sioux social relations, kinship persisted as a dominant medium of social integration."

The terrible conditions at Crow Creek, however, actively worked to undermine Dakota kinship relations, as well as their very survival. In January 1864,
in a private letter to his father, Samuel Brown charged government officials
with a widespread conspiracy to conceal the callous treatment of Dakota
women and their families at Crow Creek. He could not believe "that the officials at the Agency, and the soldiers and employees," failed to notice the dire
conditions. "I think it is for their interest that they have a systematic plan
to keep such inhuman conduct to themselves." He derided the officials for
caring more about "filling their pockets" than about the fact that the Dakota
"suffered so badly." He hoped that "the wrongs that have been heaped upon
these Indians since they have been removed from Minnesota, will some day
leak out and let those in higher authority in Washington see to the matter."

Although Brown never personally challenged this conspiracy of silence,
perhaps to protect his government position, missionaries who spent time on
Crow Creek openly condemned the inhumane conditions on the reservation
and demanded reform. They wrote letters to congressmen and government
officials, published criticisms in their mission presses and newspapers, and
finally, in 1865, testified before a congressional committee about conditions
on the reservation. In all their criticisms, the missionaries charged the government with actions that directly caused the deaths of hundreds of innocent
Dakota. They asked for better treatment for Dakota families and their removal to a new reservation.

Beginning in 1863 and continuing until their removal from Crow Creek in
1866, John Williamson, Edward Pond, Hugh Cunningham (another ABCFM
teacher), Samuel Hinman, and Henry Whipple publicized the treatment of
the Dakota at Crow Creek. For example, the ABCFM's *Annual Report* and its
monthly *Missionary Herald* published missionary letters verbatim that graphically recounted the harsh conditions. These letters described the reservation
as "a desolate region on the Missouri River, where it is impossible to sustain
life." The Dakota could eke out only "the barest of existence, with the pit-
tance which the United States Government has bestowed upon them." Even
after the February hunt, there was a "great scarcity of provisions, threatening starvation, much sickness, and great mortality." The ABCFM missionar-

ies also wrote letters to government officials, including the commissioner of Indian affairs, the Indian agent at Crow Creek, and the secretary of the interior, strongly criticizing conditions on the reservation. They reported that the Dakota could not grow crops, they were starving, and "more than one-fourth died in less than two years."

Reverend Samuel Hinman and Bishop Henry Whipple also published articles condemning the "deplorable . . . condition of these Indians." Whipple penned a self-proclaimed "fearless and honest letter" to the Bureau of Indian Affairs criticizing the conditions at Crow Creek. The government had "hurried" innocent women and children "up the Missouri to a desert country" where they "have been on the point of starvation." Whipple felt compelled to publicize these conditions, even though he knew "it will bring on my head a deep and bitter hatred but God knows I have tried to do my duty." Hinman even went so far as to state that if he had to permanently reside at Crow Creek, "I would never lay down the war-club while I lived."

In January 1864, Bishop Whipple openly and harshly criticized the entire bureau—using Crow Creek as a prime example—railing against the "crying evils" that "grew out of the Indian System." That April, he traveled to Washington, D.C., to meet with government officials about "the well-being of the Sioux Indians" at Crow Creek. In his meetings, he informed officials that Dakota were "dying like sheep on their reservation on the Upper Missouri, where there has been scarcely a drop of rain in two years." He demanded reform of federal Indian policy in general, as he had promoted for years. Whipple indicted "the Nation itself, for its wrongs to the Indians—wrongs not to the Sioux only, under this Administration, but wrongs to all tribes and under all administrations." Many did not agree with him, however, especially those in Minnesota. An article in the *Stillwater Messenger* accused Whipple of defending "the most degraded, savage, and beastly swine."

All the missionaries' public writings and meetings, as well as their private correspondence, indicated that they were truly appalled by the conditions at Crow Creek and sought to end the suffering, though not to the extent of giving up their own rations. However, their humanitarianism was always filtered through the lens of Christianity and "civilization," as it had been following the 1862 war. First, the missionaries argued that Dakota families deserved better conditions at Crow Creek because they had not participated in the war and many had rescued whites. The missionaries reminded the commissioner of Indian affairs that Dakota families at Crow Creek were innocent of "war crimes" and had even rescued 279 women and children during the war. Samuel Hinman noted that "it is hard to think that those who have been honorably acquitted and commended should so perish." Hinman made this same point again: the families at Crow Creek "deserve better things at the hands of the Government . . . [because] our people rescued the captive and broke the backbone of the Sioux War in Minnesota."

Second—and in the missionaries' estimation more important—many of the Crow Creek Dakota had "renounced their religion and customs of their ancestors and made a public profession of Christianity." The missionaries proudly stated that more than two hundred Dakota had joined their church at Crow Creek. However, the government's reservation policies actively worked against the Dakota's Christianization. Their poor "temporal prospects" hindered their "spiritual condition." The missionaries stated that the "physical trials" and starvation at Crow Creek "open wide the door for something that is worse . . . hunger frequently destroys the barriers against temptation." The Dakota needed to be removed from Crow Creek or they would "give up their faith." Moreover, conditions at the reservation forced the "best young men" to leave, which was "a great impediment to preparing young men for teachers and preachers." In sum, in the interests of humanity, justice, and especially Christianity, the Dakota needed to be "liberated" and placed with their families "where they can procure a comfortable living." Several historians have condemned the missionaries for their single-minded focus on conversion, which, according to Gary Roberts, "ironically made [them] as much the instrument of conquest as the soldiers who hunted down the Minnesota Sioux."

Despite the missionaries' pleas for the removal of the Dakota from Crow Creek in order to promote their salvation, the government did not take any action until 1865. Largely in response to the Sand Creek Massacre in Colorado on November 29, 1864, Congress created a special joint committee, headed by Senator James R. Doolittle of Wisconsin, to survey Indian affairs throughout the country. The seven-member "Doolittle Committee" worked for two years gathering evidence and eventually published an extensive report titled *Conditions of the Indian Tribes.* The committee members conducted some fieldwork but relied primarily on questionnaires sent to government agents, superintendents, clergymen, and army officers. On the basis of the fieldwork and surveys, Senator Doolittle wrote a ten-page summary of the committee's findings; information about individual tribes and reservations was published as a five hundred–page appendix. Doolittle's brief summation argued that the Native American population across the United States was rapidly decreasing. However, he offered few remedies to the reported problems, mainly diving into the debate about whether the Bureau of Indian Affairs should be located in either the Department of the Interior or the Department of War. He did offer one concrete suggestion—creating five inspection districts—but little else.

Crow Creek was prominently featured in the report's appendix. Doolittle placed Representative Asahel W. Hubbard of Nebraska in charge of surveying the Omaha, Yankton, Ponca, and Crow Creek agencies. Hubbard visited Crow Creek and also solicited testimony about life on the reservation from soldiers, missionaries, traders, and Dakota leaders. His investigation mainly focused on the winter of 1863–64. Each witness answered a series of questions that solicited information about crop failures, the supply run from Mankato, the distribution of spoiled supplies and unfit beef, the infamous cottonwood soup, and Dakota deaths from starvation during the first year at Crow Creek.

Wasuhiya-ye-dom's testimony was among the most damning. He charged that "it seemed as though they [government officials at Crow Creek] wanted to kill us." The testimonials from traders, missionaries, military officials, and missionaries all told of drought, crop failure, poor rations, corruption, sickness, starvation, and death. After his visit to Crow Creek and upon reading the testimonials, Representative Hubbard reported that he was very "disappointed in the appearance of these Indians." In his judgment, "their treatment, to speak of it in the mildest term, has not been humane." He suggested that "should crops upon the reservation fail another season, the good of the Indians and the interests of the government will imperatively demand their removal to some other location."

Also in 1865, General Samuel Ryan Curtis, as part of his duties to make treaties with tribes in Dakota Territory, visited Crow Creek. Like Asahel Hubbard, Curtis informed Secretary of the Interior James Harlan about the harsh conditions he witnessed on the reservation. Calling them the "poor Santee Sioux Indians," Curtis listed a litany of problems: "The Agency buildings are badly located. . . . The country is apparently too dry for producing corn, without irrigation, and irrigation can only be caused on a great expense.

. . . They are dependent on Government appropriations, which are squandered or exhausted in long and expensive transportation. . . . They live in the most temporary lodges." Despite these challenges, Curtis called Dakota "a better informed and better behaved clap of Indians than most of the tribes I have seen." He suggested that the Crow Creek Indians "should be sent below, probably near the Yankton Agency, where they can be supplied at less expense this winter, and with proper exertions, be prepared to raise a crop of corn next year." He also wanted the Davenport prisoners freed and reunited with their families to solve the extreme gender imbalance on the reservation.

Despite the harsh and unforgiving testimony published in the Doolittle report and Hubbard's and Curtis's recommendations for removal, Dakota families remained at Crow Creek until spring 1866. However, for the last nine months, life at Crow Creek improved slightly. First, while farming remained challenging—droughts and grasshoppers still plagued the region—the harvests were not complete failures as in previous years. Second, a new agent delivered goods from closer supply sources, instead of shipping them from Minnesota. John Williamson reported that during these months the "Indians were a little better supplied with provisions than the first year, though they never had enough to eat, and it was a low monotonous diet." Third, in November 1865, the federal government created a reservation for the Ho-Chunk in Nebraska, which "lessened competition for scarce resources and eliminated a source of tension." Although conditions improved relative to the first year, both the Dakota and the missionaries still demanded removal to a better location. Finally, in June 1866, officials moved the Dakota families from Crow Creek to a new reservation near Niobrara, Nebraska.

3 ✷ CAMP KEARNEY PRISON, DAVENPORT, IOWA, 1863-1866

On April 24, 1863, under heavy guard and chained together with irons, Robert Hopkins Çaske and his fellow prisoners, including at least one of his brothers, Hake (Fifth-Born Son), boarded a steamer that would transfer them from Mankato to Davenport, where they would continue their incarceration at Camp McClellan. In Iowa, the Hopkins brothers and their fellow inmates endured physical and emotional abuse from the commanding officers, the guards, and the citizens of Davenport. The prisoners lacked rations, clothing, blankets, and medical care. The cold winters and abysmal conditions led to illnesses and many deaths during their three years of confinement. And, of course, they endured separation from their Crow Creek families.

Robert, using skills that he had learned at the Lac qui Parle Mission before the war, wrote copiously to the ABCFM missionaries and to his relatives, telling them about the appalling conditions, sicknesses, abuses, and deaths at the prison. On May 3, 1864, he wrote that the prisoners lived "in great difficulty with little or no food." Later, in October, he agonized that "many of the prisoners are sick, and probably some will die." By winter, he noted that conditions had deteriorated further and worried that "some of us will probably freeze to death." Despite the cold, Robert reported that the guards "threw out all the stoves." Private military correspondence, meanwhile, may explain why the guards removed the only source of heat. The prison's commander, Brigadier General Benjamin S. Roberts, who was in charge of the Dakota prisoners for the first year, complained that "incompetent" Indians would "expose the barracks to burning as they are careless about fires." Although the guards eventually returned the stoves, there was "never enough heat."

In addition to physical suffering, Robert and the other prisoners endured humiliation from intrusive tourists who demanded to view them and from prison commanders who agreed to put them on display to entertain these tourists. Mostly, though, Robert missed his family. Throughout his imprisonment, he received news from missionary intermediaries about the terrible conditions and high number of deaths at Crow Creek, but he, of course, could do nothing to help his relatives. On May 3, 1864, he wrote, "I am very sad today. . . . They said my wife has disappeared, therefore I am heartbroken." A letter written by Sarah and her mother on April 27, 1864, explains that they had not disappeared but had traveled to Fort Abercrombie in search of provisions. This information, however, obviously had not reached Robert; indeed, he did not know his family's fate for months on end because of intermittent mail deliveries and the separation of more than six hundred miles. In the intervening time between letters, he could only imagine the worst.

Robert continuously asked the missionaries to help free him and his brother from prison so that they could return to their families. In spring 1864, Thomas Williamson interviewed Robert, who testified again that he had not killed anyone during the 1862 war. Robert stated that "he was sometime in the neighborhood of the town [New Ulm] but not near enough to take part in the fight." In early fall 1864, Stephen Riggs sent "a petition for the pardon of Robert Hopkins" to General Sibley. The petition worked. In September, Riggs announced that "Robert Hopkins has been set at Liberty. His free papers came about ten days ago."

Despite the promise of freedom, however, Robert remained at the prison for six more months. Some contemporary authors and historians have argued that he chose to remain at Camp Kearney to minister to the prisoners. This was not the case. He immediately wanted "to join his family," but unfortunately "there is no way for him to do it yet" because the government refused to pay for his transportation to Crow Creek. As he waited, Robert suffered from hunger because the prison commander declined to provide "rations or fuel for those who are released. . . . They say they get but one meal a day and sometimes a part of them get none."

Finally, in March 1865, "Robert Hopkins started after his wife" after enduring another winter in Davenport, without sufficient rations, halfway between imprisoned and free. Missionary correspondence indicates that the ABCFM finally paid some of his travel expenses and planned his route to Dakota Territory. He arrived at Crow Creek in March and met up with his brother, Hake, who had already been freed from prison. Both left to find Sarah and his remaining family members. President Andrew Johnson finally released the rest of the prisoners in spring 1866, a year after Robert had reunited with his immediate and extended family.

In April 1863, however, Robert, Hake, and the other prisoners did not know that their incarceration would last several additional years. At the time, they remained under guard at the Mankato prison, unsure about what would happen next. Winyan, a Dakota woman who accompanied the men to prison, described the effect of not knowing their fate: "we are suffering . . . we don't know where they will take us . . . and therefore my heart is very sad." Although these prisoners had been spared from hanging in December, they remained worried that they would eventually suffer the same fate. General Sibley stoked their fears, emphatically stating that the majority of prisoners should be hanged.

Despite Sibley's professed desire to carry out three hundred additional executions, officials decided instead to move the Mankato prisoners to Camp McClellan, an army barracks in Davenport built at the beginning of the Civil War as a recruiting and training post for volunteers. Once river navigation resumed in spring 1863, the Mankato prisoners would be placed aboard a steamer for transfer to Davenport. Sibley, however, attempted to keep the details of this plan secret until the last minute. Officials decided that "the utmost secrecy, caution and dispatch" should be used in the prisoners' transfer as "the determination had been freely expressed by numbers of citizens that the Indians should never leave Mankato alive." Because the steamer was scheduled to make a brief stop at Fort Snelling, officials also worried that the prisoners' kin would be inconsolable when they saw their husbands, fathers, sons, and brothers. Stephen Riggs agreed. "When it is known [their kin] have gone," he predicted, "there will be great wailing in the camp." To avoid angry citizens and distraught relatives, the Bureau of Indian Affairs circulated a false press release, which stated that the prisoners would be shipped to the Tortugas off the Gulf Coast. Officials hoped that this ruse would obscure their real plan to transfer the men to Iowa.

The ploy did not have much effect, and the plan to remove the Dakota to Iowa remained on track. On April 21, 1863, guards finally readied the prisoners for removal from Mankato. The group included 272 prisoners for transfer to Davenport and 48 acquitted prisoners who would be dropped at Fort Snelling and sent to Crow Creek with their families. In addition, 16 Dakota women who had worked as cooks and launderers at the Mankato prison and 4 children would accompany their male relatives to Iowa.

In the predawn hours of April 22, soldiers marched the chained male prisoners onto the steamer *Favorite*. Three prisoners were so ill that they had to be carried on blankets. The *Missionary Herald* reported the mournful and somber demeanor of the captives: "there is much to sadden the hearts . . . of these Indians . . . and more in their feelings of depression and gloom" as they were loaded onto the steamer. A group of soldiers and Joseph Brown, the commander of the Mankato prison, accompanied the prisoners to Davenport. Interestingly, the *Favorite* had crossed paths with Dakota people before the war. In 1861, the steamer had been used to bring tourists to view their annuity distributions. By 1863, however, the *Favorite*'s transformation into a prison steamer mirrored the public's changing perceptions of the Dakota themselves: from objects of interest to savages deserving punishment and exile.

While the prisoners' departure from Mankato went according to plan, the stop at Fort Snelling did not. An article in the *Goodhue Volunteer* described the scene: "As the boat neared the landing, Indians at the Fort discovered those on the boat, and made a simultaneous rush to the levee; but Col. Crooks had made preparations for them by standing a company of infantry on the levee, between the boat and those on the shore, so as to prevent the possibility of either escape or rescue." Guards on the *Favorite* quickly dropped off the acquitted prisoners, took on several more, and left Fort Snelling with the air "filled with their [families'] lamentations as if they mourned the dead." The *Daily Democrat and News* called the scene "peculiarly affecting."

The prisoners reached Davenport on April 25. Military authorities immediately assured the public that the prisoners would be "confined to hard labor . . . probably for life." Perhaps more than the forced labor, the Dakota prisoners feared for their lives, because most carried their death sentences with them to Iowa. At this time, President Lincoln had not officially announced whether further executions would be forthcoming. However, historians now know that after the Mankato hangings, Lincoln conducted another internal review of the trial records. Based on this assessment, he privately decided not to execute any more of the convicted Dakota men. Instead, the condemned men would remain indefinitely incarcerated with their original death sentences put on hold. The president also appeared open to missionary pleas to free some—especially Christian—men. However, Lincoln chose not to publicize his decisions because he did not want to further inflame midwesterners. Also kept in the dark were the prisoners, who lived in constant fear that the thirty-eight men hanged at Mankato were but "the first installment." Thus, as with his decision to decrease the number of hangings, Lincoln attempted to adopt a middle position. However, just as with the Mankato executions, he ultimately pleased not a public intent on revenge, not the missionaries who wanted to free at least some Christian Dakota, and certainly not the Dakota prisoners.

Lincoln's more tempered (albeit private) view was not shared by many Davenport citizens. Two days after the prisoners arrived, local newspapers, echoing the vitriolic language of the postwar Minnesota press, lamented the influx of the "bloodthirsty copperskins" and "murderers." An article in the *Daily Democrat and News* in July expressed "horror" that the government compelled the city to "harbor in our midst nearly three hundred of the red devils." The journalist complained that the "most beautiful camp in the West must be polluted by these fiends in human shape, fed and taken care of by the people they would not hesitate to murder and scalp at the first opportunity." Davenport citizens should not be "burdened forever with the worthless, cruel vagabonds." The article ended with a possible horrific solution that repeated the extreme rhetoric published in Minnesota newspapers: "The State of Minnesota offers $25 each for male Sioux scalp. We have over $50,000 invested in the article right here in Davenport, and the sooner the Government realizes on them the better satisfied will be the people." Another article also suggested extermination, proposing that the government "arm the Winnebago braves to hunt their enemies, the Sioux," thus saving the "expense" of imprisonment.

Despite the frenzied calls for vengeance that appeared in local newspapers, other Davenport citizens lined up not for revenge but to satisfy their curiosity about the prisoners. From about forty miles downriver, the *Muscatine Daily Journal* reported that a "large number of our citizens visited the boat to gratify their curiosity by a sight of the Indians." Bill Boldt, who was ten years old when the prisoners arrived, later remembered that "the folks stood here watching the Indians get off the boat. . . . I can see them marching now. The soldiers were there to guard them. When they marched them off-board, down the gang-plank they had them chained two by two. There were women, papooses and kids coming off the boat—all those over 12 or 14 years were chained. Soldiers lined up on each side and they marched them up hill through the swath that had been cut through the woods."

The public's fascination with the prisoners continued over the next week but took a decidedly macabre turn when the *Daily Democrat and News* reported that "a large number of Clinton and Cedar county folks had heard that the Indian prisoners at Camp McClellan were to be hanged . . . and went to town by the hundred." The Iowans wanted to witness the purported hangings, just like their counterparts in Minnesota who had traveled for miles to view the executions at Mankato. Instead of "seeing the lot of copperskins hung," however, the Iowans "hung their own heads and moved away satisfied that they had been slightly sold."

The observers who rushed to see the Indians viewed the prisoners as a collective. Articles and memoirs generally called them murderous savages, the Indians of Camp McClellan, or simply the Indian prisoners instead of by their individual names. In reality, however, the prisoners were quite diverse in age, sex, and the experiences that had led to their incarceration. The number of prisoners always hovered around 250 to 400. This number fluctuated due to deaths and transfers in (those captured during the government's punitive campaign against Dakota in the West) and out (the few Dakota released early to Crow Creek). In June 1864, there were 378 prisoners, including 30 women and 31 children. In June 1865, the population of the prison totaled 265: 195 men, 40 women, and 30 children. When it closed in 1866, the number of male prisoners had declined to 247, due to some early releases but mostly due to the prison's high death rate. The oldest prisoner was seventy-eight; the youngest, just fifteen. Most of the prisoners were men in their twenties and thirties (the average age was twenty-eight), which had lasting ramifications for the Dakota's economic survival and the growth of their population. The rolls listed Dakota women as prisoners, but they worked in the camp as cooks, launderers, and nurses. For example, upon the women's arrival, the camp commander assigned 10 women to cook, 4 to the laundry, and 2 to hospital duty.

At first the men, women, and children lived in a fenced-off portion of Camp McClellan. In December 1863, Major General John Pope ordered a further separation of the Dakota prisoners from the Civil War soldiers. Following Pope's orders, a line was drawn "along the west side of the wagon road that passes through Camp McClellan," and a "partition fence" was erected that "entirely separates the Indian business from the recruiting and instructing camp." At the relocated prison, now called Camp Kearney, all the Dakota lived in a small area that contained four thin rectangular buildings. The male prisoners lived in two of the buildings; one served as a hospital and housed the women and children; and the final one functioned as a guardhouse. Soldiers guarded the prisoners from atop a high fence with a walkway that surrounded the prison (figs. 9 and 10).

Stephen Riggs complained that the newly created Camp Kearney contained "housing of the most temporary kind." Indeed, military officials in Washington had ordered the buildings to be "small" and "cheap." Commander Roberts took this directive to heart and used substandard materials (especially green lumber) and shoddy construction for each of the four buildings. Because of their poor construction, the barracks had hundreds of cracks, which made them drafty and freezing during the Iowa winters. Dakota prisoner Elias Ruban commented that "it seems we are always in a terrible situation, there is never enough heat . . . [and] we don't have warm clothing." Riggs observed that the barracks "were so cold and uncomfortable that I would hardly stay two hours at a time." Moreover, the barracks were crowded: about 140 men shared a space meant for 100.

The prisoners and their families also suffered from insufficient rations. Initially, Roberts supplied the male prisoners with coffee, sugar, and other provisions, but orders from Washington discontinued these "luxuries" after their first weeks of incarceration. The male prisoners subsisted on "only such quantities of beef, salt, and corn as shall be found necessary for their health and the support of life." Likewise, the women received poor rations even though they worked at the camp. The children received even less—half the

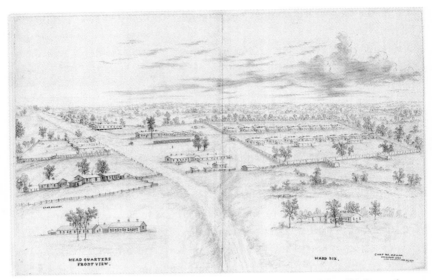

FIGURE 9. In this 1865 drawing of Camp McClellan, the "Indian Prison" is located in the upper left. Record group 92, Post and Reservation File, National Archives and Records Administration, Washington, D.C.

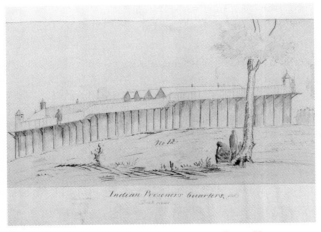

FIGURE 10. Soldiers guarded the prisoners at Camp Kearney from a raised walkway. Record group 92, Post and Reservation File, National Archives and Records Administration, Washington, D.C.

rations of an adult. At first, the guards allowed the women to supplement their own and their children's diets by gathering fruits, nuts, and vegetables outside the camp. Several farmers, however, accused them of stealing apples. Although the women protested that soldiers from Camp McClellan had stolen the apples, Roberts refused to believe them and revoked their privileges. The lack of food led to starvation among the women and children. In 1864, Stands on Earth Woman informed Riggs that she was "suffering for the lack of food" and needed "something to eat." Elias Ruban implored the missionaries to help feed the women and children, as "they are very hungry." The women and children also did not receive any clothing or blankets.

In addition to hunger and the lack of warm clothing, the Dakota children living within the confining walls of Camp Kearney were surrounded by guards and guns, which could—and inevitably did—lead to tragedy. One of the guards accidentally (at least according to a report in the *St. Cloud Democrat*) shot a little Dakota boy, between eight and ten years old, in the back of his head. The article reported that a soldier "was firing at a mark with a revolver about four in the afternoon when one of the balls glanced and hit the youth in the back of the head, inflicting a wound from which he died in a few hours." The entire camp was filled "with lamentation" due to the tragedy. Even if the boy's death was an accident, a military prison certainly was not a safe or healthy place for children.

Dangerous conditions, unheated and poorly constructed barracks, and insufficient diets led to illness, including pneumonia, smallpox, tuberculosis, and a severe eye disease that caused blindness. According to Dakota prisoner Augustin Fresneir, "there are a lot of sicknesses here . . . it is terrible here." Despite the rampant illnesses, the prisoners lacked even basic medical care. Stephen Riggs, after a visit to the prison, wrote that the "care and the surroundings are not favorable to health . . . the physician who only occasionally comes to see them wishes them all dead." Thomas Williamson reported that the sick prisoners "look very badly. The confinement and hot weather is very detrimental to their health which pleases Gen. Roberts who wishes them to die of sickness since he cannot hang them."

Twenty-seven inmates had died by December, just as their first winter in Davenport was starting. By March, the *Daily Democrat and News* reported that "the Indians confined at Camp McClellan are dying off fast. There are but about 250 left, and fifty of them are in the hospital and pest house.

Smallpox has got among them and is thinning them out rapidly." That April, eighteen more deaths were reported. When the prison finally closed in 1866, ABCFM missionaries estimated that 120 prisoners had died while incarcerated; by their estimation, about 25 percent of the total population. Given the relatively fluid nature of the number of prisoners (due to transfers in and out) as well as poor record keeping, the missionaries' percentage is difficult to confirm. Historians have offered estimates of the number of prisoners that vary from 250 to 407 men. For the purpose of discussion, if the number of prisoners is the median of these estimates (that is, about 300), and 120 died while in prison, the death rate would be much higher than the missionaries' estimate at approximately 40 percent.

The indignities continued even after death. Soldiers buried the deceased in unmarked graves just outside the prison. Bill Boldt recalled that some Iowans—including a prominent dentist—dug up the graves looking for relics, just as the Dakota's bodies had been exhumed following the hangings at Mankato. The grave robbers, however, were disappointed that "most of them [the Dakota prisoners] had been buried without anything [and] found nothing but bones." Even without the discovery of artifacts, the desecration of the graves continued for decades. In 1878, twelve years after the camp closed, members of the Davenport Academy of Natural Sciences removed several Dakota skulls from the Camp Kearney cemetery. These skulls remained part of the town's Putnam Museum of Natural History for more than a century. In 1986, the museum transferred remains in its collections to the Office of the State Archaeologist of Iowa for repatriation to the Lower Sioux Indian Community at Morton, Minnesota.

Witnessing the desecration of the graves was just one example of the abuse experienced by the prisoners. Commander Roberts stated that the men needed "to feel that they are objects of abhorrence and undergoing punishments for crimes of unexampled enormity." To achieve this goal, he implemented a series of punitive rules. First, most of the prisoners remained in chains during their first year of incarceration. Second, the prisoners were socially isolated. Roberts ordered that they could not "be visited by any parties or persons on any pretense without special authority from these headquarters." No one could "pass up on the platform or . . . hold any conversation or intercourse of any kind with them from there or elsewhere"; in other words, no one was supposed to view or speak to the prisoners. Third, the prisoners were prohibited from holding "their dances and games or amuse-ments." Finally, they were forbidden to receive "presents of food or clothing of any kind." Roberts designed each of these orders to "make [the Dakota's] confinement hourly felt as part of the retribution that is awaiting their in-human murder of men and slaughter and torture of women and children." In addition, he reminded the prisoners that they could be executed at any time. During one visit, Thomas Williamson noted that "in an interval of about 20 minutes he [Roberts] thrice repeated that if it was in his power he would have them all hung before sunset."

Most Iowans supported Commander Roberts's treatment of the Dakota prisoners. However, they challenged his decision to block citizens from view-ing the Indians. Their interest was grounded in common nineteenth-century stereotypes of Native Americans. In spring 1863, just after the Dakota's ar-rival at Camp McClellan, an article in the *Daily Democrat and News* described the prisoners as possessing "native majesty" and as "fiery . . . strong patriotic savages." Another article characterized the men as "all large and muscular, and their long black hair shines luxuriously." A journalist remembered his excitement going to view "Chief Big Eagle," as he purportedly had "a good deal of wag." Members of the public also read about the few so-called Indian princesses who lived at Camp Kearney and worked as cooks, servants, and nurses. The imprisoned daughter of Little Crow—one of the leaders of the 1862 war—received the most press coverage. She was described as a "splen-did specimen of an Indian princess," being "very agreeable in appearance—probably a decided belle among the Indian damsels. She dresses better, has finer blankets and ornaments than the rest of the females and has a really distinguished air." An article in the *Daily Democrat and News* was even more effusive in praising "Miss Crow," a "young lady of a complexion that is just a little tinged with brown, small regular features, eyes of the deepest and most melting brown, and hair jetty as a raven's wing." Miss Crow was "shy as a young gazelle" and a "pearl . . . among swine." Echoing the wording of these articles, Levi Wagoner, a resident of Davenport, planned to visit the "stalwart warriors" whom he called "models of muscular build and strength." He as-suredly wanted to see the "willowy" and "lithe" Miss Crow as well (fig. 11).

Like Levi Wagoner, numerous other Davenport residents demanded to observe these noble savages and Indian princesses. General Roberts com-plained that "strangers" constantly inundated him with requests to visit the

Little Crow's Daughters!

FIGURE 11. At least one of Little Crow's daughters lived at the Camp Kearney prison. Visitors came from far and wide to see the "Indian princess." Courtesy of the Blue Earth County Historical Society.

prison. He lamented that "the prison at Camp McClellan has become a sort of Menagerie, where all the idle and curious people [want] to congregate and amuse themselves with the antics of these savages." Stephen Riggs confirmed that whenever he visited the prison, "there were a good many white people about the doors." Indeed, Civil War recruits at Camp McClellan spent so much time viewing the Dakota prisoners that they failed to perform "their proper duties." A side trip to the prison "became a matter of course" for those passing through Davenport on steamers. Journalists traveled from Chicago and beyond "to have a few words with the fascinating Miss Crow." Even Iowa's governor, Samuel Kirkwood, and his family made a point of visiting the prison to view the "curiosities." These local citizens, soldiers, tourists, journalists, and politicians became so intrusive that Commander Roberts (reluctantly) rescinded his ban on visitors and allowed the public to stand on the platform and look down on the prisoners for two hours every afternoon except for Sunday.

While Roberts begrudgingly allowed tourists to view the Indians, Captain Robert M. Littler, the overall commander of Camp McClellan, promoted the spectacle, especially for children. On May 6, 1863, the *Daily Democrat and News* published a short paragraph about the Dakota prisoners, saying that Littler had experienced "a good deal of trouble and annoyance from repeated requests of the [city's] young folks to go in and see the Indians." To halt these frequent appeals, he promised to "make arrangements to receive all the children and the teachers of the different Sabbath Schools in the city on Saturday afternoon of this week. This will be a rare chance for the young folks, and they should turn out *en masse*." Littler allowed the young observers to stand on the raised walkway that surrounded the prison grounds and gaze down on the Dakota. Later, children from the "2nd ward school" in Davenport, who perhaps had missed Littler's arrangements, had a private opportunity to view the prisoners when guards brought some of the men to their school. Reportedly, the Indian prisoners "afforded much entertainment to some of the pupils, were an object of terror to others, and disgust to nearly all." Another boy remembered that Littler allowed the guards to bring several prisoners to his house to dine, "for the simple reason that [his father] enjoyed seeing how much they could eat." More than sixty years later, Catherine and John O'Connor still told their grandchildren stories about their childhood encounters with the "Indians of Camp McClellan."

For those children and their parents who did not have an opportunity to visit the prisoners in person, Littler suggested fitting "up a car on the 4th of July in which he will place about twenty Indians in 'full dress,' the whole surmounted by a gay bower of flowers, with a young girl perched on the top representing the 'Goddess of Liberty.'" I could not find any evidence that Littler had actually implemented this plan. His proposed float, however, would have symbolically portrayed the Dakota as defeated and under the control of the United States; the commander, perhaps not aware of the irony of this, wanted to dress the prisoners according to his specifications and place them literally under Lady Liberty. Indeed, the proposed float illustrated the prisoners' position in Davenport in general—because the Dakota had been defeated militarily and imprisoned, they had been redefined as harmless objects of fascination. Thus, Roberts's and Littler's actions were two sides of the same coin—one commander attempted to keep the Dakota subservient through punishments and restrictions, while the other used humiliation and symbolism to achieve the same goal.

Although both commanders ultimately had the same objectives, the War Department initially sided with Roberts over Littler. In June, just before the planned parade, the War Department reinstated Roberts's tourist ban, ordering Captain Littler "not to allow any visitors to enter the Indian prison . . . [instead] the prisoners be kept at hard labor as much as possible." Even this order, however, had caveats to assuage the public's desire to view the Indians; citizens would be allowed to see them "when they came down to bathe."

This restricted order, however, appears never to have been implemented. About a month later, the people's desire to see the Indians reached a new pinnacle. Two thousand people from around Ottawa, Illinois, organized a "huge excursion" to Camp Kearney to celebrate the Fourth of July. The organizers planned to hold "a pic nic on the Island, and visit Post McClellan for the purpose of seeing the Indian prisoners confined here." They "ordered thirty cars for the trip" and hoped to use "the proceeds of the excursion . . . to aid in the completion of the new Baptist church at Ottawa."

Throughout their confinement, the prisoners continued to be treated as a spectacle. However, material conditions within Camp Kearney had improved somewhat by early 1864. Most important, General Roberts left by spring 1864, turning over command to others who were somewhat less strict. For example, subsequent commanders ordered the removal of the prisoners' irons. Some prisoners were allowed to leave the camp during the day. These first expeditions, however, were limited to performing forced labor for the prison or nearby farmers. Several prisoners, along with a small guard, left Camp Kearney "to cut wood, carry up water from the river, and, in general, to do the work of the camp." By August, some prisoners also left to work on the harvest for local farmers; they received nominal wages for their labor. This practice continued over the next two years, and "during hoeing and harvest times, squads of prisoners were sent out to the farm-houses around, with or without a guard."

Over the months, the prisoners' time outside Camp Kearney extended beyond work details. Some men went out "frequently . . . even to the city." On several occasions, "a dozen Dakota men would be permitted to go out on a deer-hunting excursion, with but a single white soldier accompanying them." As they spent more time outside the prison, some of the men entertained the idea of escaping. When a group of elders, including Robert Hopkins, learned of the escape plans, they convinced the prisoners that running away "would result in their all being more severely dealt with, and perhaps they would again be reduced to chains; and, finally, that it would put off the time of their hoped-for release." They also worried about retribution against their families at Crow Creek for infractions committed within the prison. Moreover, escaped prisoners faced the daunting challenge of traveling more than six hundred miles without food, supplies, or transportation to reunite with their families. Finally, Four Lightning wrote that "the white men were maybe afraid we would try to escape, but we would never do that, because we would not leave the children [who lived in the prison] behind."

Even though the prisoners ultimately chose not to run away, not all members of the public agreed that the Dakota men should have loosened restrictions and time outside the prison. An anonymous "tax payer" wrote to the *Davenport Daily Gazette* demanding to "know why the Indian prisoners of Camp McClellan are escorted about the city by a small guard and allowed to enter private gardens and congregate before stores to the great annoyance and fright of women and children." The letter argued that Iowans already labored "in the harvest field and on the streets to furnish taxes to pay for the food of these murderers of defenseless and innocent women and children," and having their "homes invaded and disturbed by them" added insult to injury. The author insisted that the "idle prisoners . . . be placed at labor on some of the Government works and be made useful, at the same time relieving the guard at the camp for duty in the field." Another unidentified "tax payer" also complained about the "laxity in allowing the Indians to be out of camp." The prison commanders, however, reassured the public that the men were compelled to "do as much work as possible," and they left the prison only to "obtain water from the river." At all times, guards accompanied the prisoners to ensure that "nothing shall be permitted that in any way annoys our citizens."

The enmity of some members of the public illustrated the Dakota's precarious position in Davenport. Despite the 1864 reforms, the daily indignities and misery of prison life continued into 1865 and beyond. "The confinement of nearly four years, and the uncertainty which had always rested upon them like a nightmare," Stephen Riggs wrote, "had all along produced many cases of decline." They were "too much afraid to hope." After visits to Camp Kearney in September 1865 and January 1866, he commented on the prisoners' continued hardships. On the first trip, he noted that the prisoners still suffered from pulmonary consumption as well as "opthamalia," which led to blindness, and smallpox. In December 1865, he reported that the men did not have wood for fires and were "not very comfortable." In January 1866, five prisoners died, as "the waves of cold prove[d] to be waves of death to the sick." Also that year, the cheap construction came back to haunt officials when "one of the buildings in the Indian camp fell down—being pressed by a weight of snow . . . fortunately no one was injured by its fall." The remaining three barracks were "in a miserable shackley condition, and during a storm . . . one of [the remaining barracks] had to be propped, to prevent its being blown down." The crumbling buildings were just one indication of the general decrepit nature of Camp Kearney after three years of use.

Members of the public also continued to view the Dakota prisoners as human spectacles. Some even treated them as "animals" to be "petted." Nothing illustrates this better than the horse-versus-Indian races held at a local racetrack in Muscatine in October 1865. Local newspapers, such as the *Davenport Daily Gazette*, enticed their readers to attend, noting that "it would be *very* funny to see a half-naked human trying to outrun a beast." The races would be "excellent" and "lots of fun." The *Daily Davenport Democrat* also publicized the "exciting" "Indians vs. Horses" races. During the two days of competition, guards transported several prisoners to the racecourse and assigned them stereotyped names in English, including Deerfoot and Fleetwing. For a purse of $1,000, the Dakota racers ran a little over four miles, while racehorses brought in from Chicago covered eight miles at the same time. A series of mile-long man-versus-horse races were also run with prizes of $500, $100, and $50. Spectators watched a horse win the longer race, but Dakota runners won some of the shorter contests. While the prize money was not insignificant, no amount of money could compensate for the fact that such races exploited the Dakota for entertainment. Even the *Davenport Daily Gazette* later questioned the morality of the races. An editorial in the *Gazette* criticized its rival paper, the *Democrat*, for calling the races excellent. While "there is some excuse for trying the speed . . . of horses," the article chided, there is "none for matching a man against a brute." The *Daily Davenport Democrat* responded by defending the races as "dignified" and an "excellent sport."

While spectators may have enjoyed watching the Indian-horse races, they did not want Dakota living among them. In March 1865, articles appeared with increasing frequency in the Davenport press complaining about Indians "lurking" and "prowling around their houses." This spike in complaints corresponded with the months when several prisoners, including Robert Hopkins, had been freed but could not afford to travel to Crow Creek. Residents complained about "Indian depredations" and called the soldiers to task for not watching over the freed prisoners. They demanded that Captain George E. Judd, the commander of Camp Kearney at the time, "give the matter prompt attention, and save the people much anxiety and some little ammunition." After both the guards and local citizens became "a little sassy," Judd called a public meeting on March 22, 1865, to "consider the best method of refuting the false charges . . . of negligence of duty as guards over the Indians." At the meeting, the guards defended the released Indian prisoners. They argued that "the popular prejudice existing against them [the Indians] is unjust, and unworthy of an enlightened and Christian people." Despite this, articles continued to protest the sight of Dakota men walking freely around town.

Throughout their time at Camp Kearney, the prisoners held a strange in-between status for Davenport citizens. On the one hand, the *Daily Davenport Democrat* called them "Indians with the Indian taken out of them." For the most part, Iowans no longer feared Dakota; they saw them as defeated, which rendered them relatively harmless. On the other hand, the prisoners were still not entirely "civilized," which made them exciting to watch. Outside of the races and parades, however, most members of the public agreed that the Dakota men needed to remain in prison. They certainly did not want to encounter Indians around their stores or near their homes.

Whether members of the public feared or were fascinated by them, most stereotyped them as Indians, not as individuals with their own stories, families, and personalities. The prisoners were princesses, savages, fascinating entertainment, or nuisances, not fathers, brothers, sons, or daughters like Robert Hopkins, Augustin Fresneir, or Winyan. These continuing traumas led to "a feeling of depression and gloom" that rested, "like a dark cloud, upon many of them." A Dakota prisoner named Frost wrote a letter memorializing the family members he had lost since he had been imprisoned at Mankato. His story was just one of many: "Since they put me in prison, from that time, I am very sad every day. You will hear about what saddens me. At the place called Black Bank [near Mankato] one of my younger brothers died. Then they also hung one of my cousins by breaking his head off. Also at the same place they killed three Dakota children. . . . Then at the mouth of the Minnesota River, a child of mine died. And from the time we came to this land, my older brother, Walks among the Clouds, died. And one of my uncles died. My father's brother and also my brother-in-law died, his name was Kills Thunder. Those three relatives of mine died here, also six more relatives died—it is so. My brother, I am alive here with only one brother, therefore, every day my heart is very sorrowful."

Although nothing could compensate for his loss of kin, Frost and the other prisoners fought to take care of their remaining relatives despite their incarceration. Like their mothers, sisters, and wives at Crow Creek, the prisoners attempted to fulfill their traditional kinship obligations to their *tiospaye*, their extended family. Beginning with their arrival in Davenport, they had noted the public's fascination with them. By 1864, they had taken full advantage of this fascination by selling handmade items to the public. Throughout the second half of their confinement, they were allowed to gather such materials as shells, wood, feathers, and stones during their expeditions outside Camp Kearney. The women and children living at the prison also collected shells and other materials from the banks of the Mississippi. The prisoners used these supplies to establish "a brisk business in making finger rings from clam shells." In September 1864, Stephen Riggs reported, "every one [was] busy

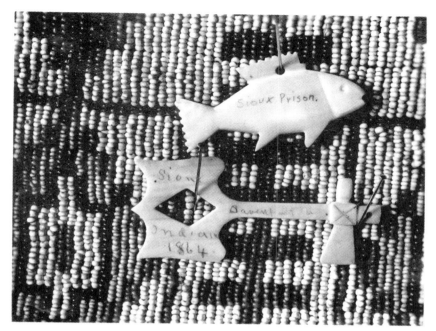

FIGURE 12. Dakota prisoners at Camp Kearney made and sold items to the public in order to raise money to help themselves and their kin. These items were made in 1864. Hauberg (John Henry) Papers, Special Collections, Augustana College.

making rings, crosses . . . watch chains, etc. They have presented me with about fifty rings, a dozen hatchets, and a few fish, and also a couple of large birds." The prisoners then added moccasins, beadwork, crosses, and "other ornaments" to their repertoire (fig. 12). They were so industrious that they continued their production on the Sabbath, leading to a strong rebuke from staunch Presbyterian Thomas Williamson, who demanded rest on Sundays, just as his son at Crow Creek had enforced rest on the Sabbath during the winter buffalo hunt. The prisoners, however, ignored Williamson's appeals and continued to manufacture their goods.

The prisoners also made bows and arrows, which appealed to little boys. Boys clamored for their parents to buy them "Indian bows and arrows," which sold for "four bits a piece." Fifty years later, J. Ed Kuehl still remembered giving some of the Dakota men hickory saplings from his father's woodpile so that they could make him bows and arrows. An article in the *Daily Daven-*

port Democrat, however, cautioned parents, noting a huge increase in injuries among little boys who shot out their eyes with the "immensely popular" Indian bows and arrows.

The prisoners expanded their range of customers to include returning Civil War soldiers, many of whom were flush with cash. Stephen Riggs reported that "the Indians here are in possession of more money than at any time previous when I have been here. Many Iowa soldiers are returning and have plenty of money, which makes quite a demand for their trinkets." The prisoners even sold their goods to "the soldiers who guard them." The ABCFM missionaries extended the prisoners' market beyond Iowa. After a brief visit to the prison, Alfred Riggs, Stephen Riggs's son, received "a quantity of rings . . . for the sale of the prisoners" that he likely sold in Chicago, where he attended seminary school. During a trip to Washington, D.C., Stephen Riggs promised to "scatter [the Dakota ornaments] along my path in the East."

While the missionaries frequently sold their goods, at times the prisoners made the sales themselves. These transactions, however, were often humiliating. For example, a journalist climbed atop the fence surrounding Camp Kearney to view the Dakota prisoners. As he took notes on the spectacle below, he dropped his pencil into the prison yard. He tied a string to his handkerchief and lowered it, yelling at the prisoners to return his pencil. After sending it up, several prisoners used this system to deliver "two or three purchases which they fastened to the line." In return, the observers "threw postage currency to them." Although the journalist reported that the prisoners "enjoyed this" and "showed delight," this was likely far from the truth. Certainly the prisoners took every opportunity to sell their items. However, as in this particular example, the buyers treated them as less than human when they gazed down at them, took notes on them, and eventually tossed a few coins into their "pen."

Not everyone supported sales of the prisoners' goods. One Davenport citizen "wondered at the eagerness with which they were sought. We would receive none of them from such bloody hands." Another article labeled the sales "an abomination." The author complained about "five or six great, ugly, good for nothing Indians loitering about town peddling bows and arrows, with a smart, active white man to guard them." The cost of the guards was too expensive, and the prisoners should be "banished beyond the pale of civilization."

Those who spoke out against the prisoners' goods were in the minority, however, and some citizens even took it upon themselves to hire prisoners to perform "Indian dances." Stephen Riggs noted that the prison sutler, "for the purposes of making money," hired several Dakota prisoners to dance in the camp center. He ordered them "to dance at different places, and four or five different times, for the amusement of the white people." For their efforts, the sutler "furnished them food and drink and paid them $2 each." In September 1865, "the soldiers persuaded Antoine Leblanc to get up a dance. In this there was some twelve engaged." In December, "Arnold the settler" hired a "party of the young men to dance Indian dances at the County Fair." Missionaries like Riggs railed against these dances, not because the sutler, the soldiers, and the settlers exploited the Dakota—which they did—but because Indians should not participate in such "savage displays." Certainly the settlers used the Dakota for their own gain and amusement; as prisoners, the men could hardly refuse. Still, the Dakota added the compensation they received from the dances to the profits they made from the sale of ornaments, bows and arrows, and other items.

Compensation aside, the prisoners "said very frankly that they liked to dance—they had grown up with the love of dancing." These hired dances gave them time outside the prison and allowed them to perform something that had formerly been forbidden, especially under Commander Roberts. Interestingly and likely unknown to the public, the prisoners may also have used the dances as a way to help the sick. When "Arnold the settler" hired the young men to dance at the county fair, the "'wapiyapi' [medicine man] led the dance to help the sick left behind at the prison." Upon questioning by Stephen Riggs, the dancer defended his choice of dance, stating that it "was right to heal the sick and to keep men from dying." Thus, the dance can be viewed from multiple perspectives. The sutler, soldiers, Arnold, and county fair participants were entertained by it; as a Protestant missionary, Stephen Riggs derided the dancers for publicly exhibiting "superstition" and "heathenism." The dancers themselves, however, may have viewed their dance as a way to save the lives of their fellow prisoners.

Wamditanka (Jerome Big Eagle) and perhaps other prisoners as well also insisted on payment for another request: standing or sitting for a portrait. W. W. Hathaway, the assistant commissary at the prison, wanted to take a formal portrait of Wamditanka dressed in his "Indian clothing." According to an article in the *Davenport Weekly Democrat*, "Big Eagle put on all his finery and paraphernalia and we went down to the studio of a photographer. . . . Everything went well until we neared the place when Big Eagle began to remove his finery. We asked him what the trouble was and he said he would not pose unless we paid him $15," approximately $215 today (fig. 13). According to historian Stephanie Pratt, in addition to asking for payment, Wamditanka transformed the portrait into "a means of self-expression and self-representation." In the photograph, he wore six eagle feathers and held a gunstock club (although the blade had been removed), which signified his importance as a warrior. He posed without a gun, thus insisting "on a more Native based understanding of warfare and indigenous signification systems." On several different levels, Wamditanka made the best of a situation that at first glance seemed only to stereotype him. However, the photographer eventually came out ahead; once Wamditanka received his payment, the store profited by selling his image, even running advertisements in local papers offering "Photographs of 'Big Eagle,' an Indian brave" for sale.

Even if the photographer ultimately profited from Wamditanka's image, the amount of money collected from all these sources was quite substantial. Compensation for dances and photographs tended to bring in one-time payments. Sales of the handmade items, however, were especially lucrative. Forays into Davenport to sell them could earn as much as $80 to $100 a week — $1,150 to $1,440 today — and sometimes more. For example, "in the last week of their imprisonment, the [prisoners] worked in real earnest, making bows and arrows, which the women and boys took down to the town to sell." By Saturday, they had raised $80. Another week netted them nearly $90 ($1,300). In one month, Stephen Riggs reported, the prisoners raised more than $230 ($3,300) of "their own money." Their profits were quite large for the time; for example, in 1860 a farmhand in Iowa earned approximately $13.18 a month; a day laborer, only $.99 a day. As another point of comparison, the ABCFM missionaries received salaries of $400 to $500 a year, approximately $30 to $40 a month.

These extensive funds helped the prisoners survive their confinement. Although conditions had improved somewhat after 1863, inmates at Camp Kearney still lacked blankets, clothing, and food. The money they raised helped fill some of these gaps. At times the prisoners shopped for themselves, although some members of the public complained about this. It was

FIGURE 13. Wamditanka (Jerome Big Eagle) asked for and received payment for this portrait and staged the image himself. Courtesy of the Minnesota Historical Society.

easier, then, to have intermediaries, especially Protestant missionaries, make purchases for them. In June 1864, Thomas Williamson wrote that he spent "four to five or six hours a week in going to the city and making purchases for them." Over the months, Williamson used the Dakota's money to purchase spectacles, clothing, blankets, "light" (one would assume lanterns), and other "sundries." He also bought them "all the bread they eat, as Government only furnishes them with meat and corn, or cornmeal." It appears that Williamson shopped not for individuals but for the larger prison community, who then shared the food and goods.

Missionaries like Williamson and Riggs certainly knew how much money the prisoners made through their sales. In 1865, Stephen Riggs decided that the ABCFM should benefit as well. "In this state of their finances, I thought it best to put the New Bibles on sale" for a dollar or two each. After making his rounds at the prison and tallying the number of Bibles purchased, Riggs called his sale "a perfect success," raising a total of fifty dollars. However, the prisoners may have purchased the Bibles for a different reason; when they handed over their money, the men informed Riggs that they longed "to be released. They want exceedingly to get back to their people."

The prisoners also attempted to help their kin by sending supplies and money, just as their relatives sent them goods and money in return. In 1865, several prisoners mailed their relatives at Crow Creek "a supply of clothing." A prisoner called Joe Allord sent twenty dollars to his wife in 1864. Another prisoner entrusted Thomas Williamson to give ten dollars to his family. When John Williamson visited Davenport, he reported that a "man gave me a blanket and coat for his brother" at Crow Creek.

This system, however, would have broken down without the assistance of the Protestant missionaries. The missionaries sold the prisoners' products, purchased goods for them with the proceeds, and sent money between their missions in Iowa and Dakota Territory. Of course, the missionaries did not plan to serve as economic intermediaries; they came to Davenport to proselytize, as illustrated by Riggs's Bible sales. Indeed, throughout these years, a rotating group of ABCFM and Episcopalian missionaries attempted to convert the prisoners to Christianity. The elderly Thomas Williamson traveled to Davenport directly after the prisoners' transfer from Mankato and remained near Camp Kearney for most of the next two years. Stephen Riggs visited the prison in 1863 and 1864 and relieved Williamson at the end of June 1865.

Alfred Riggs spent several weeks in Davenport attempting to conduct singing classes; John Williamson left his station at Crow Creek twice to visit the prison. Episcopalian Samuel Hinman also visited the prisoners, although he never stayed long. Likewise, Bishop Henry Whipple spent little time at the prison due to illness, although he did write to the prisoners.

While the missionaries' goal was conversion, the press, prison officials, and members of the public accused them of working to release all the prisoners. This broad characterization, however, was untrue. The missionaries were actually divided over who and how many of the prisoners should be released. Thomas Williamson, for example, supported the release of most—if not all— of the prisoners throughout his time in Davenport, while Riggs and Whipple favored freeing only a few select Christian Dakota. Even Williamson, however, touted the prisoners' adoption of Christianity in advocating for their release. On April 27, 1864, he wrote to President Lincoln listing six reasons why the Davenport prisoners should be released. His first three points reiterated common themes that the missionaries had stressed since 1862: many of the prisoners had rescued settlers during the war; they had already been punished enough; and they (and their families) had lost everything when they had been driven from Minnesota. In addition, he argued that the men should be freed for religious reasons, because "most of these prisoners are Christians and members of the Christian church." He proudly reported that most of the Dakota prisoners had converted to Christianity either before or during their time at Camp Kearney.

Thomas Williamson worried that conditions within the prison might cause these converts to forsake their newfound faith. He complained that the amount of work required by the Camp Kearney commander left the prisoners little time for schooling or worship. Because they were required "to do so much of the labor around the camp, the facilities for teaching them are not quite as good as they were last year." The prison guards also kept the men and women "at work during meeting time." Another time, several men could not come to meetings because they were "being kept as servants by the officers and soldiers of the camp." The immorality of such actions aside, Williamson worried that the prison environment clearly did not support a continued acceptance of Christianity. As at Crow Creek, Camp Kearney's poor material conditions and the constant hard work hindered the Dakota's "spiritual condition."

Williamson's criticisms and efforts to free the prisoners angered Commander Roberts. In July 1863, Roberts banned him from the prison. Roberts angrily claimed that Williamson indoctrinated the prisoners "with the ideas that they are not guilty of any atrocities usual in Indian wars." He also accused Williamson of being "insubordinate and untruthful." For these "crimes," Roberts ordered that "the intercourse of Rev. Thomas S. Williamson with the Indians is unauthorized by any authority." Roberts also banned Alfred Riggs for trying to teach singing to the prisoners. Riggs complained bitterly that Roberts "refused utterly to let me in" because "the prisoners were to be allowed no amusements." Samuel Hinman reported that the commander's decision was "very generally approved [of] by the people."

The ABCFM missionaries and its governing board flew into action to overturn the ban. Alfred Riggs published several articles in East Coast newspapers denouncing Roberts. An article filled with hyperbole published in the *Annual Report of the ABCFM* called Roberts's actions "an offense against Christianity and humanity of the age." The ABCFM's board of directors sent a strongly worded letter to "Washington for a reversal of the order." Following the evangelical backlash as well as Stephen Riggs's appeal to General Sibley to reverse the order, Roberts begrudgingly allowed Williamson access to the prison.

Despite his confrontation with Roberts, Williamson continued to advocate for the prisoners' release. In 1864, he received ABCFM funds to travel to Washington, D.C., to speak in person with President Lincoln. Using some of their funds to collectively fight for their freedom, the prisoners contributed eighty dollars to help defray the cost of his trip. That March, Williamson arrived in Washington. He initially failed to make any progress, reporting that he had "been here almost two weeks and have as yet effected very little." When he finally met with the commissioner of Indian affairs, William Dole, and President Lincoln, he asked for the immediate release of at least one-third of the prisoners as well as an investigation into all the prisoners' trials. Although Williamson ultimately failed to obtain the release of the number of prisoners he had requested, Lincoln issued an order pardoning twenty-five, including Robert Hopkins's brother. He also promised Williamson that "others would be set at liberty, at a no distant day."

Williamson's efforts to free the prisoners, however, made him an outlier even among Protestant missionaries. Stephen Riggs admitted that "he and

Dr. Williamson differed considerably on the question of criminality in the condemned Dakotas." Williamson thought that they should all be freed, but in "this respect I am satisfied he was mistaken." Riggs frequently admonished Williamson for his plan to free all the prisoners, lecturing him that it did "not strike me favorably." He called his colleague's plan "impracticable," because it would free convicted murderers, and "convicts don't have the privilege of living with their families." Likewise, while Williamson was in Washington, Bishop Whipple refused to support his efforts to free the prisoners. According to Williamson, "Bishop Whipple told me that while he sympathized with me in my object of getting the prisoners released he thought it would be better for me to prosecute it myself without him taking part in it or even making known that he was desirous of . . . the same thing."

While Williamson made his rounds in Washington, Riggs continued his own fight for the release of a small number of Christian Dakota. In spring 1864, he wrote numerous letters to General Sibley asking for the release of "E-yo-jan-jan, Ta-ho-hpe-wa-kan, Ta-pay-ta-tan-ka, and Wee-yoo-ha" — all Christians who had rescued whites during the war. Sibley granted the release of these four prisoners. Riggs also successfully advocated for the release of Robert Hopkins that fall.

Although Riggs, Williamson, Hinman, and Whipple differed in their ideas about who should be freed, members of the public and press treated them all the same, derisively calling them friends of the Indians. Samuel Hinman wrote that because he supported Dakota, he was "persecuted and almost ashamed to walk the streets." He promised, however, that "God helping me I will never give up till I have made my point." One time, "some white roughs" even beat Hinman "until he was insensible" because he supported the prisoners. Bishop Whipple also stated that he was "bitterly abused" for being "an Indian sympathizer." Although he knew that the "Indian officials resented [his] interference," he promised to continue his fight for justice even if it "brought much hostility upon himself." In addition to his conflict with Commander Roberts, Thomas Williamson also antagonized the *St. Paul Press*. The newspaper "was put into quite an agony the other day on hearing that efforts were being made to . . . [free] the prisoners at Davenport." A military commander criticized the missionaries for obtaining the release of "some of the greatest scamps" from Davenport merely "because previous to the outbreak, [they] had occupied a small corner in the church." Of course, the missionaries' troubles in no way equaled those of Dakota, a point noticeably absent in descriptions of their often self-proclaimed persecution. That said, the missionaries faced hostility from the press, government officials, and prison commanders, who viewed them as working to free all the prisoners.

Certainly, the criticism faced by the missionaries indicated a larger public disdain for the Dakota prisoners. This opposition, as well as Lincoln's assassination, kept the prisoners confined to Camp Kearney until 1866. In 1864, President Lincoln had assured Williamson that all the prisoners would be released soon. The president's assassination on April 14, 1865, put this promise on hold. Some of the prisoners lamented Lincoln's death; at least he had kept the majority of them from the gallows before and after they arrived in Davenport and had made a vague promise of imminent release. Moses Many Lightning, for example, worried that without Lincoln the cavalry soldiers might kill them. While the president had mainly ignored them after their removal from Minnesota—partially because of the Civil War and partially because presidents generally delegated Indian affairs to federal and local officials— the prisoners knew that things could always get worse. Although President Andrew Johnson ultimately stayed their execution, he ignored the prisoners for another year, leading to "the bitterness of 'hope deferred.'" In the meantime, the prisoners and their kin continued to work to survive, even if survival involved adopting or adapting to new ways or forming further conflicted alliances with Protestant missionaries.

4 * RESILIENCE, RESISTANCE, AND SURVIVAL: LITERACY

In the three years following the war, the separated Hopkins family struggled to survive. Whether in prison or on the reservation, the Hopkins family—and many others—enlisted the ABCFM and Episcopalian missionaries to help them obtain food and supplies; they also used them as intermediaries to fight for their freedom. In addition, many appropriated missionary-taught literacy as a way—although imperfect—to maintain kinship ties. Robert and Sarah wrote letters to each other to help bridge the hundreds of miles between Camp Kearney and Crow Creek. Robert also wrote letters to the missionaries asking them to help him return to his family. After 1862, hundreds of other Dakota also wanted to use literacy to help themselves and their kin, and they turned to Robert, Sarah, and other literate Dakota to teach them to read and write in their own language, for their own uses. This indicated a major shift from the prewar years, when the majority of Dakota had rejected both English and literacy as tools and symbols of missionary and government oppression.

In the years before the war, Protestant missionaries had attempted to teach Dakota men, women, and children to read in their own language in order to promote conversion. Members of the extended Hopkins family were some of their star pupils. Robert, Sarah, Catherine Totidutawin, Lorenzo Lawrence, Joseph Kawanke, and young Samuel all learned to read and write in the Dakota language at the ABCFM mission schools. Indeed, the ABCFM missionaries touted Catherine Totidutawin as the first Dakota woman to learn to read. In the 1840s, Catherine Totidutawin even sent her older son, Lorenzo Lawrence, to Ohio for a year (although she was told it would be only a few months) to learn "American customs and language." In 1856, Robert, Joseph Kawanke, Lorenzo Lawrence, and several others joined the Hazelwood Republic, a community established by Stephen Riggs and a group of "civilized" Dakota that focused on farming, Christian worship, and literacy. The Dakota founders, with Riggs's input, even wrote and published a constitution in the Dakota language. Although members of the small republic were some of the few Dakota who had learned to read and write in their own language prior to the war, only Lorenzo Lawrence could fluently speak, read, and write in both English and Dakota.

Following the war, when hundreds of Dakota desired lessons in reading and writing from literate Dakota, Robert took the lead in establishing schools at the Mankato and Camp Kearney prisons. At Crow Creek, women like Sarah informally taught both the young and the elders how to read and write in the Dakota language. Samuel attended the ABCFM mission school on the reservation. Dakota of all ages clamored for reading and writing lessons to help bridge the separation created by imprisonment and exile. The Presbyterian and Episcopalian missionaries supplied religious reading materials, slates, chalk, and paper and ink, but Dakota teachers provided most of the instruction, especially at Mankato, Fort Snelling, and Camp Kearney.

Historians have debated whether adopting literacy helped or harmed Native American peoples like the Hopkins family. On the negative side, some historians have argued that literacy destroyed oral traditions. John Peacock, for example, correctly points out that literacy "was ultimately intended by missionaries to destroy Dakota oral culture." By translating the Dakota's oral language into written form, the missionaries intended "first to own and then to disown the Dakota language." Others have offered a more positive evaluation of native literacy. While agreeing with Peacock that the missionaries wanted to destroy oral culture, these historians note that often there was a disconnect between what the missionaries intended and what actually happened. Some Native Americans appropriated literacy to achieve their own goals. In these cases, literacy became a tool of empowerment rather than oppression. The Dakota's adoption of literacy in the postwar years provides evidence for this second interpretation: many Dakota did not reject oral tradition as much as they added another form of communication to help them survive imprisonment and separation. As Gwen Westerman asserts, the Dakota's postwar literacy is "a testament to their ability to adapt and to survive."

This is not to say, however, that literacy did not bring problems. Government officials criticized several aspects of Dakota literacy. Those in charge of Indian policy deemed native languages inferior and uncivilized; English was the language of civilization. This meant that federal officials demanded that all instruction take place in English. While a handful of Dakota could read and write in English, the vast majority of literate Dakota—like most members of the Hopkins family—could read and write only in the Dakota language. Furthermore, federal officials worried that literate Dakota might use their skills to plan further rebellions or escape from Camp Kearney. This fear led government officials and the Protestant missionaries to monitor and censor the Dakota letters. Missionaries may even have informed government and military officials about the location of Indian camps in Dakota Territory based on letters they read from their congregants.

Before the war, the missionaries certainly did not foresee themselves becoming embroiled in a debate over literacy, censorship, and how Dakota chose to use literacy. Indeed, beginning in the mid-1800s, the ABCFM and Episcopalian missionaries had established schools at each of their stations solely to promote conversion to Christianity. As Rufus Anderson, one of the most important ABCFM theorists, noted, the object of schools was "first, the conversion of pupils and secondly, the procuring of native Christian helpers." In every instance, ABCFM mission schools were "always subordinate to the preaching of the gospel." Missionaries were exhorted to "labor and expend money in educating . . . only with reference to the extension and establishment of vital Christianity." In his instructions to Samuel Hinman, Bishop Henry Whipple ordered him to gather Dakota children "into a day-school, where they should have Christian teaching." Reverend Hinman confirmed that his "entire and only work is to preach the gospel to the heathen, and the sole object of this work is that these heathen be convinced of sin, converted, and finally saved through Christ."

The schools' curriculum focused primarily on literacy because the missionaries believed that the ability to read and write directly promoted conversion. Steffi Dippold, in her work on Wampanoag literacy in the colonial period, comments that orthodox Protestant missionaries believed that "spiritual rebirth . . . required alphabetic literacy." If Indians were "to be able to individually encounter the gospel of salvation," they "needed to learn how to read." Similarly, in her study of Tsimshian Christians, Susan Neylan argues that the missionaries' "central focus on the Bible resulted in a heavy emphasis on the importance of literacy." The missionaries proselytizing to the Dakota fully embraced this long-standing, widely accepted philosophy, affirming that students "only needed a Bible and the ability to read its pages to realize that its life-saving truth came directly from God." This meant that the missionaries viewed literacy as a means to achieve a religious end, not as a goal in and of itself.

Surprisingly, given their focus on religious conversion and "civilization," both the ABCFM and Episcopalian missionaries taught students to read in the Dakota language rather than in English. They argued that teaching literacy in English was a difficult, very slow process because students needed first to learn an entirely new language. Because speed was of the essence to promote conversion, the missionaries needed to teach them to read in Dakota, thus eliminating the time needed to study English. Alfred Riggs summarized the importance of teaching in Dakota: "It has been our belief that to reach the people at large you must get to them through their own language."

To teach literacy in Dakota, the missionaries needed to translate the Dakota's oral language into a written one. In the mid-1830s, ABCFM missionaries Samuel and Gideon Pond created the Pond alphabet, based on the Roman alphabet. They first linked all vowels in the Dakota language, as well as most consonant sounds, with a corresponding letter in the English alphabet. However, several Dakota sounds were unknown in English and did not correspond to any letter. Because oral Dakota did not use the letters *c, f, g, j, r, v,* and *x,* the Pond brothers assigned these letters to unique Dakota sounds. For instance, they used *c, j,* and *x* to represent *ch, zh,* and *sh,* respectively.

After the Ponds created the alphabet, the ABCFM missionaries worked tirelessly to translate and publish religious texts in Dakota (fig. 14). From 1836 to 1860, they collectively published a dictionary containing more than 15,000 words, classroom materials for children, portions of the Bible, and hundreds of hymns. The translation process continued into the second half of the nineteenth century and eventually comprised the entire Bible (1879) and numerous other religious texts. Examples of these works include the *Dakota Spell-*

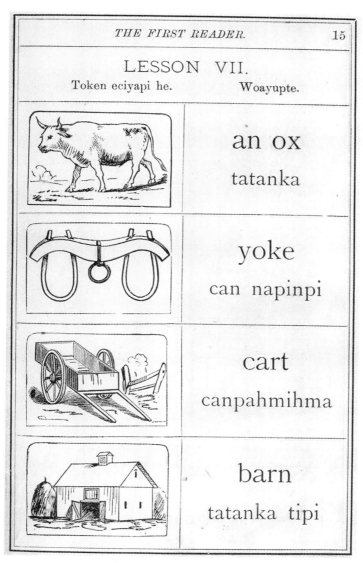

LESSON VII.

Token eciyapi he.   Woayupte.

an ox

tatanka

yoke

can napinpi

cart

canpahmihma

barn

tatanka tipi

FIGURE 14. This page from Stephen Riggs's *Model First Reader—Wayawa Tokaheya* illustrates the way that the missionaries linked Dakota words with images of objects they considered to be "civilized," such as an ox (*tatanka*) or a barn (*tatanka tipi*). Courtesy of Augustana University, Center for Western Studies.

ing Book (1836), *The Dakota First Reading Book* (1839), the third chapters of Proverbs and Daniel (1839), *The Second Dakota Reading Book: Consisting of Stories from the Old Testament* (1842), *Wowapi Mitawa* (1842), the Acts of the Apostles, the Epistles of Paul with the Revelation (1843), *Grammar and Dictionary of the Dakota Language* (1852), *The Pilgrim's Progress* (1858), *Dakota Odowan* (1868, comprising 113 hymns), and *Model First Reader—Wayawa Tokaheya* (1873). Mission teachers primarily used *Dakota ABC Wowapi* (1866) to teach basic literacy. The ABCFM missionaries complained that the Episcopalians relied on their translations throughout the 1860s. Eventually, however, Samuel Hinman learned enough of the Dakota language to translate and publish the Episcopal Book of Common Prayer, its catechism, and a hymnal.

Despite the availability of reading materials in the Dakota language, very few students attended the mission schools before the war. Both ABCFM and Episcopalian missionaries sent their national boards monthly tallies of the number of students. These numbers are tricky to interpret, however, because the missionaries tended to highlight their total attendance rather than the students' daily attendance. The overall figures included those students who attended a mission school for a day or two and never returned; the missionaries also counted students who came for longer periods but then left for months to hunt with their families. Thus, the daily attendance was almost always lower than the total count. Even if the exaggerated numbers are used, however, school attendance was quite low. For example, in 1862, just prior to the war, the ABCFM claimed to have fifty students enrolled at the Yellow Medicine school, but their average attendance "scarcely exceeded sixteen." The Hazelwood boarding school had only eighteen pupils, while the Lower Sioux Agency did not have an ABCFM school. Bishop Whipple claimed to have fifty students in his newly established school on the Lower Agency but did not provide average attendance records.

Clearly, by the missionaries' own numbers, most Dakota rejected the ABCFM and Episcopalian mission schools before the war. Surprisingly, given their desire to promote "civilization" among the Indians, most government officials also criticized the mission schools. Most important, officials disliked the missionaries' decision to teach in the Dakota language using translated texts. Government administrators called Indian languages (including Dakota) childish and incapable of expressing abstract ideas. English was the language of civilization. As such, literacy must be taught entirely in English.

One official lectured that "their barbarous dialects should be blotted out and the English language substituted." This English-only policy would reach its apex in the government boarding schools of the late nineteenth and early twentieth centuries.

Like government officials, the postwar press also depicted the Dakota's language as inferior. Iowa and Minnesota newspaper articles printed invented quotations from Dakota warriors that characterized their language skills as primitive; the words and sounds attributed to Dakota also stereotyped them as unintelligent. For example, after the Mankato hangings, an article published in the *St. Cloud Democrat* reduced the last words of those executed to a series of odd, meaningless vocalizations—"boo, woo, woo, woo"—which "hit the ears of the spectators as a noise like the breaking loose of Pandemonium." At Camp Kearney, an "old chief" gave a speech to a visiting general. The *Davenport Daily Gazette* sarcastically printed "a full copy of the speech," which consisted solely of three grunts—"Ugh, ugh, ugh." Several articles also portrayed the Dakota's attempts to speak English as broken and simplistic. An article in the *Daily Democrat and News* quoted a "big Injun" as saying, "I jun lost!" But, recovering himself, he struck "his breast," grunting, "No, Injun not lost . . . Injun here!" Commander Benjamin Roberts condescendingly spoke to the prisoners using this same broken English, gruffly lecturing, "Ingin no work. Ingin no eat." In sum, the press and some military commanders depicted Dakota as a highly infantile language unworthy of translation into written form. Moreover, Dakota men and women probably could never learn to read or write in English, because their attempts to speak a "civilized" language resulted in ungrammatical utterances.

Ironically, given the government's and the public's widespread acceptance of the supposed inferiority of the Dakota language and their assumed inability to learn English, some government officials nonetheless worried that Dakota men and women might use both of these skills to organize further resistance. First, writers could send encoded letters in the Dakota language to their relatives planning raids or military campaigns. The agent at Crow Creek was concerned that letters written in Dakota might contain "secret communication" that would induce the women at Crow Creek to "go off and join [the hostiles]." Adjunct General Nathaniel B. Baker (in charge of raising militia in Iowa) also complained that the "convicted Indians are in constant communication with their tribes," which allegedly allowed them to orchestrate raids on the Minnesota frontier from prison. Second, the few Dakota who could read English (like Lorenzo Lawrence) might learn of planned military actions from English-language newspapers. General Alfred Sully, in his punitive campaigns following the war, could not figure out how some encampments knew about his troop movements in advance. Remembering that his plans had been published in several Iowa and Minnesota newspapers, he wondered whether these papers had "found their way [to the Dakota] . . . and thus notice be given to the Indians to be on the lookout?"

While the government's fear that Dakota would use literacy as a military tool was by and large speculation, one letter has been found that validates this concern; potentially more exist as well. In 1866, Major Joseph Brown received a letter from the Red River Camp during the volatile period of military expeditions against Dakota. Brown was immediately suspicious of the letter. While it was supposedly sent by Canadian officials, he noted that it was written in "poor French." Also, it attempted to delay his arrival at the camp, which he had planned for four days later. Brown concluded that the writers were actually Dakota who intended to postpone his arrival, thus giving the camp time "to gather provisions to take them north."

The desire of Dakota to mislead soldiers certainly served as an incentive to learn to read and write. Most Dakota men, women, and children, however, wanted reading lessons so they could communicate with their relatives during their forced separation. Indeed, following the war, a "perfect mania" for reading began even before their exile from Minnesota. At Mankato, the "three hundred and thirty men in prison" desired instruction "in letters." Observers who visited the prison reported that they witnessed "from ten to twenty groups or circles, reading. These circles average about ten persons and each one usually has its teacher. All over the prison you will see men engaged in writing, some with slate and pencil and others with pen and paper." Likewise, at Fort Snelling, all "except the oldest Dakotas, attempted to learn to read and write." Even women "sixty years of age are learning to read." Stephen Riggs was elated by the desire for education that followed in the wake of the war. "As much progress has been made during the present winter in reading and writing," he proudly announced, "as was made during the twenty six or seven years preceding, by all the Dakotas." Education took hold "with an enthusiasm which is amazing" after years of opposition to the missionaries' schools.

While the missionaries offered rudimentary instruction in literacy, they mainly distributed instructional materials, including spelling books and readers in the Dakota language, along with slates, chalk, pens, ink, and paper. Riggs reported that he handed out more than four hundred copies of "the little spelling book . . . and the demand is not satisfied either at Mankato or at Fort Snelling." In one day alone, he dispensed "100 copies of these A.B.C. books" in the Mankato prison. However, the new readers advanced so quickly that they soon outgrew the first readers and demanded higher-level texts. The demand for the ABCFM's readers at all levels became so great that the missionaries placed an emergency order to print hundreds more in Minneapolis. The Episcopalians also budgeted $283.20 "for the publication of books in the Dakota language."

After receiving writing materials and books, literate Dakota instructors, including Robert Hopkins at Mankato, took over the lessons. The missionaries admitted that they exerted little effort teaching at Mankato or Fort Snelling, because the Dakota's "teachers have all been from themselves." For hours each day, Robert and the "more advanced [readers] . . . instructed new beginners in their letters or tracing a few words on the slate as they copy." In this way, "with little or no instruction, except what they gave each other, many . . . were soon able to read fluently, and to write a beautiful hand."

The demand for instruction in literacy only increased after the Dakota's exile from Minnesota. At Camp Kearney, the ABCFM once again started a school and distributed reading and writing materials, and literate Dakota, again including Robert, served as the main teachers. These instructors were very successful: by 1864, more than two hundred prisoners had learned to read. Thomas Williamson proudly stated that "there are more good Dakota readers now in prison here, than were ever to be found at any one time previous to the outbreak." He hastened to add, however, that "more than 100 could read the scriptures correctly and fluently."

At Crow Creek, meanwhile, the missionaries followed a more traditional educational model; both the ABCFM and Episcopalian missionaries established schools that focused on instructing Dakota children. By all accounts, the demand for seats in these schools exceeded the supply, again signifying a major shift from the prewar years. At first, John Williamson ran the ABCFM school himself. By mid-1863, however, the demand for education was so great that he hired Edward and Mary Pond and Hugh Cunningham (all children of first-generation Minnesota missionaries) to teach at the school. In December 1863, Williamson wrote: "Edward Pond commenced his school last Monday week. He has 161 names enrolled, and a good many come whose names are not enrolled." Two years later, the school still attracted many students, averaging "120 or more" each day. The Episcopalians also established a school at Crow Creek, which "had more children than we could care for."

In part, the popularity of the schools at Crow Creek can be attributed to conditions on the reservation. To put it simply, the schools kept children nominally warm during the freezing winters. Although the ABCFM missionaries initially held their school under a hastily constructed arbor, they convinced the Dakota's agent, Clark Thompson, to build a more permanent structure. The agent, however, did not insulate the building or provide heat; John Williamson finagled ABCFM funds to insulate and reinforce the walls and to install a small stove. After the modifications, many Dakota parents would have seen the school as a relatively safe, warm place for their children to spend several hours each day. The heat would have been especially welcome in the context of poor winter clothing, shelter, and illness. Williamson admitted that a larger stove would have attracted more students. In addition to keeping students warm, the Episcopalians occasionally provided them with food, which helped counter the rampant starvation. Samuel Hinman also hired Dakota workers at Crow Creek to build "two rooms for schools," which provided some income. At Camp Kearney, the reading lessons likely helped distract the prisoners from the terrible conditions, the abuse by Commander Roberts, and the stress bestowed by gawking tourists.

Even if students initially attended the schools for material reasons or as a distraction from hardship, they quickly learned to read and write. The missionaries boasted that "teaching Indians to read and write in their own language . . . is very easy." Of course, the missionaries attributed their students' accomplishments to their own efforts, including their instruction (no matter how limited), the Pond alphabet, and their numerous religious translations. Historians have argued, however, that Dakota students quickly learned to read because they connected traditional Dakota pictographs with the missionaries' English alphabet. According to Gwen Westerman, "Writing was not a new concept to Dakota people in the nineteenth century. Before explorers and missionaries came to this area, Dakota people were recording information on bark skin, wood, and rocks. They used pictographs and other symbols." When he first arrived in Minnesota, ABCFM missionary Samuel Pond witnessed the Dakota's use of symbols. Pond saw evidence of Dakota "picture-writing" all around him with figures drawn "on bark or on a tree that they had peeled." In this way, they conveyed "to others considerable information." Samuel Hinman also commented on the Dakota's "picture-writing," which he described as very sophisticated. According to Hinman, their symbols could represent a thing or an event (a bear or a battle), but they could also stand for an idea or an abstract quality (love or goodness).

Dakota used picture writing for many purposes, including telling stories. Stephen Riggs explained that they drew "figures of men and horses . . . with coal or cut in bark, [which] told the story of a war-party." He also described pictures "of pipes and horses feet, with other such hieroglyphs," that "told a man's history." They drew symbols to sign their names and to indicate the location of their villages and burial mounds on maps. Traders used picture writing to keep their accounts. In the 1840s, some Dakota even used pictographs to protest the churches of the ABCFM missionaries. In a letter to a fellow missionary, Thomas Williamson complained that "the devil is very industrious about here this winter. The boys have been on every occasion *carving* . . . obscene figures on the benches and with coals marking them on the walls." Samuel Pond also noted that the "walls of the front hall" at his home "were adorned with choice specimens of their famous picture-writing as high as the tallest of them could reach."

Although young boys likely used the pictographs to show their disapproval of the ABCFM churches, the missionaries still encouraged Dakota to link their pictographs and symbols with literacy. Dakota called their pictographs *wowapi*. When translating English into Dakota, the missionaries used the word *wowapi* to mean "book." In this way, they facilitated the adoption of new ideas by presenting them in cultural terms that Dakota understood.

Even if the missionaries openly linked Dakota pictographs with literacy, they still sought to use reading to promote Christianity following the war. Indeed, Stephen Riggs praised imprisonment because it "had been a good school for them." Certainly, the prisoners did not share Riggs's benign evaluation of imprisonment, nor did they endorse his sole focus on Christianization. Even the missionaries admitted that the Dakota's main "motive to the acquiring of knowledge . . . has been that they might communicate with their friends." The widely scattered Dakota "could only be heard from by letter."

Letter writing allowed women at Crow Creek to communicate "with a father, a brother, or perhaps a husband."

The volume of mail illustrates the importance that Dakota men and women placed on communicating with distant family members during their Minnesota imprisonment. In early March 1863, Stephen Riggs carried three hundred letters from Fort Snelling to the prisoners at Mankato. He returned from the prison with about the same number. In late March, he delivered more than four hundred letters to the prison. Another time, he carried more than five hundred letters to Fort Snelling. Riggs also brought fifty daguerreotypes of friends and relatives to the prisoners. Family members read these letters and contemplated the pictures over and over again. The letters that passed between Mankato and Fort Snelling created "a kind of electric sympathy existing between the two places. Communications were numerous and frequent."

The prisoners asked the missionaries to do more than just carry their letters; they also requested their help at both Mankato and Fort Snelling. Henihda (Louis Walker) wrote Bishop Whipple that "he was in jail and I do not no what for. . . . Oh my friend could you not help me in my distress." Capeduta (Scarlet Beaver) wrote Thomas Williamson from the Mankato prison, informing him that "I with all my fathers people are in distress." Likewise, Sarah Marpihdagawin (Mrs. White Dog) implored Whipple to help obtain the release of her son. "My boy," she wrote, "had never harmed anyone, [and] is very anxious to return here and this now is the thing that I long for. . . . I am very anxious to hear from you in regard [to] the prospects of my boy in getting" released from prison. Mary Renville sent a letter to Stephen Riggs, asking him to "see what can be done. don't let them stay in that camp till they all die."

The amount of mail increased once the federal government exiled families from Minnesota and more people learned to read and write. Once again, the men at Camp Kearney and their families at Crow Creek used the missionaries to facilitate their correspondence. Before the establishment of an official post office at Crow Creek, mail service was spotty at best, with times between delivery and receipt as long as three weeks. To circumvent the slow postal service, the missionaries hired letter carriers or carried the mail themselves between their missions in Iowa and Dakota Territory. In July 1863, John Williamson informed his father that "two days ago I sent about 18

Dakota letters to your care and today I put up about 30 more." A month later, John sent nearly a hundred letters to his father's care in Davenport. Also in 1863, Samuel Hinman traveled between Davenport and Crow Creek, taking "a large number of letters" with him.

By 1864, the postal service had become more regular, and Crow Creek received mail about every ten days. While the missionaries continued to send letters between their missions, they also mailed letters for Dakota women at the newly established post office. In January 1864, the ABCFM missionaries facilitated "a large mail . . . from their friends on the Missouri, and a few days after, they sent 280 letters to the post office." Each time the mail arrived, the missionaries posted and received between one and three hundred Dakota letters.

The amount of money the prisoners spent purchasing writing supplies and stamps provides further evidence of the letters' importance to them. As I discussed in the previous chapter, the prisoners spent some of the money they raised selling items to tourists on blankets, food, and other material goods. However, they spent the largest percentage on letter-writing materials and postage. In 1863, John Williamson, from his post at Crow Creek, used Dakota money to mail forty-eight letters, at a cost of twenty-five cents each, for a total of twelve dollars. In May 1864, Thomas Williamson "purchased for them stationery, including postage stamps, to the amount of between twenty five and thirty dollars, with their own money; and I suppose that, through the soldiers who guard them, they have purchased a larger amount in the same way." In a visit to Camp Kearney, Stephen Riggs also bought them "considerable" paper and other writing supplies "with their own money."

Recipients at both ends eagerly awaited the arrival of letters from their relatives. Some letters contained welcome news. One of the first things Wamditanka did after learning that he could leave Camp Kearney was to send a letter to his relatives telling them the good news. Likewise, Elias Ohan Manyakapi immediately wrote to his relatives about his impending release: "I rejoice and am glad because . . . I am to be released [from prison]. Most of all I truly give thanks to God that I shall again on this earth behold my family and my relatives." In 1865, rumors swept through the prison that everyone would soon be released. Although the report proved to be false, the prisoners immediately sent letters "home that they had been told . . . that they were all coming home in the spring."

Unfortunately, most of the letters contained neither positive nor welcome news. In this way, the correspondence was a double-edged sword: Dakota men and women wanted to hear from their relatives but dreaded what they might learn. In fact, the news was generally grave. For example, many of the letters sent from Fort Snelling to Mankato contained heartbreaking news. Waniyhiyewin dictated an emotional letter to Thomas Williamson for her husband at Mankato. She told of the physical and emotional tribulations she and their children endured at Fort Snelling. "I am now with my children in a suffering condition," she said. Their son Andrew "is not right well yet. He still purges blood sometimes." She also could not stop thinking about her husband, which made her sad all the time. "Because of my sadness I am not strong and seem as if I would be sick. I am continually considering what will become of me." She concluded that "I have no one upon earth to whom I can turn for support and am miserable, but I always remember you because I know you love me. I always remember you." Unfortunately, Waniyhiyewin's husband was powerless to help. He must have dreaded that the next letter would bring news of Andrew's death and his family's continued suffering.

Many of the letters continued to contain grim news following the Dakota's exile from Minnesota. In 1863, the prisoners worried that they would receive letters telling them that their families at Crow Creek had starved to death during the winter. Sarah Marpihdagawin wrote that "three us have died and now are lying on hills of the Missouri. . . . We have lost everything. My niece who was so good, is now dead and I shall never look upon her face again in this world." In 1865, at Camp Kearney, Nina-iyopte received a letter from scout Daniel Renville telling him of the death of one of his relatives at Crow Creek. Another Dakota prisoner, Good-Good, also received distressing news from Crow Creek. A letter informed him that "the people are starving this winter, there they are dying from starvation. This saddens me very much my relative." Ruban Tahohpi Wakan worried that every time he received a letter from Crow Creek he would "hear bad news." From prison, he was powerless to help his relatives, who were "scattered and separated, they are pitiful, and I think this is terrible." Stephen Riggs summarized the anguish that accompanied the letters: "They all seemed to be in pretty good spirits until yesterday when a great quantity of letters came to them from their friends on the Missouri. The prospect of their families starving or suffering from want this winter, cast a gloom over them."

Likewise, the families at Crow Creek worried about receiving dreadful news from Davenport. In 1864, a young prisoner wrote a letter to his grandmother at Crow Creek. He simply began, "I am in trouble." He continued: "Grandmother now for three seasons I have not seen my mother nor my sisters nor any of my nephews. I have not seen you for a long time. Grandmother I wish to say to you many things but if you will give me a letter then I will give you another. I wish you all my kingdom to give me a talk."

While letters from both Camp Kearney and Crow Creek frequently contained distressing news, the absence of letters further increased anxiety. Without information, families undoubtedly feared the worst. At Crow Creek, the missionaries reported that women rushed to the post office whenever the mail arrived, eagerly awaiting the distribution of letters. Those who did not receive letters suffered. When almost all the letters had been handed out and "the prospect of her getting anything diminishes . . . [her] expression changes . . . and her countenance seems to assume a perfect blank." Those women who had not received letters could be heard in the evening "bewailing [their] long unheard of friends."

Even those who received letters, however, could never be certain that their content was accurate because government officials monitored and censored the letters, especially at the Mankato prison. Stephen Riggs reported that "Major J. R. Brown, who has special charge of the prisoners," was "required to read all the correspondence." It is questionable whether Brown actually read every letter that passed through the camp, given the reported volume of correspondence, which could total hundreds of letters per week. However, Brown spoke fluent Dakota (he was married to a Dakota woman and had served as the Dakota's Indian agent before the war) and could read and write in the language, so it is certainly possible that he read at least a portion of the letters and censored those he found problematic.

Even if Brown did not scrutinize every letter, some of the writers practiced self-censorship to avoid potential problems. Because they knew that their letters might be read, most prisoners "generally state that the writer 'is well cared for and well fed, is in good health, had been baptized and joined the church, says his prayers three times a day, and had taken the sacrament,' together with various items of prison life." Although the letters may have reflected carefully worded statements designed to pass Brown's inspection, at least their relatives knew that the writers were alive.

Government officials openly and unapologetically censored Dakota letters. ABCFM missionary John Williamson also quietly censored at least one Dakota letter. In an undated letter, he informed his father that Icarapi, a prisoner at Camp Kearney, wrote to his wife at Crow Creek. In his letter, "Icarapi says to his wife that he will see her either in the harvest or in the fall. I couldn't make anything else out of it but that he intended to run off [from Camp Kearney]." Williamson asked his father to look into this matter. He also "scratched it off as I thought it would cause talk among the Indians." Williamson's comments indicate that he read the letter, censored it, and asked his father to investigate Icarapi's possible plans to escape.

Icarapi's letter raises some important questions. First, the prisoners took great pains to convince the guards, missionaries, and members of the public that they would not escape. Indeed, by all accounts they never attempted to leave Davenport, even when granted time outside the prison. However, Icarapi's letter indicates that he may have planned to run away and return to his family at Crow Creek until (perhaps?) he was stopped by the missionaries. It is uncertain whether he was an exception to the rule, or whether other escapes were planned and executed but have not surfaced in the written record. In addition, no record has been found telling how Thomas Williamson responded to his son's request to look into the matter. Did he inform the camp commander, or did he remain quiet about the potentially volatile situation? Where, ultimately, did the missionaries' alliances fall?

Second, John Williamson's motive for censoring the letter remains unknown. Was he doing the government's work by exposing and attempting to stop a plan for escape? Was he trying to protect Icarapi and his family from retaliation if he had carried out his plan? At the very least, Williamson violated Icarapi's trust by reading and then altering the letter. Because only one missionary-censored letter has been discovered, it is uncertain whether the missionaries read and altered other Dakota letters. An intriguing sentence in one letter, however, suggests that the practice was more widespread than just this one example: in 1864, John Williamson informed his father that he spent considerable time "fixing up the Indians' letters that are to be sent off." What did he mean by "fixing up"? Correcting grammar and spelling? Editing the letters' content? Scratching out information? Either way, Williamson admitted to reading and altering the letters. Even if his changes were relatively benign, he violated the senders' trust by reading the letters instead of simply mailing them. In the worst case, he deleted information that he judged to be inappropriate, as he did with Icarapi's letter.

A letter written by Joseph Brown provides another example of the missionaries' troubling use of the Dakota's letters. In a letter to Gabriel Renville, who served as head of the Dakota scouts, Brown complained that family members at Crow Creek "are constantly writing down to Mr. Riggs and others" about the scouts (see chapter 6). Brown cautioned Renville to tell the writers to "keep quiet for every letter they send down there on the subject . . . [draws] attention to them." The writers "had all better keep their paper than to write to anyone on the subject." This indicates, once again, that the missionaries read the Dakota letters and (possibly) relayed the information beyond the Dakota community. In this case, it appears that the information potentially harmed the Dakota scouts by discussing their location and actions. Again, this is just one example, but it does call into question the dynamic of letters that not only served as one of the few ways for Dakota to maintain contact with their kin but also imperiled those same ties if the letters were used against them.

The missionaries' probable censorship of Dakota letters provides a concrete example of how literacy became a contested battleground among Protestant missionaries, government officials, the public, and Dakota in the postwar years. Government officials feared Dakota literacy, missionaries wanted to use it as a tool to promote Christianization, and members of the public viewed Dakota as unintelligent and unable to communicate in the English language. For Dakota, however, literacy, as Barbara Monroe argues with regard to the Plateau Indians, was "not a tool of civilization and assimilation, as the white men had hoped, but a tool for cultural preservation and political activism."

While many Dakota appropriated literacy for their own purposes, the extreme climate of the postwar years guaranteed that it would remain a limited tool for resistance. Dakota men and women could read about the dreadful conditions in their relatives' letters, but they could do little to change those circumstances from within the confines of Camp Kearney or from their isolated reservation. Literacy also could be used against them if private information was read by government officials or Protestant missionaries. Thus, literacy played an important but ultimately conflicted and restricted role in the Dakota's attempts to survive the postwar years.

5 ✳ RESILIENCE, RESISTANCE, AND SURVIVAL: CHRISTIANITY

Prior to the U.S.-Dakota War, most Dakota rejected missionary-sponsored schools and instruction in literacy. Likewise, very few Dakota chose to convert to Christianity. Once again, members of the Hopkins family were a notable exception; they not only learned to read and write in the Dakota language but also became part of the small number of Christian Dakota. Robert's interest in Christianity began decades before the war. In the 1840s, he attended the Lac qui Parle Mission church, eventually converting to Christianity and even becoming a church elder. At Lac qui Parle, he met and married Sarah, another early Christian convert, which integrated him into one of the main Dakota Christian families at the time, including Sarah's cousins from the large Renville family, centered around Joseph Renville, a mixed-blood trader. Robert also lived at the Hazelwood Republic, Stephen Riggs's small settlement of Dakota Christians, in the mid-1850s. By the 1860s, he served as an elder in Thomas Williamson's Pajutazee Mission on the Upper Sioux Agency in Minnesota.

Following the war, Robert continued his affiliation with the ABCFM, becoming its main religious liaison to the prisoners first in Mankato and then at Camp Kearney. The missionaries noted that while "some of us have preached to them [the Mankato prisoners] every Sabbath, the work has seemed to be carried chiefly through his [Hopkins's] instrumentality." They proudly stated that "Robert Hopkins, the ruling elder, [spoke] in a manner highly appropriate and edifying, far beyond what could have been expected of one with no more education and experience in public speaking." Robert was "the ruling spirit in the prison—the spiritual bishop there."

After the prisoners' removal to Davenport, Robert continued to play a central role in promoting Christianity. An article in the *Daily Democrat and News* observed that at Camp Kearney "the great majority belong to the [ABCFM] Presbyterian order of Protestants." Robert contributed to these conversions by holding "religious ceremonies in one of the barracks three times each day . . . in the Sioux language." He also performed marriages and administered the sacraments. Even the guards called him "the Minister." Stephen Riggs summarized Robert's importance to the ABCFM's mission: he was "the leader in all that pertained to worship." At Crow Creek, Sarah, her mother, and her brothers also played active roles in the ABCFM church.

Because he was a lay minister and teacher, Robert and his family were afforded opportunities—though still limited—unavailable to non-Christian Dakota. For example, John Williamson admitted that he favored Robert and worked for his freedom more than that of other Dakota. "I have inquired more particularly into Caske's case, as he was an elder in the church at Pajutazee," Williamson acknowledged, "one of the most active young Christian men, my father's neighbor, whom we all loved most dearly, and who assisted my father in his escape, as a son." Once the missionaries had helped free Robert from prison, they asked the ABCFM's board to "furnish him with transportation to the Missouri this fall." When he arrived at Crow Creek, Riggs suggested employing "him as a native preacher giving him such remuneration as may be agreed upon with the committee at Boston." The ABCFM eventually authorized the payment, which provided Robert with an income at a time when few opportunities existed for work on the reservation.

Robert's close and continued ties to the ABCFM missionaries as well as the benefits he received from that relationship, however, set him apart from the other prisoners and even led some of his Dakota peers to question his loyalty. Thus, at the same time that many prisoners desired to learn to read and write or expressed an interest in Christianity, they also remained profoundly wary of both the missionaries and their main converts, including Robert, as they had in the prewar years. In May 1863, soon after his arrival at Camp Kearney, Four Lightning penned a lengthy letter to General Sibley. "There's one named the 'First Born Son' [Çaske], who wrote a letter to S. R. Riggs, no matter what he says, he's not truthful," he stated. "There's some men who consider themselves friends of those on the outside, but the Dakota are afraid of them, we are thinking, maybe they said something bad about us, that's why we are continually writing to you. In our opinion, you shouldn't listen to those persons." Letters have not been translated that indicate whether Robert informed against his fellow prisoners to Stephen Riggs or any others. However, his ties to the missionaries and, through them, government officials certainly led prisoners like Four Lightning to question his loyalty. According to Waziyatawin, this division between Christian and non-Christian Dakota was "one of the most insidious characteristics of colonization [in] the way in which it divides the colonized."

While several prisoners worried about Robert's ties to the missionaries, many cautiously followed his model and affiliated with the Presbyterian or Episcopal Church after the war. Indeed, missionary records tallied an impressive number of conversions that totaled in the hundreds in Minnesota, Iowa, and Dakota Territory. These numbers alone, however, do not tell the story of the Dakota converts. Evidence from Dakota and missionary letters indicates that at least some men and women at Camp Kearney and Crow Creek converted to Christianity to procure material support or aid in obtaining their freedom. This went against the missionaries' very strict definition of what it meant to become and remain a Christian. The fact that some Dakota may have converted to obtain benefits, however, is meant neither to privilege physical over cultural survival nor to imply that Dakota religious beliefs and practices could not provide spiritual strength during this time of hardship. Conversely, it is not intended to question the beliefs of those who remained affiliated with one of the Protestant churches, including subsequent generations. Rather, the focus on material aid highlights the undeniable fact that conditions were so poor in the postwar years that basic survival was the primary concern of most families. As should be abundantly clear by this time, the missionaries favored and supported Christian Dakota over all others. Some Dakota men and women used this to their (albeit limited) advantage, even switching denominations if it helped them in some way. Others converted to Christianity in prison but left the church (much to the missionaries' disappointment) once they received their freedom.

For some Dakota, practicing the missionaries' religion helped them to survive the postwar years; those who did so are the main focus of this chapter. It is important to note, however, that for others, any alliance with the missionaries signified an acceptance of all they had fought against in 1862. Robert Hopkins illustrates the uneasy path that he—and many others—navigated among Christianity, ABCFM and Episcopalian missionaries, and his fellow Dakota. Unlike the practice of selling items in Davenport to raise money or even learning to read and write in the Dakota language, the topic of Christianity was much more controversial and is fraught with tension and conflict into the present day.

Before and after the war, the missionaries offered a very strict definition of what it meant for Dakota men and women to convert to Christianity. Both the ABCFM and the Episcopal mission boards demanded that Indian converts meet the same strict set of requirements for church membership as Euro-American congregants; in other words, they needed to give up their previous religious beliefs entirely as well as many of their cultural practices. In the case of the ABCFM, Indian converts needed to read and understand the Bible, attend weekly meetings, and experience a change of heart or a conversion experience. Once potential members met these criteria, a committee of missionaries tested them on their knowledge of the scriptures, commitment to Christian morality, and validity of their conversion experience. As Stephen Riggs explained, converts needed to offer "substantial evidence that they are born again" before making "a profession of religion." Riggs understood that these requirements might be difficult for Indian converts to achieve, but "our God is a jealous God, and the religion of the Bible is an uncompromising religion."

In part due to this uncompromising definition of conversion, very few Dakota chose to accept Christianity prior to the war. Although missionary publications used optimistic phrases such as "planting seeds for the future," in the months prior to the war the ABCFM counted a total of only eighty-three Christians at their three mission stations—Hazelwood, Yellow Medicine, and the Lower Sioux Agency—and many of these converts did not attend church on a regular basis. Years later, Robert Hopkins's obituary would summarize those lean years: "The white ministers worked for 27 years in the . . . Minnesota land, [and] for 27 years made [only] three churches." Likewise, the Episcopal mission, which Bishop Henry Whipple opened in 1860, had yet to attract many members. Although the missionaries worked with "diligence and fidelity," at best their missions euphemistically experienced "quiet progress."

Strong opposition to the missionaries' message certainly contributed to the low number of conversions before the war. In 1860, Bishop Whipple visited Wabasha, one of his early converts, to discuss the widespread hostility to his mission. Whipple was especially worried about "the opposition of the medicine men to the mission. Lately they have taken pains to get up a dance on every Lord's Day to keep the people from the church." He wanted Wabasha to offer advice on how to counter this opposition. The ABCFM missionaries also reported resistance to their presence in Minnesota, again especially during their Sunday church services. One day, a group of Dakota men even shot "at the church bell as a target [and] . . . cracked it so that it would not ring" during a Sunday meeting. Stephen Riggs was so "affected that he cried" in front of his small congregation. After Catherine Totidutawin converted to Christianity, she was subjected "to divers sort of persecutions. . . . There were times when all were forbidden to attend public worship at the mission."

Because of these strong challenges to Christianity, when the war broke out most missionaries worried that they would finally need to concede defeat and leave Minnesota. To their surprise, the opposite occurred, and hundreds of Dakota men and women converted to Christianity at Mankato and Fort Snelling. The "results of almost thirty years of previous toil," the ABCFM missionaries boasted, "have been eclipsed by the success of a single-year." For the first time since their arrival in Minnesota, the missionaries reported large numbers of converts. On February 3, 1863, the ABCFM missionaries recorded 275 "extraordinary baptisms" in the Mankato prison. That number grew exponentially to about 300 a few weeks later. Likewise, at Fort Snelling, the ABCFM "congregations have been large [approximately 300 to 500 attendees], measured only by the capacity of the place." They counted 140 converts. The Episcopalians also confirmed about 100 Dakota converts at Fort Snelling (fig. 15). In addition, Thomas Williamson, Father Augustin Ravoux, and Stephen Riggs baptized many of the condemned men prior to their executions. All these conversions led the missionaries to rejoice that "God's Spirit has been working mightily among them."

The missionaries continued to report conversions after the Dakota's exile from Minnesota. Evangelicals were thrilled to read missionary reports of Dakota families singing "hymns of praise ascending to Jehovah" as they

FIGURE 15. Bishop Henry Whipple (center) confirmed about a hundred Dakota in the Episcopal Church at Fort Snelling in 1863. Courtesy of the Minnesota Historical Society.

left St. Paul for Dakota Territory via steamer. Upon reaching Crow Creek, these families reportedly continued to attend services in large numbers and to "show that they have given up heathenism for Christianity." Thomas Williamson marveled at the conversions, calling them "one of the most remarkable displays of God's grace of which we have any record." While the ABCFM claimed the majority of the converts, the Episcopalians also reported numerous church members at Camp Kearney and especially at Crow Creek. In 1864, Samuel Hinman, who visited the Davenport prison several times but focused most of his efforts on Crow Creek, claimed to have baptized 270 adults and 317 children, confirmed 108, and gathered 200 communicants.

ABCFM and Episcopalian hyperbole aside, the large numbers of reported converts fail to convey the entire story. Even the missionaries themselves questioned the sincerity of these conversions. Of all the missionaries, Stephen Riggs agonized the most over "the genuineness of their professions." He asked whether "all these Indians [should] be regarded as genuine converts?" He answered his own question: "Probably not." He worried that the prisoners may have used Christianity as a means to an end, for example, to obtain their freedom or material aid. Other ABCFM missionaries, however, were cautiously optimistic. While acknowledging that some of the converts might be insincere, the ABCFM's corresponding secretary, Selah Treat, found it "gratifying to hear that there is so much evidence of piety among the prisoners. I have always supposed that there would be considerable 'weeding out', at some time; and the reports thus far are quite as good as I expected." John Williamson agreed, noting that "there are no tares among this wheat, it is not reasonable to expect. But as it has only just sprung up, we do not see the tares as yet, only the wheat; and we rejoice in that." Most rejected Riggs's cynicism and chose to believe that the "Spirit of the Lord is among them."

Outside the tight missionary circle, however, the subject of the Dakota converts was even more controversial. Members of the public, journalists, and government officials commented extensively on the issue of Dakota and Christianity. A visit to the prisons at Mankato and Fort Snelling, a stop at the banks of the Mississippi River as the Dakota traveled to Crow Creek, or a call at Camp Kearney to see the prisoners invariably produced commentary— some laudatory but most negative—about their religious practices. Immediately after the war, journalists rushed to see the prisoners at Mankato and Fort Snelling. Some confirmed the missionaries' excitement about the conversions and commented on the piety and religious devotion of the prisoners. An article in the *Goodhue Volunteer* called the missionaries "eminently successful" and confirmed that the Dakota converts "spoke confidently of their hopes of salvation."

Other articles, however, viewed the Dakota's professions of religion as a ploy to evade the punishments they so richly deserved. An article in the *St. Cloud Democrat* blamed the missionaries for saving many of the convicted men from hanging. The missionaries "have had such 'a season of prayer' with their red brethren, have given them so many primers and testaments and have published such touching accounts of their piety and progress of their pursuit of knowledge that the President . . . could scarce be expected to break up this academic grove by hanging all of the pupils." But according to the paper, their piety was false—merely a means to an end. "After they have finished their education," the journalist warned, those supposed Christian Dakota "will be able to make their next massacre . . . much more horrible than the last." A reporter for the *Semi-Weekly Wisconsin* also complained that Dakota Christians at Fort Snelling were "anything but the 'good Indians' that we read about in missionary works. The only nobility we could discover consisted of half dressed bodies with ugly, devilish faces." During his visit to the prison, this reporter denied witnessing any "of the devotional exercises for which the Sioux were so celebrated."

Several newspapers also made sure to note that Dakota families sang hymns as they departed Fort Snelling for Crow Creek. An article in the *Goodhue Volunteer* confirmed that the singing occurred and praised Dakota families for embracing Christianity. "It was a thrilling and suggestive sight to witness these savage children of the wilderness . . . singing praises to the white man's God in Old Presbyterian tunes." These hymns "touched the heart of the hearer and spectator." Indeed, the reporter called this "strange spectacle of Christian worship . . . one of the most remarkable episodes in the history of the Indian war." Again, however, not all comments were positive. An article in the *St. Cloud Democrat* scoffed at reports of prayer meetings on the steamer. The journalist claimed that the "entire sketch [in the *Goodhue Volunteer*] is evidently written by some reporter connected with the [missionary] establishment." Reports of singing were "nonsensical, high falluting stuff." If by some chance the prayers and singing had occurred, the "bloodstained devils" did so only because this was "a most effective means of saving guilty wretches from everlasting punishment." For their part, Dakota families on the steamer disliked the attention; they found the "whites" who gathered to hear their singing "very unpleasant."

The Dakota prisoners continued to undergo religious scrutiny upon their arrival in Iowa. Some Davenport journalists effused about the prisoners' piety and marveled at their transformations under the missionaries' tutelage. One journalist commented that the prisoners were "nearly all religious— the most of them believing in the Presbyterian creed. They have an Indian preacher among them. . . . They hold divine service twice a day and have prayers morning and night." Another visitor attended one of the prisoners' religious meetings "through the politeness of Captain Littler." He reported that "the greater portion of the prisoners are professing Christians . . . [of] the Presbyterian order of protestants. . . . Rev. Cas ke-a [Robert Hopkins] dispenses the gospel in the Sioux language . . . in the usual style of the Presbyterian Church. . . . We never attended a meeting of more devout people, as far as we could see."

Like their counterparts in Minnesota, however, other commentators were more cynical with regard to the prisoners' adoption of Christianity. One visitor to Camp Kearney specifically denigrated Robert's sermons. The Dakota prisoners "were called out in line . . . and required to listen to a 'talk' from one of their orators. We have read something of the 'native eloquence' of the red man, but here our vision failed. . . . We could see no evidence of nobleness or dignity of character, but rather evidence of treachery and cruelty." Another observer accused the prisoners of being "very religious" only "because they entertained a 'well-founded hope' of fair treatment in the spirit land" despite their "feats in scalping." An 1866 article in the *St. Cloud Democrat* questioned whether any Indian could become a "civilized Christian," especially those Dakota men who were "guilty of the worst crimes during the outbreak." "There are instances where a civilized Indian has turned out a Christian and a useful member of society," the author lectured, "but they were like 'hens' teeth,' very rare."

At Camp McClellan, Commander Roberts concurred with those who questioned the religious sincerity of the prisoners. He also intensely disliked the ABCFM missionaries' religious services and the daily meetings convened by Robert Hopkins. The commander called their prayer meetings a farce. Instead of Christian worship, he saw "powwows . . . got up . . . under religious names." These "heathen displays" were a "nuisance" and made "Camp McClellan intolerable." Like Roberts, some members of the public also criticized the prisoners' "powwows." An article in the *Daily Davenport Democrat* described East Davenport as "a delightful place to retire to after the toils and cares of the day." However, the arrival of the "big Injuns at Camp McClellan" changed everything. They reportedly held all-night "pow-wows" that disturbed the residents' "repose before morning." While the missionaries witnessed "earnest Christian devotion . . . [and] a high standard of Christian character," Commander Roberts and some members of the public perceived religiously sanctioned heathenism and savagery.

Despite these negative comments, the missionaries proudly reported the conversion of hundreds of Dakota men and women. Letters written to the missionaries by Dakota prisoners seemed to back up the missionaries' optimism, as many referenced an interest in or acceptance of Christianity. In 1864, Ruban His Sacred Nest wrote Riggs that he believed "God is most Great and Good," although he acknowledged that "several said it [Christianity] is terrible." Also that year, Old Iron Man informed him that the prisoners were "thinking about the Holy Spirit and His Word with all our heart. I am always in prayers, so the Holy Spirit will help us. And I always depend on the Holy Spirit, my relative, and I am letting you know that." Similarly, Iron Flyer Flying By knew that the Bible "is supposed to be good" and promised Riggs that "we instruct ourselves in his word." As one of the translators of the letters notes, "some of the prison writers seemed to be very apt disciples of Rev. Riggs." Likewise, the Episcopalians received letters from Dakota men and women professing their Christian faith. In a letter to Bishop Whipple, Good Thunder discussed his Christian beliefs. "We were once wild men," he wrote. "We are now Christians. It was you who led us to the light." Hapon Taopi (the widow of a Dakota Episcopal minister) also informed Bishop Whipple that she met "on the Praying day, in prayer for you . . . and we do not fail to remember you ever in our daily prayers."

After their release from Camp Kearney in spring 1866, several freed prisoners and their relatives from Crow Creek continued to affiliate with either the Presbyterian or the Episcopal Church. Some even became ministers. Stephen Riggs extolled the fact that "three of the men who were in prison are now preaching the gospel as licentiates, and two as ordained ministers, co-pastors of the native church at Niobrara." Bishop Whipple also discussed the familial ties of two generations of Dakota Episcopalians. The father, George Whipple St. Clair, was a preacher; his son, Henry Whipple St. Clair, "like his father, he counts it joy to tell men the love of Christ, and is full of the desire to work for his people, who hold him in deep affection and respect." Like the St. Clair family, many Christian Dakota passed their religious beliefs to their families and subsequent generations.

Even if families remained within the church, evidence indicates that a desire to obtain material benefits played a role in some (perhaps the majority) of these conversions. Both the ABCFM and Episcopal missionaries distributed food and clothing to their church members. In particular, the Episcopalian Hinman "watched over their temporal as well as their spiritual interests." Hinman excelled at fundraising and sent letters to the East Coast requesting monetary donations to feed the starving Dakota. In his appeal, he pleaded for contributions to help "these poor people, neglected, abused, and robbed, [who] are proper subjects for Christian charity; and every American ought to blush with shame, if he be not willing to give them every blessing that they need." He raised "large contributions of money . . . for the benefit of these loyal Santee Indians." Hinman used this money to send provisions to Man-

kato, Fort Snelling, Camp Kearney, and Crow Creek. In addition, Hinman
and Whipple contacted authorities in Washington, D.C., and received per-
mission to send "moccasins, leggings, shirts . . . and food" to the prisoners
at Mankato and Camp Kearney. Likewise, as discussed earlier, the ABCFM
missionaries, especially Thomas Williamson, shopped for the prisoners to
supplement their meager rations and facilitated the procurement of clothing,
moccasins, and blankets.

In 1864, Stephen Riggs also gained control of a small amount of government funds that he marked for distribution to Christian prisoners. He wrote
a letter to Thomas Galbraith, the Dakota's agent during the war, asking
about "relief" funds for "certain Indians." Galbraith sent Riggs back blank,
signed checks and told him "to fill out in such sums as in your opinion the
present necessities of the Inds. warrant." The sum, however, was not to ex-
ceed twenty-five dollars. Riggs distributed the checks to Christian Dakota at
Camp Kearney.

Dakota men and women could not help but note the obvious link between
acceptance of Christianity and receipt of missionary or government funds
and supplies. Indeed, Dakota writers frequently referenced both Christianity
and requests for aid in the same letter. For example, Elias Ruban asked the
missionaries to send food for the women and children at Camp Kearney. At
the end of the same letter, he requested "one of those nice Bible covers." In
another letter, Flies Twice promised the missionaries that he was preaching
to others about the Holy Spirit. He next mentioned that the food was "terrible" and noted that "you the white people are powerful, you can do something about this."

Even more than they wanted material aid, the prisoners hoped to reunite
with their families. Some converts may have envisioned Christianity as a way
to obtain release from Camp Kearney. Certainly, they realized that the missionaries fought for the liberation of prominent Christian prisoners such as
Robert Hopkins. Dakota prisoner Henry Now informed Stephen Riggs that
he had "been terribly imprisoned for three years." However, he informed the
missionaries that he "did not point a gun at the soldiers, and did not take the
soldiers' belongings . . . and here I am in prison here, and that is why I want
you to speak for me." Similarly, Mr. Uses a Cane wrote Riggs a letter "seeking your help, my relative, we want to see our relatives, and we need your
help to talk for us, that's the purpose of our letter." In the first part of his

letter, another prisoner, Antoine Provencalle, promised that "in the future I will join in communion"; in closing, he asked Riggs to "see Major [William H.] Forbes" and tell him that "I have not participated in any bad things our Dakota have done." The missionaries themselves noted the close relationship between Christianity and freedom, writing that "very few had ever attended Christian worship till after they were condemned and imprisoned." John Peacock likewise argues that a correlation existed between Christianity and freedom: "at least some of the writers may have been writing to their 'father' and 'relative' missionary Stephen Riggs to convert to or to reaffirm their Christianity in exchange for help getting released."

The Camp Kearney prisoners also implored the missionaries to assist their relatives, again highlighting kinship as one of the Dakota's guiding principles. Robert Hopkins wrote Riggs that he would "be so thankful" if the missionaries facilitated the "release [of] my younger brother from prison." Frost also asked the missionaries to help free his relative, as "he did not kill a white man. So now they will make him suffer terribly. . . . My relative was then in the badlands with sore eyes and could not shoot any gun—it is so." Another prisoner at Camp Kearney wrote Riggs asking him to help "the women . . . over on the Missouri. They are hard up. They are all dying." Above all else, the missionaries remarked, the prisoners "pray for their families."

Long-standing rivalry between the ABCFM and Episcopalian missionaries also provided an opportunity for Dakota men and women to potentially play one Protestant denomination against the other. Beginning in 1860, the ABCFM missionaries complained bitterly about the Episcopalians infringing on "their" mission territory in Minnesota. They accused the Episcopalians of using "books prepared by our missionaries," singing hymns translated by the ABCFM, and reading "our translations of the Scriptures" to potential converts. However, "in their publications and public speeches, [the Episcopalians] altogether ignored our work among the Dakotas." Bishop Whipple scoffed at the ABCFM's complaints about his nascent Minnesota mission, arguing "that there was no mission of any kind" on the Lower Sioux Agency, although Reverend Riggs "seemed to think it an intrusion on [his] territory thirty miles distant."

This rivalry intensified following the war, when the ABCFM missionaries accused the Episcopalians of attempting to steal their converts at Fort Snelling and Mankato. John Williamson stated that the Episcopalians' work at

Fort Snelling troubled him "ten times as much as the Catholics" because "they work things sharper. They have been working around Paul [Mazaku-temani, an ABCFM convert prior to the war] again and I am afraid they are going to get them." Of course, Williamson denied any agency on the part of Mazakutemani to choose whether to affiliate with a particular church (or not to affiliate at all); his remarks implied that the Episcopalians could easily ma-nipulate him.

The competition between missionary organizations further increased at Crow Creek and Camp Kearney. At Crow Creek, John Williamson again accused Hinman of attempting to steal his converts, including Paul Maza-kutemani, Simon Anawangmani, and Antoine Renville. Hinman allegedly offered these men money to leave the ABCFM. Mazakutemani informed Wil-liamson that "Mr. Hinman had told him he would give him money" to join his church. In 1863, with few opportunities for work at Crow Creek, Hinman paid starving Dakota to construct two meetinghouses. The following year, he also divided three hundred dollars among his Dakota catechists and helpers. The ABCFM missionaries alleged that Hinman's bribes "produced something of a rivalry among his followers who remember how many things he used to give them."

Likewise, Stephen Riggs complained that "some thirty or forty of the men in [Camp Kearney] prison have gone off to the Episcopalians. H[inman] was over there a few weeks ago and [gave] money largely it is said. In this kind of work we do not profane to compete with him." In 1866, John Williamson grumbled that Hinman had "figured out the cheapest way" to obtain con-verts: "stay away and let us teach them till he wants to make some use of them, and then come back and lay claim to them . . . by being lavish of little means." According to Williamson, Hinman's small payments did not equal the ABCFM's expenditures on schools and religious materials. The ABCFM, however, was not the only denomination to malign its rivals for allegedly using underhanded methods to obtain converts. Hinman wrote to Bishop Whipple complaining that "the ABC[FM] Missionaries are making every effort to alienate the Indians from our influence. . . . [They] refuse to give Books and Writing Materials or Instruction to any who do not join their Church. The same system is being pursued here [at Crow Creek]. I have never acted in this principle and never will."

Certainly, the Dakota witnessed and commented on this interdenominational rivalry. It is possible that some Dakota used this competition for souls to their advantage by switching denominations to obtain assistance. It is telling that Hinman achieved his greatest success after offering work and support to starving Dakota. This charity is something that John Williamson did not always reciprocate. In 1864, families at Crow Creek asked the ABCFM missionaries help them as well. Williamson wrote, "The Indians have told me he [Hinman] had written letters to all the churches soliciting money to keep them from starving, and they asked me to do the same, but I have not done it because I feared it would not succeed in time to do any adequate good, though I do think they will be starving here all the time till next May." Williamson's refusal to follow Hinman's lead must have seemed callous to the families at Crow Creek. It may also have encouraged them to join Hinman and the Episcopalians.

If some Dakota switched churches to obtain assistance, they may have believed that they would remain Christians in good standing even with a change in denomination. The missionaries held that if converts truly understood Presbyterian doctrine and joined the Presbyterian Church, for example, they would not turn to the Episcopalians. Dakota, however, saw things differently. Clifford Canku, a Presbyterian minister and one of the translators of the Dakota prisoner of war letters, comments on the lack of divisions in traditional Dakota religion. "In the ancient ways of worship, we had only one religion," he explains. "And we didn't distinguish between denominations." As such, a Dakota man or woman may not have seen any problems with switching from Presbyterian to Episcopalian.

The Dakota converts and the missionaries likely viewed church denominations in different ways; they also diverged over what it meant to become and remain a Christian. For the missionaries, converting to Christianity meant renouncing all Dakota cultural and religious practices. Many Dakota converts, however, rejected this all or nothing definition of conversion. Two examples best illustrate this difference in opinion: the debate over polygamy and what the missionaries called medicine or *wakan* dances. Many converts refused to leave their polygamous marriages, even when ordered to do so by the missionaries. Others refused to give up their spiritual ceremonies when faced with disease and death. Dakota converts argued that these practices helped them survive; if the missionaries truly loved their converts, they would allow these practices to continue. The missionaries, on the other hand, refused to see that what they considered to be heathen practices played any role in the Dakota's survival. Indeed, they believed that such practices hastened the Dakota's spiritual demise.

From the time they arrived in Minnesota in the 1830s, the ABCFM missionaries told potential converts that polygamous marriages were antithetical to Christianity. Some Dakota men practiced sororal polygamy, where a man married two (or more) sisters. There was some dispute among the missionaries about the prevalence of polygamy among Dakota. Samuel Pond reported that "polygamy was not general among the Dakotas, a single wife being the rule, and polygamy the exception." He calculated that perhaps "no more than one-twentieth had more than one wife at a time." Bishop Whipple agreed, noting that "polygamy is permitted, but is not common." Stephen Riggs, however, wrote that polygamy was "quite a common thing." Thomas Williamson was somewhere in the middle of his colleagues, estimating that "more than half of the men with whom I am acquainted have two or more wives." Numbers aside, most of the missionaries believed that even one polygamous marriage was too many. ABCFM missionary Moses Adams called polygamy a "licentious and vile sin" and stated that the "social relations of the Dakotas are rotten to the core with this vice." Riggs linked polygamy with a litany of other sins, including infanticide and war.

Because polygamy was "an iniquitous state," the missionaries demanded that a man involved in these marriages "put away one of his wives, and be married to the other according to the Christian mode." For example, when Catherine Totidutawin first met the ABCFM missionaries, she was part of a polygamous marriage with Left Hand and another woman called Rachel. The missionaries lectured Catherine, Rachel, and Left Hand that it was "not a good custom to have two wives"; indeed, Left Hand would need to give up one of his wives before joining the church. When he refused to choose one wife, Catherine Totidutawin eventually decided to leave her husband. After she left the marriage, Left Hand told all "others not to join the church."

Following the war, many shared Left Hand's anger over the missionaries' continued refusal to sanction—or at least overlook—polygamous marriages. The war and its aftermath led to the loss of many male lives, the division of families between prisons, and the striking gender imbalance at Crow Creek. Even though Dakota men and women argued that polygamous marriages helped ease these gender disparities, the missionaries continued to demand that all converts leave polygamous unions. In the Mankato prison, Stephen Riggs feared "trouble . . . in connection with the subject of polygamy among the new converts." To deal with this "trouble," he made a list of nineteen potential converts involved in polygamous marriages. He lectured these men on the sin of polygamy and made those who "had more than one wife c[o]me forward and select one—forsaking the other." After compiling his list of women who would be "put away," he traveled to Fort Snelling to tell the women of their husbands' decisions, reporting (perhaps disingenuously) that in all cases "the women promised to be willing to be put away." The same process happened at Camp Kearney: the missionaries demanded that their converts renounce all wives except one. The prisoners were then expected to write letters to their "put away" wives, letting them know of their decision. Riggs failed to consider what happened—both socially and economically—to those women who were cast off by their husbands. It is ironic that he claimed to support the sanctity of marriage, yet his policies compounded the trauma of the war and its aftermath by treating some women and their children as inconsequential collateral in the larger war against heathenism.

Many Dakota men, however, rejected the missionaries' negative evaluations of polygamous marriages and refused to "put away" their wives, especially after their release from prison. Following Tunkaknamane's discharge from Camp Kearney, for example, he went back to "both of his old wives." John Williamson also informed his father that "you will be sorrowed to hear of the fall of Mazakutemani. He has taken another wife." While Williamson wrote him "several admonishing letters," Mazakutemani "refused to come to trial before the session." Similarly, Samuel Hinman complained about "most if not all of the half-breeds having from two to four wives—Indian women that have come from the Missouri. These women should be returned and the men brought to order."

While some converts openly violated the missionaries' ban on polygamous marriages, others attempted to covertly protest this policy by, ironically, using the literacy skills taught them by the missionaries. John Williamson asked Stephen Riggs at Camp Kearney to "remind the prisoners that their agreement to give up polygamy must extend to word as well as deed." He found out that some "who have promised to put away one wife have written letters to that woman trying to get her to wait for them." For instance, "Pejutska had two sisters for wives and promised [us] to put away the younger,

[but] has for some time been writing to both." Pejutska told both women to wait for him until he returned to Crow Creek. Williamson also informed his father that "there is one thing the Indians in jail do which I do not think is right." They refused to give up their wives as promised, "and then write to them as such." These letters are telling for two reasons. First, they illustrate that the Dakota prisoners used missionary-taught literacy to protest one of the ABCFM's religious policies. Second, Williamson obviously had read these letters, probably without the recipients' knowledge, because he knew content that certainly was not meant for his eyes. He then forwarded this information to his father, urging him to admonish Pejutska and others for their resistance.

In addition to subverting the missionaries' ban on polygamy, many converts refused to halt what the missionaries derisively called their medicine dances. The prisoners at Camp Kearney openly continued to practice this traditional ceremony. Stephen Riggs complained that the men were "*conjuring*, or doctoring the sick after the Indian manner." When he reprimanded the men for performing the dances, they switched to holding them at night after Riggs had left. The soldiers guarding the prisoners, however, provided Riggs with lists of "those engaged in each of these misadventures. . . . The white soldiers told me there has been of late a good deal of noise in the camp at night from their conjuring."

After learning of their continued nightly ceremonies, Riggs again told the converts that they needed to abandon all their heathen practices. "I explained to them that the religion of Christ, in its march through the earth, found many customs which were wrong, and consequently inconsistent with its profession." As such, they must "*abandon* all wrong customs." The prisoners, however, strongly protested this ban, especially in light of the sicknesses and lack of medical care. They confronted Riggs, telling him that "their friends were sick and dying. The white doctor did not care if they did die. . . . It was not wrong to heal the sick." Another prisoner also "took issue on it squarely. He said he had conjured the sick and he thought he did right. It was surely not wrong to heal the sick. . . . One hundred had died since their imprisonment. Their sick were neglected by the white Doctor. He did not care if they did die. They did not know how to cure disease in any other way."

Riggs's own letters and reports backed up the men's reports of widespread illnesses, the lack of medicine and a doctor, and the high death rates at Camp Kearney. However, he refused to see the men's actions and ceremonies as legitimate responses to dealing with these critical issues. Indeed, he decided to submit the issue of "conjuring or Dakota doctoring" to the Camp Kearney board of twelve Dakota elders. The board members conferred and reached a decision. Two of the elders refused to ban the "medicine dances." The first argued that "men had been sick—men were sick now—and men would be sick in the future and die. We could not say that it was wrong to endeavor to heal the sick and keep men from dying." The second used the missionaries' own teachings to question Riggs's call to ban the healing ceremonies. "Was it not right to alleviate suffering and heal the sick and keep them from dying?" he asked. "Jesus did that on earth." Despite this strong dissent, the other ten elders voted to ban the practice.

In the case of the medicine dances, the majority of elders sided with the missionaries. However, in other situations the board of elders, Dakota preachers, and female religious leaders had more latitude in making decisions without direct missionary interference. Both the ABCFM and the Episcopalian missionaries relied on preachers "of their own nation" out of necessity; there simply were not enough missionaries to cover all of Iowa and Dakota Territory. Of course, at Davenport, the ABCFM missionaries counted on Robert Hopkins. In 1866, at Crow Creek, they licensed Simon Anawangmani and Peter Tapaytatanka to preach. Reverend Hinman and Bishop Whipple also used "shepherds from among their own people." At Crow Creek, Hinman chose Paul Mazakutemani and Daniel Oldman as catechists. The small number of male preachers, however, could not reach all the scattered families around Crow Creek, so the ABCFM missionaries "found it expedient to appoint 'deaconesses' whose special duty it was to conduct prayer meetings and to take charge of classes of women." John Williamson also selected twelve Dakota women to travel "from tent to tent" preaching Christianity. Likewise, Bishop Whipple lauded "the loyal women who have been my helpers in this blessed work." Two Dakota women—Maggie Good Thunder and Madaline Mumford—joined their male counterparts as catechists for the Episcopalians. These Dakota men and women led church services and Bible study groups, often without oversight.

The missionaries admitted that these "native preachers may be more effective than we ever were or ever could be." Stephen Riggs commented that Indians "will listen to men of their own nation telling their own experiences . . . when they would not listen to us." Religious historian Bonnie Sue Lewis agrees with Riggs, writing that Native American preachers "knew the language, the customs, and the cultural values that enabled them to present the Christian message in terms that made sense to other Indians." Native American preachers did not need "language training or cultural orientation." Dakota ministers preached in their own language and could tailor sermons to cover topics important to them. For example, ABCFM preacher Artemas Ehnamani consistently preached that the Lord was sent not to "the grand and mighty" but to the "poorest little boy here." Lewis convincingly argues that "Ehnamani and his people, especially following the Dakota War, could identify with the indigent." Dakota preachers also chose not to focus their sermons on the subject of sin (much to the missionaries' chagrin), because they did not view "sin . . . as persons trained in Christian lands." Finally, because they had experienced postwar suffering themselves, Dakota preachers could offer comfort to congregants. Robert Hopkins, for one, "spent some whole nights conversing and praying with the anxious." Elden Lawrence, a descendant of Lorenzo Lawrence, comments that native preachers "were called . . . to have compassion toward their fellow man."

In addition to offering comfort, Dakota preachers at Camp Kearney organized their "classes according to their former clans or villages." They appointed *Hoonkayape* (elders) to lead these classes. According to the missionaries, these accommodations were necessary. "The large numbers added after the outbreak, both in the prison and camp, and their entire want of Christian training, required that they be placed under a special . . . instructor. This we found could be best accomplished by making . . . *Hoonkayape* class leaders." While exigency created this policy, John Williamson commented on the importance of following Dakota cultural practices by honoring elders with positions of authority: "those whom I talked with said White men may be able to listen to a young man but a young man can't stand before this people." However, the missionaries' accommodations went only so far. When the elders focused too much on the community (according to traditional Dakota cultural practices) rather than on the individual, the missionaries attempted to "oppose this tendency."

Despite the existence of Dakota preachers and elders who could (and did) ignore missionary dictates, evidence shows that many of the prisoners—and their kin at Crow Creek—chose not to remain within either of the churches after their release. Stephen Riggs complained that after leaving Camp Kearney, "not a few have fallen and dishonored this profession." John Williamson concurred, stating that "the Sioux young men who came home [from Camp Kearney] are nearly all dropping back into the evil habit." In 1863, he expelled five members and suspended twenty-four from the ABCFM church at Crow Creek. In 1865, he noted that "of 225 members on our church roll, about one-third have not been here for nearly a year; another third have been here but a few days at a time, once or twice; and a part of the other third have been away." In 1866, "of the 157 who were received on the Roll from Davenport last summer only 36 were at Class Meeting." The depleted 1866 rolls included Wamditanka (Jerome Big Eagle), who informed John Williamson that "he is not indebted to God for his release and so we need not expect his assistance."

The changing and depleted church rolls indicate that missionaries and Dakota men and women in the postwar period had differing goals and perspectives. Members of the public and military officials also offered contradictory evaluations of Dakota Christians. The missionaries interpreted (or wanted to interpret) the majority of conversions as real—as the natural outcome of their decades of hard labor and devotion. They pointed to the large number of initial converts at Mankato, Fort Snelling, Camp Kearney, and Crow Creek as evidence that a large percentage of Dakota had finally accepted Christianity, although they fretted when some of these conversions failed to endure. Commander Roberts and many members of the public, however, viewed the conversions as fake, manipulative, and even manifestations of missionary-supported heathenism. One military commander in Dakota Territory scoffed that Christian Dakota "have about as much religion as a buffalo bull."

The Dakota also had multiple perspectives. Some undoubtedly accepted Christianity as a way to deal with the years of incarceration and the bleak conditions at Crow Creek. Others, understanding that the missionaries would help them if they belonged to their church, used this to their advantage. Still others appeared to accept Christianity but continued to practice several cultural and religious practices—some covertly until caught and admonished—which the missionaries viewed as disqualifying them for church membership. The missionaries seemed surprised when converts did not wholly give themselves over to Christianity and completely abandon all other cultural and religious practices. John Williamson complained that his church members "never understood that they belonged to us. I told them they couldn't have been made Elders if they did not belong to us, but they did not seem to understand it." Each of these perspectives was not mutually exclusive, and many converts undoubtedly fell into all three categories at the same time or moved among categories at different times.

With all these different permutations, it is problematic to suggest that the Dakota converts "had only one choice: Either they were true converts, or they only pretended to give up their traditional gods in hopes of extricating themselves from jail." Perhaps there is not only one truth, as the missionaries framed Dakota acceptance or rejection of Christianity, but as John Peacock argues, "great variation between what those multiple accounts claim to be true." Whether Dakota men and women converted to Christianity, selectively incorporated some of their traditions into Christianity, or used the missionaries to fight for their and their relatives' freedom, "Christianity served as [one] resource in communal survival" in the context of multiple and continuing hardships.

6 * RESILIENCE, RESISTANCE, AND SURVIVAL:
THE DAKOTA SCOUTS

ollowing the U.S.-Dakota War of 1862, much of the Dakota Oyate was divided geographically into unequal groups. Around 1,300 people were exiled to Crow Creek; a fluctuating number—although never less than 200 men and 20 women and children—were imprisoned at Camp Kearney; and at least 150 Mdewakanton warriors and 2,800 Sisseton and Wahpeton who had not participated in the war had fled from Minnesota to regions north and west. The final group—totaling close to 300 men before the program ended—served as scouts for the U.S. military in its punitive campaigns against Dakota. Since colonial times British, French, and American armies had used Indian scouts as guides, informants, and auxiliary soldiers. In the postwar years, General Henry Sibley followed this long-standing practice. Sibley primarily but not exclusively recruited Sisseton and Wahpeton scouts to capture all so-called hostile Dakota who had fled from Minnesota. He ordered the scouts to "take no prisoners."

Robert Hopkins, his family members, and associates from the Hazelwood Republic were represented in each faction of the divided Dakota Oyate after the war. Of course, Hopkins was imprisoned in Davenport, while his immediate family lived in exile at Crow Creek. Robert's neighbors from the Hazelwood Republic, including Henok Mahpiyahdinape (Cloud-Appearing) and his father, Wamdiokiya, had fled to Manitoba. Beginning in 1863, his brothers-in-law, Lorenzo Lawrence and Joseph Kawanke, and Sarah's cousins, members of the large Renville family, all served as scouts. This initial group of scouts consisted of mixed-blood Dakota, like the Renvilles, who had been affiliated with traders or Protestant missionaries prior to the war. Others, like Sarah's brothers, were full-blood Dakota men who had either attended a mission church or school or joined the Hazelwood Republic. Most of this group could read and write in Dakota. A few, like Lorenzo Lawrence, could also speak, read, and write in English. These early scouts mainly consisted of mission-educated Dakota men who had rescued settlers during the war. However, as the number of scouts increased over the next several years, military officials likely impressed other Dakota men into service. Their larger number and the method of their recruitment meant that the later scouts were more diverse in terms of their backgrounds, ages, and experiences.

The subject of the Dakota scouts is a contentious topic. At the time, the scouts received criticism from other Dakota, Protestant missionaries, and military officials. Dakota scouts, by their very definition, existed to inform against their own people. As such, they faced strong opposition from those Dakota men and women who viewed them as traitors. Missionaries worried that soldiers would corrupt those scouts who had converted to Christianity. Military officials relied on Dakota scouts but often treated them as expendable, assigned them hard labor around their camps, and failed to distribute pay and rations. Into the present day, the scouts remain an extremely controversial subject. Several contemporary Dakota activists and scholars have called them "traitors" and "betrayers" of their own people. Other historians have described them as "renegades, traitors, and mercenaries." Thomas Dunlay summarized this strain of historiography: scouts "consciously and deliberately betray[ed] their own people to serve their own selfish interests." However, Curtis Dahlin makes the opposite argument, calling the scouts "heroes rather than traitors to their people."

As I researched this chapter, I increasingly found myself unable to offer an overall evaluation of the scouts that accurately captured the experience of each individual. Certainly, my research leads me to challenge those scholars who have uncritically lauded the actions of the scouts; this interpretation reflects a colonial view that rewards only those Dakota who informed or fought against their own people. On the other hand, I hesitate to join those scholars and activists who condemn the actions of all scouts. Many (unfortunately fragmented) documents from that time present a more complicated picture of the scouts' collective experience, especially for those who worked as scouts after 1864. First, between 1864 and 1866, at least some of the scouts were likely impressed into service against their will. Second, some viewed service as scouts as a way to obtain their own release from prison or the freedom of their relatives or, at least, as a way to provide their families with rations or money. As Major Joseph Brown, one of the main military officials in charge of the Dakota scouts, admitted, many of the Dakota scouts enrolled "more to their own advantage than to that of the service." Finally, even those who signed up to work as scouts faced difficult assignments, and some occasionally refused to carry out orders. These points are not meant to defend the scouts or absolve them of their military actions against other Dakota. Rather, they illustrate the fact that each of the approximately 280 men who eventually worked as scouts had varied reasons for joining (or, in some cases, lacked the ability to choose), and all made different decisions during their years of service.

The use of Dakota scouts arose in the context of continued retaliation and military campaigns against Dakota. In the weeks following the war, many Dakota fled north and west, including approximately 150 Mdewakanton warriors as well as many Sisseton and Wahpeton who had not participated in the war. Government officials, military commanders, and settlers worried that these so-called escaped Dakota would return to Minnesota to launch further attacks against frontier settlements. Rumors also circulated that Dakota warriors would form alliances with other tribes in Dakota Territory and beyond, and together they would continue to wage war against the United States. Henry Sibley warned President Lincoln that Dakota might combine with "the powerful bands of Upper Sioux . . . to renew the scenes of murder and desolation, of the past year on a grander scale, along the whole border." The fear of attacks, as well as the desire to continuously punish Dakota for the 1862 war, led to a two-pronged war on Minnesota's frontier and in Dakota Territory. Primarily individuals and small groups carried out the war on Minnesota's frontier, while generals planned more traditional military operations in Dakota Territory. Dakota scouts played roles in each of these campaigns.

On the Minnesota frontier, military officials and Minnesotans worried about warriors "prowling about" on the frontier, attacking unprotected settlements and isolated farms. In the months after the war, local newspapers sounded alarms about alleged sightings of Dakota warriors. The *Goodhue Volunteer* claimed that "Sioux spies" had infiltrated Wright County northwest of Minneapolis. Another article also warned that "Indian camp fires have been seen in several places in Hennepin county. . . . It is also said that a party of seven Indians were seen at Lake Manison, in Hennepin county, last week, by a farmer and his son, and that their trail was followed to within six miles of Minneapolis." Along with sightings of Dakota came several reports of attacks on settlers. In July 1863, the *St. Cloud Democrat* proclaimed that "citizens are being murdered in different portions of the State by bands of Sioux that lurk in the timber." In 1864, rumors continued to circulate of "roving bands of hostile Indians, who seem ever present and ready to steal horses and stock of settlers, and kill the owners." As late as 1865, Major General John Pope reported that "the Sioux Indians have been attacking everybody . . . [with] several raids into Minnesota [and] one along the Iowa border."

Some newspapers, however, claimed that reports exaggerated the number of hostile Dakota. An article in the *Goodhue Volunteer* noted that while there may have been sightings of Dakota encampments on Minnesota's frontier, "we greatly doubt it. In times of excitement people have strange fancies. A cow boy is deformed and multiplied into a dozen Indians, and the well known cow-path assumes the shape and form of a secret Indian trail." Soldiers assigned to guard the frontier confirmed the fact that accounts of large numbers of Dakota warriors often proved to be untrue. Lewis Paxson, who maintained a diary during his military service on the frontier, reported numerous false alarms, including one instance in which Dakota warriors turned out to be cattle.

Despite several erroneous reports, in early 1863 some Dakota men stole horses and killed several settlers. These raids increased tensions on the frontier, and farmers living in isolated settlements demanded protection for "their homes and punish[ment for] the butchering devils." At first, settlers living in western counties took matters into their own hands, forming "secret societies" whose "avowed objects are to hang or shoot every Indian suspected of having a hand in the recent murders." In October 1862, Samuel Hinman had confirmed the existence of "secret organizations" created to "exterminate the Indians." By summer 1863, these secret societies had come out into the open and received official sanction. At this time, the Minnesota adjunct general authorized the mustering of "sixty-day scouts." Advertisements appeared in newspapers announcing the recruitment of Euro-American scouts who would "scour the woods from Sauk Centre to the line of Sibley County. They will go in squads of five under their own chosen leader. Each man will arm, equip and subsist himself. Compensation, $1.50 per day, and $25 for every Sioux scalp taken." In September, "General Orders No. 60" increased the number of scouts, allowed them to independently patrol outside of a squad, and raised the price paid for each Dakota scalp to $200 (approximately $4,000 today). Legal historian Colette Routel has called "the Minnesota bounty system . . . illegal from its inception." Even at the time, some spoke out against using "barbarous warfare" against Dakota. An editorial in the *St. Paul Pioneer* called paying for scalps "peculiarly barbarous" as it violated "our common humanity." Even critics, however, stated that "extraordinary circumstances" justified the bounties.

Citizens rushed to serve as scouts, despite the program's questionable legality and morality. Two weeks after the order's publication, all available slots for scouts had been filled. After recruitment, newspapers covered the actions of the scouts in detail. One article described them having "a lively hunt in Lesueur county. . . . Fifteen Indians were seen there [the] day before yesterday, and the settlers have turned out in force to kill them." Four scouts ultimately collected bounties. In February 1864, the *St. Cloud Democrat* reported that "a splendid specimen of a Sioux scalp was yesterday deposited with the Adjunct General, by Oscar A. Horner, an independent scout. . . . The bounty of $200 was at once paid to Mr. Horner."

Newspapers especially covered the most famous scalp taken under the bounty system—that of Taoyateduta (Little Crow), one of the leaders of the 1862 war. On July 3, 1863, Nathan Lamson and his son Chauncey were hunting near Hutchinson, Minnesota. They came upon Taoyateduta and his sixteen-year-old son, Wowinapa (although the Lamsons did not know who they were at the time), who were picking berries. Nathan Lamson opened fire, wounding Taoyateduta. While Lamson and his son ran to find reinforcements, Wowinapa remained with his father until he died, then fled. The next morning, a group of soldiers and civilians retrieved the body, which they scalped and brought back to Hutchinson. They initially placed the body "near McGraw's store where all the village might see it." Later that day, in a particularly gruesome desecration, children filled the body's ears and nostrils with firecrackers for the town's Fourth of July celebration. In the following weeks, numerous newspaper articles debated whether the body was actually that of Little Crow, with many weighing in on "*Little Crow*, or not *Little Crow?*' that's the question." In March 1864, after the body had been identified as that of Little Crow, Nathan Lamson received five hundred dollars from the state of Minnesota; his son received seventy-five dollars.

As tensions grew on the Minnesota frontier, Major General Pope ordered punitive expeditions into Dakota Territory to hunt down fleeing Dakota. He also wanted to prevent Dakota warriors from forming a feared (although at the time untrue) "large army of Indians" with other Great Plains tribes. To achieve these goals, Pope ordered two expeditions into Dakota Territory in summer 1863: General Henry Sibley would travel northwest from Minnesota, while General Alfred Sully would move up the Missouri River from Sioux City, Iowa. Pope hoped to "create a pincer movement ensnaring the hostiles."

While Pope, Sibley, and Sully touted the success of their punitive campaigns, many historians are less positive in their assessments. Much of the criticism surrounds what Pope and his commanders called battles but what many subsequent historians term massacres. These massacres resulted from the fact that military commanders often could not determine whether an encampment was hostile or friendly or whether it had any relationship with Dakota warriors who had fled from Minnesota after the war. Commanders and soldiers alike saw all Indians on the Great Plains as hostile Sioux. Indeed, Sully admitted that his soldiers "cannot tell one Indian from another."

The inability to distinguish friend from alleged foe led to tragic results. In September 1863, under Sully's leadership, soldiers attacked a village of between 3,000 and 4,000 inhabitants, mostly Ihanktonwan (Nakota) and Hunkpapa (Lakota), at Whitestone Hill in present-day North Dakota. Soldiers massacred 300 men, women, and children and captured another 250 women and children, who were subsequently relocated to the Crow Creek Reservation. The troops burned and destroyed everything in the village, including tipis, wagons, clothing, tools, weapons, dogs, horses, and sixty tons of dried bison meat. With regard to Whitestone Hill, Samuel Brown, an interpreter at Crow Creek, warned the public back in Minnesota "not to believe all that is said of Sully's successful expedition against the Sioux. I don't think he ought to brag at all." Sully did "what no decent man would have done; he pitched into their camp and just slaughtered them." Brown stated that Whitestone

Hill was filled with "friendly" Indians, but after Sully's attack "many turned against the United States."

Before troops destroyed the village at Whitestone Hill, however, Adjunct General Nathaniel Baker appropriated several "trophies" for his personal collection, including a council robe ("which will fit the General remarkably well"), a pipe, bows and arrows, a tipi, and a "beautiful saddle cloth." "These specimens are all worth having and will make a fine addition to the General's cabinet of war trophies." In a bizarre development, on December 9, 1864, the *Davenport Daily Gazette* reported that General Baker traveled to Camp Kearney and presented Wamditanka (Jerome Big Eagle) with "a great wigwam or Indian lodge, captured by the 6th Iowa Cavalry, at the Battle of White Stone Hills." After the presentation ceremony, which was witnessed by various Davenport dignitaries and the Dakota prisoners, Wamditanka set up the tipi near the prison barracks and lived in it for the winter. The next spring, however, Baker returned to Camp Kearney and demanded that Wamditanka return his trophy. It is unclear what Baker did with the tipi after he reclaimed his prize. In the context of Whitestone Hill, the lodge certainly sent a message to the Dakota prisoners about the futility of further resistance. It also served as a cruel symbol of the Dakota's subjugation as well as Wamditanka's continued imprisonment.

In addition to looting villages for prizes, the military commanders also received several requests for Indian skulls for study. A "scientist" known only as J. Pitcher, from Detroit, sent several letters to General Sibley requesting "skulls both male and female" from his campaigns. Pitcher wanted the skulls preserved and shipped to him in Detroit; the soldiers who sent the skulls would "be paid at the Detroit Savings Bank." It appears that he did not receive his requested skulls, however, because a year later he asked Sibley if he and several other "scientists" could attach themselves to Sibley's expedition to Devil's Lake to obtain "specimens" themselves. Pitcher's requests illustrate another example of the desecration of Indian skeletons for studies that began after the Mankato hangings and continued with the Camp Kearney prisoners and Little Crow. These studies invariably produced "evidence of the Indians' inferiority" and thus served to further justify the ongoing military campaigns.

Bolstered by evidence that seemingly cast Dakota as inferior, the punitive expeditions continued during the summer of 1864. Once again, Major Gen-

FIGURE 16. Part of General Sully's army near Fort Berthold, North Dakota, during his summer 1864 punitive expedition. Courtesy of the Minnesota Historical Society.

eral Pope feared that Great Plains tribes would join "the Lower Indians" and continue their "attacks . . . by land and water." This meant that Pope continued to target encampments perceived as having ties to hostile Dakota. In July 1864, soldiers with "nerves strung up to a high tension" attacked an encampment of approximately 2,000 Hunkpapa, Sans Arc, Miniconjou, Blackfoot, and Yanktonai as well as a small number of Santee Dakota at Killdeer Mountain in present-day North Dakota. Sully's troops killed an estimated 150 Indians. As at Whitestone Hill, the majority of those at Killdeer Mountain had no ties to the Minnesota war. Also similar to Whitestone Hill, Sully ordered his soldiers to burn the village (1,800 lodges) and all its supplies (around 200 tons). Some of the men who survived were sent to Camp Kearney, while their families were held in prison camps near government forts—like Forts Abercrombie and Berthold—across Dakota Territory (fig. 16).

Battles like Whitestone Hill and Killdeer Mountain brought peaceful tribes into the conflict and increased volatility on the western frontier. Stephen Riggs, who served as a military interpreter on the expeditions, stated that "the present result of our campaign is that the Ehanktonwans and Yankto-

nais have been engaged in the [war], as very likely the Tetonwans will be also."
Historian Paul Beck agrees, commenting that the "columns of vengeance" of
1863 and 1864 inflicted destruction "not only on the handful of resisters, but
also on those who favored peace and had no part in the war." By 1865, as historian Robert Utley argues, the punitive campaigns against Dakota had "set
off a chain reaction that . . . locked Sioux, Cheyenne, Arapaho, Kiowa, and
Comanche in a war with the whites that overspread the Great Plains from the
upper Missouri to the Red River." Indeed, in summer 1865, Major General
Pope planned to move into present-day Montana and Wyoming, far beyond
his original campaigns in Dakota Territory. Thus, a relatively short and isolated war in Minnesota became one—although not the only—of the precipi-
tating events in the overall war for the western plains that did not end until
the massacre at Wounded Knee in 1890.

Dakota scouts participated in all the military campaigns that followed the
U.S.-Dakota War. General Sibley authorized the first group of scouts in late
winter 1863, after Gabriel Renville (held at Fort Snelling) recommended ap-
pointing himself and nine of his fellow prisoners as scouts. By spring, the
number of scouts had increased to approximately thirty men. Members of
this initial cohort had similar backgrounds. Many shared kinship ties. For
example, nine of the scouts had the last name of Renville, including Gabriel
(who served as head of the Dakota scouts), Joseph Akipa, Victor, Antoine,
Michael, Isaac, and Daniel Renville. Others also had kin ties to the Renville family, including Red Iron, Amos Ecetukiya, Solomon Two Stars, and
Lorenzo Lawrence and Joseph Kawanke (Sarah Hopkins's brothers). Many
of these scouts had been affiliated with the ABCFM in the prewar years, including Lorenzo Lawrence, Joseph Kawanke, Paul Mazakutemani, Simon Anawangmani, John Other Day, and Joseph Napayshne. Stephen Riggs noted
that "more than one half—perhaps about three fifths of all our old church
members are in this little band" of initial scouts. Other scouts belonged to the
Episcopal Church, including Good Thunder and Wabasha. Many had long-
standing affiliations with traders, including the Campbell, LaFramboise, Fre-
niere, More, and Robertson families. Many had connections to all three of
these categories: the Renvilles, Protestant missionaries, and traders. Many
scouts were older: in 1863, Joseph Akipa Renville was sixty-eight; Simon
Anawangmani, forty-nine; and Paul Mazakutemani, fifty-seven. Finally, ac-

cording to Riggs, during the war all these scouts had "showed themselves to be on the side of the white people."

After 1863, the number of Dakota scouts increased, especially during 1865. By 1866, when the scouting program ended, approximately 280 men had served as scouts. As the number of scouts grew, their backgrounds correspondingly became more diverse. Many still had kin who worked as scouts or had ties to the missionaries or traders. However, the names listed on the scout rolls included fewer English names, and many lacked ties to the Renvilles or to Protestant missionaries. These scouts also tended to be younger than the initial group, with many being in their twenties.

More important, fragmented documents and records suggest that coercion played a role in recruiting these later scouts; in other words, at least some did not volunteer like the initial cohort. In 1864, Bishop Whipple sent a scathing letter to General Sibley, accusing his soldiers of illegally kidnapping Indians and forcing them to serve as scouts against their will. These soldiers procured "Indians for the army in a way which will, or may bring sorrow to ourselves. The way is, to get the Indians, (often minors) drunk, then cut their hair, put on a white mans dress and ship off the" new scouts to the battlefield. Whipple demanded that these scouts "ought to be discharged." While Whipple specifically mentioned Ojibwe men, in the latter portion of his letter he implied that the coercion may have been more widespread, including forcing Dakota men to serve as scouts against their will.

Other evidence also indicates that Sibley forced prisoners captured on his punitive expeditions to serve as scouts. By 1865, the military held Dakota families captured during the previous year's campaign at "Scarlet Plum's Camp" near Fort Abercrombie. In spring 1865, Sibley ordered Major Robert H. Rose to "make 100 scouts." Samuel Brown, who worked with the scouts as an interpreter, carried out this order; he went to Scarlet Plum's Camp "to make some scouts, we made 31." The next day, "we finished the Scouts we got passed 99." Later, Brown returned to Scarlet Plum's Camp for "three more men." Certainly, as captives, the men had very little say in their fate. Brown's choice of words—"make" instead of "volunteer" or "agree"—likewise implies a lack of choice. Military commanders may also have used captured family members as hostages to force men to serve as scouts. John Williamson remarked that "as long as they keep their [relatives] in jail they will have a hold on them." Perhaps due to their impressment or the treatment of their family members, Joseph Brown described this new group of scouts as "deceptive" and questioned their loyalty, calling them "almost useless," unable "to go five miles . . . without getting lost." Brown suggested relying instead on the cohort of scouts formed earlier under Gabriel Renville.

Even without direct coercion, many prisoners saw scouting as one of the few ways to obtain their release from prison; indeed, the issue of freedom runs through many of their stories, whether they (or their relatives) were captured or imprisoned at Fort Snelling, Camp Kearney, or Scarlet Plum's Camp in Dakota Territory. The initial small group of scouts, led by Gabriel Renville, obtained their release from Fort Snelling by volunteering to serve with Sibley. The Camp Kearney prisoners, hearing of their success, also attempted to obtain their freedom through scouting. In spring 1863, Riggs received a letter written to General Sibley from the prisoners at Camp Kearney; he translated the letter and forwarded it to Sibley. The prisoners asked "to be placed on his list of scouts in his campaign against Little Crow." Sibley denied their request. In fall 1863, more than 250 prisoners—especially those in the hospital—again tried to "enlist as soldiers." Riggs reported that "they have all entered into it, with only perhaps a half dozen exceptions." Sibley again refused their application. Given their repeated requests to serve as scouts, the prisoners obviously viewed military service as one of the few ways to leave Davenport.

When Sibley refused to allow the Camp Kearney prisoners to work as scouts, their scout relatives attempted to use their own service to free them. Gabriel Renville informed Sibley that he had "always done what you have commanded me to do and now I beg of you a favor. My nephew . . . I wish that you would release him for me." In 1864, several scouts presented Sibley with a list of sixteen names of prisoners they wanted pardoned. In an 1865 letter to Bishop Whipple, a scout named Pay Pay wrote that he had not seen his imprisoned son for three years. Pay Pay asked Whipple to intervene with Sibley so that he could "see some of my children alive that are in prison returned home once more." It appears, however, that Sibley denied most of these requests. Pay Pay accused him of "tell[ing] a lie and I am always sad."

Some of the scouts even tried to purchase their relatives' freedom from prison. In 1865, Thomas Williamson sent a letter to George E. H. Day, special commissioner to the Indians of the Northern Superintendency, with the scouts' offer to "pay to the amount of 160 dollars for the release of their friends." He forwarded Day a sheet listing the name of each scout, the names of his imprisoned relatives, and the amount they would pay for their release. For example, Joseph Kawanke and Lorenzo Lawrence each pledged ten dollars for the release of three of their relatives from prison; Pay Pay pledged ten dollars for his three sons. In addition to this list, Williamson sent Day "a little box of beautiful [Indian] ornaments." While Day promised to look into the matter, the prisoners remained at Camp Kearney. Finally, however, Williamson reported that "you will rejoice with me Judge Day says in a letter received last evening that it is determined to pardon all the Indian prisoners confined near Davenport except Godfrey [an African American man married to a Dakota woman], though it may be some weeks before arrangements are completed for taking them away."

This correspondence among Williamson, Day, and the scouts is perplexing. What was the scouts' money supposed to pay for? Evidence does not indicate that the prisoners hired lawyers, nor did they pay for character witnesses, for example. Moreover, only the president or Sibley could grant pardons for the prisoners, so Day simply needed to present their case; there were no fees involved. Was the money a bribe to Day? This would be quite ironic, because Day had railed against corruption in Indian agencies in the prewar years. It is also interesting that Williamson stated that the scouts had pledged $160 to free their relatives, but in his letter he offered Day only $130. Did Williamson take a fee for serving as an intermediary? Moreover, it is not known if these funds were actually transferred to Day. It does not seem like the money made a difference anyway; as Williamson noted, Day did not act quickly, and the prisoners remained at Camp Kearney for at least an additional six months after he made their requests.

While the scouts' offer of payments likely had little effect on releasing their relatives from prison, they also attempted to care for their kin at Camp Kearney and Crow Creek by sending them money. Thomas Williamson received "a draft of $20" from scouts Paul Mazakutemani and Amos Ecetukiya for two of their relatives at Camp Kearney. Both scouts asked their relatives to spend some of the money on postage to write them letters. Paul Mazakutemani also sent Mary Renville $25 for caring for his children during his time as a scout. Scout Red Iron's commander seemed incredulous that he "expended all the money he had ($160 I think!) in necessaries for his family" at Crow Creek, even though the commander admitted "they were all . . . in a very destitute condition."

In addition to sending money to their relatives, scouting also allowed some of the men (especially the initial cohort of scouts) to feed and even remain with their families. These options were unavailable to nonscout families at Crow Creek. Indeed, the punitive expeditions made things exponentially worse for families at Crow Creek because Sibley cut off support from the Yankton, for example. Catherine Totidutawin wrote that "General Sibley made the Yanktons suffer by war and no one helped us." When faced with diminishing opportunities for survival due to the punitive expeditions, the wives of scouts received rations from the military for their husbands' service. These provisions supplied families with at least minimal sustenance, while others who remained at Crow Creek came much closer to extreme starvation. Some scout families even lived together, especially in the winter months. In December 1863, scouts Paul Mazakutemani, Joseph Kawanke, and Scott Campbell, among others, "all have their families with them and are well." Of course, this set them apart from other Dakota families who faced extended separation in the years after the war.

Even when the scouts left for Dakota Territory on the punitive campaigns, their families still received benefits unavailable to other Dakota. Approximately thirty to forty families were allowed to remain in Minnesota during their husbands' service as scouts. Gabriel Renville's family lived at Traverse des Sioux during his time with the campaigns. Joseph Brown's Dakota wife and children resided in Henderson. The families of scouts "Paul, Simon, and Otherday" also remained in Minnesota. Bishop Whipple moved several scout families to Faribault, where they farmed on land owned by a mixed-blood trader named Alexander Faribault. Many of the families living at Crow Creek wanted to leave the reservation and join their scout relatives in Minnesota, including Sarah Hopkins. She wrote that she was "always praying that we will come home with my brother and his family." In 1864, four or five families from Crow Creek who had kin among the scouts—including Robert Hopkins's family—lived with their scout relatives in Minnesota. The military clearly stated, however, that the families' stay was temporary: "These [scout] families had no permanent residence or planting-grounds, but were removed from place to place under the direction of military commanders." Moreover, by 1865, the families who had left Crow Creek to join their scout relatives "were under orders to return."

For many Dakota, the fact that scouts and their families received these benefits for fighting against their own people made them traitors "against their own kindred." Traditionally, Dakota had used ridicule, ostracism, and even violence as a way of challenging those perceived as working against their kin or community. Indeed, scouts like Joseph Kawanke and Lorenzo Lawrence had encountered ridicule and ostracism due to their prewar affiliation with Protestant missionaries. The scouts continued to face similar hostility for their work with the military. Joseph Brown reported that Dakota scouts were "scoffed and ridiculed by those connected with the hostile camp." They were called names such as "white Sioux" and "Dutchmen" (after German settlers living around the reservation before the war).

Some scouts even faced violence because of their close affiliation with the military. In November 1864, "two hostile Indians belonging to Six's and Red Leg's bands" attempted to "take the life of Gabriel Renville, chief of scouts." In part due to these threats, Renville was "allowed 4 men as his body guard." In 1866, when the military began to muster scouts out of the army, Bishop Whipple pleaded with Sibley to "make some special provision for Taopi and family and possibly a few others. He was a principal witness against the hostile Indians and his course would never be forgiven. I feel sure it would cost him his life." Samuel Brown summarized the difficult position held by the scouts: "For a Sioux to show his loyalty by taking up arms against his own nation . . . he risks the chastisement from his own people."

Certainly, the scouts' military assignments placed them into direct conflict with their fellow Dakota across the western frontier of Minnesota and into Dakota Territory. As one of their main jobs, a contingent of Dakota scouts patrolled the Minnesota frontier, stopping all so-called hostiles from making their way back into Minnesota. Joseph Brown was convinced that "a considerable number of the Sioux engaged in the outbreak of 1862 are still determined upon continuing their hostile raids upon the white settlers on the frontier. I deem it important that preventive measures be adopted upon this subject." To solve this perceived crisis, Brown assigned a small number of Dakota scouts to protect the border in 1863 and 1864; their number increased in the winter and spring months during their hiatus from the punitive campaigns. Beginning in 1865, the majority of scouts operated from a series of small camps on the frontier to prevent incursions into Minnesota.

Brown ordered the scouts stationed on the border between Minnesota and Dakota Territory to observe "the movements of any party of hostile Indians on their way to the settlements . . . and report at once to the Commanding officers of the nearest military posts. Should a party smaller than your own in numbers be found you will attack and capture or drive them back." Numerous examples exist of scouts following these orders and informing against and even capturing or killing Dakota who attempted to enter Minnesota. In April 1863, Joseph LaFramboise, one of General Sibley's scouts, apprehended Red Cloud a few miles above Fort Ridgely in Minnesota. In May 1865, "thirteen Indians, who were on their way to depredate against the whites were killed at different times by these friendly Indians while acting as scouts for the protection of the frontier." Also in 1865, in perhaps the most tragic incident, scout Solomon Two Stars encountered several Dakota men on the frontier. Under strict orders "not to take prisoners," he killed his favorite nephew. Two Stars reported that he executed his sister's son "before my tears could blind me" in what he called the "awfullest moment of his life." A newspaper article describing the incident failed to mention his grief. The *St. Cloud Democrat* merely stated that "ten scouts, under Two Stars, had met five Indians returning from the frontier, and killed four of them." In addition to challenging and even killing their own relatives, the scouts by their actions "expedited the resettlement of huge areas of Minnesota" by Euro-Americans.

Dakota scouts also carried out orders that prevented their fellow Dakota, especially starving Crow Creek hunters, from killing buffalo. To prevent any Indians from traveling into Minnesota, Major General Pope created a large restricted area on the eastern border of Dakota Territory at the James River (also known as the Dakota River). In 1865, a small hunting party from Crow Creek spotted buffalo. Unfortunately, before "they had succeeded in procuring any considerable supply of meat, the buffaloes crossed to the east side of the Dakota [River]." When the hunters attempted to cross the river in pursuit of the buffalo, they were stopped by "a party of Brown's Indian scouts," who commanded the "Indians to remain on the west side of the Dakota, stating that they had orders . . . to prevent, by force if necessary, all Indians of this agency from crossing the Dakota river." The Crow Creek agent strongly protested this policy, arguing that the starving Dakota needed the buffalo to survive. His plea failed, and the hunters returned to the reservation without meat.

In addition to patrolling frontier areas, Dakota scouts accompanied Pope's punitive campaigns during the summers of 1863 and 1864. On these expeditions, they performed numerous tasks traditionally associated with Indian scouts, including reconnoitering, discovering and following the enemy's trail, locating encampments, and verifying the tribal affiliation of villages. Soldier Frank Myers commented that Dakota scouts "always marched or scouted ahead of the command." In both summer campaigns, the "scouts led the way, followed by pioneers, a detachment of cavalry, the artillery, wagon train, and infantry, with more cavalry bringing up the rear." Sibley and Sully ordered the advance scouts to "ascertain if there were any recent signs of Indians."

Throughout the summer campaigns, scouts brought news of Indian encampments. In July 1863, before it was known that Little Crow had been killed, Sibley received a report that "Little Crow and his warriors were at Devil's Lake intending to take a stand. Sibley has sent Indian scouts in to ascertain whether the reports are true." In July 1864, "Paul Mazakutemani, who marched some distance in advance of the main party, reported having seen seven lodges in the vicinity of a large lake some three miles east. He was satisfied . . . that the camp was a large one and the main portion of the lodges hidden from view by an intervening ridge of land." The scouts' reports about Little Crow and the location of lodges guided the army's military engagements. As such, some of their information led to tragic results. For example, Frank Myers, who took part in the massacre at Killdeer Mountain, wrote in his memoir that scouts came "back on the dead run . . . reporting a large Indian camp a few miles ahead of us. After a short conversation with the commander, through the interpreter, the scouts" prepared for battle. It is unclear why the scouts did not realize or failed to mention that Killdeer Mountain did not contain many hostile Indians. The result, however, was the destruction of a largely peaceful encampment.

Scouts also followed Pope's orders to help negotiate peace treaties. Beginning in 1863 and lasting into 1865, scouts "who had accompanied the expedition, were sent out to visit the various tribes, to assure them of an earnest desire on the part of the whites for peace, and invite them . . . to make a treaty." In a letter written in Dakota, Joseph Brown ordered Gabriel Renville to "give good advice to all you see. Those who have not murdered the whites need not be afraid (to come in and treat with us), and all who are not murderers of white people should move away (and separate themselves from the hostile camp). The Government does not want to fight (or harm) those who have not murdered the whites."

Specifically, the scouts were charged with convincing the Sisseton to sign a treaty with the United States. In February 1864, Renville and Brown presented "plain and simple" terms to them. To make peace, the Sisseton needed to promise not to hunt in the "restricted area." They also "must deliver to the government, or drive from your camp, all Indians who have been guilty of the murder of the whites." Finally, they needed to move to Devil's Lake (called Spirit Lake today). If they did not "immediately and fully accept" these terms, they would "be regarded as enemies and be pursued and shot by the troops next spring and summer . . . and if necessary, the whole Sioux nation will be exterminated." Paul Mazakutemani also spoke with the Sisseton about a peace treaty, informing them that they "were not implicated in the war of the Lower Sioux with the white people." Thus, he urged them to formalize a treaty with the United States so they "could return to what was good." Despite this combination of threats and diplomacy, by 1866 the majority of Sisseton still had not signed a treaty. At this time, Brown and Renville again demanded that they "must surrender." If they chose not to do so, "they will be pursued summer and winter with fire and sword."

In addition to carrying out tasks traditionally associated with Indian scouts, Dakota scouts performed a myriad of other tasks that histories of scouts generally fail to mention. For example, military correspondence indicates that the scouts spent much of their time performing labor at the military camps and forts, constructing temporary and permanent military buildings, barns, and icehouses. In 1864, Major Robert Rose ordered Dakota scouts to "put up a good stockade." They hauled hay, cut timber, and gathered ice and fuel. In 1864, Brown reported that the scouts were mainly "employed in procuring timber for the Agency . . . [and] putting up hay." They even planned and constructed roads between the forts. These activities bring to mind those of African American soldiers serving in the Civil War during this same period, who often were tasked with hard labor in Union camps.

The military also used Paul Mazakutemani, Charles Crawford, and many other scouts to deliver the mail. This task was not easy because the Dakota mail carriers needed to "run the gauntlet to get through the hostile country." In addition to traveling along dangerous routes, mail carriers often faced the wrath of commanders if they did not deliver the mail quickly enough. Major Rose was extremely angry when his mail was delayed. He fired off a letter demanding that Samuel Brown (the scouts' interpreter) "find out the name of the scouts who failed to make connection so as to have had the mail here yesterday, and report to me either this evening or tomorrow morning." When the scouts finally arrived with the letters, they stated that they had been delayed because their horses had "played out." Rose did not accept this excuse and fired off another letter telling Brown that he would "not again receive such an excuse for not getting the mail here on time, as a horse playing out. Let them know that I intended to have discharged the two who failed, but upon your request and recommendation concluded to give them one more chance."

The reprimand that the Dakota carriers received for late mail was just one example of the perils associated with scouting. Although the scouts performed tasks essential to the military's missions, many soldiers and commanders still viewed them as suspect, disloyal, and even as so-called bad Indians. Even Joseph Brown failed to trust all his own scouts. In 1864, Brown was camping with some of his scouts. One night, a group of Indians approached the camp. They immediately informed Brown that they were "friends of the whites" and were "in the employ of Genl. Sully" as scouts. Brown lashed out that they "were not good Indians when they attempted to get into my camp at night, and that when they acted as bad Indians they must expect to be treated as bad Indians." He lectured the scouts that he would receive "a white man" if one accompanied the group; otherwise, "the Indians could not come even after telling me they were good Indians." Condescending and threatening, Brown's words clearly indicated that white officials were in charge and that the scouts could not act on their own. He divided them into good and bad scouts, even though they all worked for the U.S. Army.

While the standoff between Brown and the so-called bad scouts ended peacefully, other misunderstandings did not. For example, in 1863, Chaska, a scout, saved the life of George A. Brackett (a beef contractor for the expedition), but rumors circulated that he had killed him. Some soldiers wanted revenge, and "a member of the 6th Minnesota Infantry obtained poison from a hospital clerk and administered it to Chaska." He died. In another case, in 1865, General Sully imprisoned Alexander LaFramboise for "interpreting wrongly." John Williamson defended LaFramboise, stating that the problem lay with Sully, whose "ideas of making peace are not such as would suit the Indians and probably the principal trouble is there."

Problems also arose because many officers and soldiers were unable to tell Indians apart, including their own scouts. Both in military engagements and on the Minnesota frontier, the potential existed for scouts to be mistaken for hostile Indians. For example, during the punitive expeditions, John Other Day "incurred great danger, not only from the fire of the savages, but from our own troops who repeatedly discharged their muskets at him, mistaking him for one of the hostile Indians." Those scouts stationed on the Minnesota border also risked being challenged by Euro-American scouts hunting for bounties. In both areas, Dakota scouts attempted to find ways to quickly indicate their status as friendly Indians. During the punitive expeditions, they "changed from their Indian costume for soldiers' uniforms . . . so they would not be confused with hostiles." When stationed on the frontier, they carried written passes from Brown indicating their status as friendly Indians. Of course, the volatile situation on the frontier meant that scouts might not have time to show their letters before being fired upon.

Dakota scouts endured the dangers and indignities of scouting in order to receive pay and rations to help support themselves and their kin. When General Sibley appointed the first contingent of scouts in 1863, he promised them "$40 per month [for food] for our horses and rations for ourselves and family." By 1865, however, after complaints that the scouts were paid too much, the amount was decreased to "thirty-five ($35.-) dollars per month and one ration per day, or one dollar per day and a ration of flour (or bread) pork (or beef) coffee (or tea) sugar, soap and salt to the scout and each member of his family." However, in practice, many of the rations were of poor quality or inedible. One scout complained to Samuel Brown that "the flour that you left for us had been wet and it was so mouldy we had to feed some to the pigs." The scouts also protested that "the most prominent ingredient of . . . [their] cursed coffee" was "essence of cat." Joseph Brown agreed that the "coffee" should "have been thrown in the Minnesota [River]."

In addition to substandard or spoiled rations, most scouts and their families did not receive supplies for the winter months. Moreover, the military confiscated the scouts' "public horses" for the winter. Military officials timed their dismissal in the worst possible way: they waited to send the scouts into winter quarters without rations until it was too late for them to hunt. Even if they wanted to hunt, they often did not have horses of their own. Joseph Brown complained that his scouts were "retained in service until December, and then after the seasons for hunting fine furs has passed, when their horses had been all worn down in the service, and the snow covered the ground, they were turned loose to shift for themselves." The lack of rations led many of the scouts to lose "all confidence in those having control of their affairs." Brown chided military officials for underestimating "the intelligence of by far the greater number of the scouts." They wanted to be "properly appreciated." Of course, more than appreciation, the scouts wanted their promised pay, rations, and horses, especially during the winter months.

While Joseph Brown spoke out in defense of the scouts and demanded that they receive rations and respect, behind the scenes he may have been one of the biggest perpetrators of fraud against them. The *St. Cloud Democrat* published a lengthy and scathing indictment of Joseph and his son Samuel: the elder Brown was an "evil genius in all Indian matters," a "graceless scamp whose name is synonymous with everything that savors of rascality." As one of his many sins, he allegedly cheated the scouts out of all their pay. In great detail, the journalist charged the Browns with stealing the scouts' pay vouchers. "So far as I have been able to learn, not one of these vouchers has ever gone into the hands of the scout, where it properly belonged, but into the hands of Brown's son, who brings into the Quartermaster's office, an order founded by the classic X of Paul and Agrippa, directing that the officer turn over the same to the bearer Brown." The *St. Paul Press* also received eleven affidavits from scouts employed by Brown charging that "sly Old Joe . . . has been in the habit of employing the scouts . . . largely for his personal use and behoof" and "had traded considerably in vouchers, paying the scouts goods instead of money." The *Press*, however, did not publish the affidavits in their entirety because "the subject is not interesting enough to most of our readers." Historians have confirmed that Gabriel Renville and twelve other Dakota scouts were not paid for at least five months of arduous service on behalf of the federal government; the swindle likely was much more widespread. The scouts were not reimbursed for this missing pay until twenty-five years later, in 1891, when Congress finally passed a law settling with them for $136,022.

The lack of pay and rations and the daily perils certainly led some Dakota scouts to resist following orders; others may have failed to discharge their duties because their loyalty ultimately lay with the Dakota Oyate rather than with military officials or the Browns. Scouts who were caught resisting, however, faced harsh punishments, including imprisonment or even death. Resistance—and punishments for that resistance—took multiple forms. Some scouts failed to carry out orders. In 1863, for example, a white soldier "shot a half breed soldier for disobedience." Other scouts chose to abandon their jobs entirely. In 1865, a "deserter from our service . . . stole several horses and joined the Santees, trying to get them to make war." Other scouts may have informed encampments in Dakota Territory about the troops' movements to give them time to escape or plan an attack. General Sully was convinced that some of the scouts "give the Indians information in regard to the movements of the troops." In 1865, at least five scouts were confined in the stockade at Fort Abercrombie for various infractions. Even Gabriel Renville, head of the Dakota scouts, was ordered (although it appears the command was never carried out) "imprisoned in the Guard House" because he "exerted his influence to prevent the Indians from engaging as scouts."

One of the most startling acts of resistance (at least from the missionaries' perspective) came from Henok Mahpiyahdinape (Cloud-Appearing), who may have helped derail peace negotiations between the Sisseton and the United States. Judged by his background, Henok appeared to be one of the least likely of the Dakota scouts to work against the government. Henok's father, Wamdiokiya, was one of the first Dakota men to learn to read and write from the ABCFM missionaries. Although he never joined the mission church at Lac qui Parle, Wamdiokiya worked as an itinerant teacher and helped the missionaries translate the Bible into Dakota. He also encouraged close ties between the missionaries and his son. As a child, Henok attended the ABCFM church and school, where he learned to read and write in Dakota. In the 1840s, he traveled to Ohio with Lorenzo Lawrence and Simon Anawangmani (both became fellow scouts) to study English. In the 1860s, he served as secretary for the Hazelwood Republic. Following the war, Henok and his family escaped to Manitoba.

In December 1863, it appears that Sibley called Henok back from Manitoba to help him negotiate peace with the Sisseton. In a letter, Sibley asked Henok to "see the Indians who have not killed whites to make arrangements by which they may separate themselves from the bad Indians and not be hunted and killed by our soldiers." He ordered Henok to "tell them that they can meet me and the military officers here for the purpose of making peace and putting themselves under the protection of the Government."

By 1866, however, the Sisseton still refused to sign a treaty. In part, officials blamed Henok for the lack of progress. In a letter, scout Charles Crawford informed Joseph Brown that while the Sisseton wanted peace, "they have been prevented by reports put in circulation by 'Henok.'" Allegedly, Henok told them about "barbarities to which the Indians are subjected by the military authorities." In addition, when the "Light band" of Sisseton started to travel to Fort Wadsworth to make peace, "'Henok' sent a messenger after them to tell them they must not think of surrendering, and if they went near any of the forts, they would be hunted like wolves." Henok was accused of informing them that, for amusement, soldiers had killed several Dakota chiefs. His warnings supposedly kept the Sisseton from surrendering. Upon reading this letter, Brown immediately sent Crawford to the Sisseton to undo Henok's damage. He ordered Crawford to "tell them not to believe any of the reports that bad men have put in their ears. They are all lies." Crawford informed the Sisseton that Henok had told these lies for his own benefit.

Henok's story illustrates some of the difficulties of making generalizations about the scouts. His background—which included extensive ties to Protestant missionaries and "civilization"—fit the profile of many who worked for the United States military against Dakota. Instead, he chose to challenge government and military policy in Dakota Territory. Others with Henok's same background—including Gabriel Renville—made different choices and mostly carried out orders, although even Renville conflicted with his commanders at one point. Like Henok and Renville, each of the approximately 280 men who eventually served as scouts had diverse backgrounds, motivations, and experiences that defy easy characterization. Some volunteered to serve as scouts, while others were likely impressed against their will. Many carried out their orders, while others did not. Some were treated as heroes by settlers and military officials, like Renville, while others were called bad Indians and accused of taking plunder by Minnesota newspapers. Some had the support of their extended families; others were ridiculed, ostracized, and challenged for their ties to the government, as they had been since the early 1840s.

Even if they volunteered or had the support of their families, Dakota scouts faced a series of irreconcilable conflicts and contradictions. Arguably, many of the men who served as scouts wanted to help take care of their kin. However, their duties as scouts often set them against other Dakota and even their own extended families. They sent money to their relatives at Crow Creek, but they also followed orders that kept their Crow Creek relatives from hunting buffalo and cut off access to the Yankton, which they had used to stave off starvation. While some of their own families could remain in Minnesota, they patrolled the frontier carrying out orders to keep all other Dakota out of the state. In at least one tragic incident, a scout took the life of his own relative as he guarded the border. Their defense of the border also expedited the resettlement of lands by Euro-Americans, which in turn led to the removal of those scout families who had been allowed to remain in Minnesota. Some translated incorrectly, warned their relatives of forthcoming attacks and unfair treaties, and deserted; they were imprisoned or killed if caught. At other times, however, scouts provided reconnaissance that contributed to the tragedies at Whitestone Hill, Killdeer Mountain, and other locations. There were no easy answers or choices for Dakota in the painful years following the war, which included bounties on Dakota scalps, the desecration of Little Crow's body, and punitive campaigns on the western frontier. The scouts fit uncomfortably into the larger narrative of resilience, resistance, and survival that characterized the years after 1862 for all Dakota.

7 ✳ CONFLICTS CONTINUE, 1866–1869

I n spring 1866, President Andrew Johnson finally ordered the release of all
the Davenport prisoners. The men—and the women and children who
still resided at Camp Kearney—could finally reunite with their Crow
Creek kin on a new reservation near Niobrara, Nebraska. When they
learned of Johnson's order, the divided Hopkins family must have felt optimistic—at last, they could put the war behind them and live together, taking
care of their immediate and extended kin. The promised reunification, however, proved elusive, and the cultural and geographical divisions that both
predated and were exacerbated by the war continued. Once again, the Hopkins family stood at the crossroads of the divisions and conflicts faced by all
Dakota families even after their promised reunification.

In March 1865—more than a year before the rest of the prisoners—Robert
Hopkins departed Camp Kearney and traveled to Crow Creek with assistance
from the ABCFM missionaries. He quickly learned, however, that Sarah and
Samuel had left the reservation. The previous summer, they had moved to
the Minnesota frontier to live with the families of Sarah's brothers, Lorenzo
Lawrence and Joseph Kawanke, who served as scouts. Instead of immediately reuniting with his family, Robert worked with the ABCFM as an itinerant preacher; certainly, the salary provided a strong incentive for his decision.
His status as a released prisoner likely kept him from the Minnesota frontier
as well.

In spring 1866, members of the Hopkins family briefly reunited in Nebraska after the government forced most Dakota living in Minnesota to leave the state. Their reunification, however, was short-lived, and various members of the extended Hopkins family soon resided hundreds of miles apart in various locations. In 1866, Sarah's brother Lorenzo Lawrence made a precarious living after being "hired by some white men to travel with them among the white people." Their "old and frail" mother, Catherine Totidutawin, accompanied him. In 1867, Catherine Totidutawin and Lorenzo Lawrence's family moved to the newly established Lake Traverse Reservation in present-day North and South Dakota. Also in 1867, Robert Hopkins accompanied the ABCFM missionaries on a lengthy trip across the Great Plains. During this trip, Thomas Williamson praised Robert's devotion to the church and missionary work. "I cannot speak too highly of Hopkins," he enthused. "We could not well have done without him on the journey. He is equally at home chasing a buffalo or an antelope, in mending a broken wagon, and preaching the gospel to his people."

Despite his continued work with the ABCFM, Robert and his extended family remained divided, living in Nebraska, on the Lake Traverse and Devil's Lake Reservations in Dakota Territory, at a small settlement near Flandreau in present-day South Dakota, and ultimately in Montana. Members of the Hopkins family suffered from poverty, starvation, and disease in all these locations. As they had in the years immediately following the war, they penned letters describing their plight. On March 20, 1868, Catherine Totidutawin wrote a letter to Jane Huggins Holtsclaw, a longtime ABCFM missionary acquaintance, telling her about the poor conditions on the Lake Traverse Reservation and asking for help (fig. 17). Catherine Totidutawin wrote that she and her family "are badly off for food. Day after day they knock off bark and eat it." Faced with starvation, she asked Holtsclaw for assistance with a little girl she had been raising. "I have brought up another girl, but as I am now so helpless I wish you to have her," she explained. "She is called Nani, and she is five years old. I wish that she might grow up hearing God's word. . . . I am unable to do it. . . . I wish you to have her as long as you live, and if you agree to it you will write me a letter."

Catherine Totidutawin's heart-wrenching letter serves as a counter to the optimistic narratives often used to describe the Dakota's reunification after

FIGURE 17. Catherine Totidutawin and her son Lorenzo Lawrence, Lake Traverse Reservation, Dakota Territory. Courtesy of the Minnesota Historical Society.

1866. When government officials promised the Dakota Oyate a new reservation in Nebraska, they predicted that "the darkest period in the history of the eastern Dakota would be past." Stephen Riggs called Nebraska "the promised land" and wrote that after 1866, "all the Dakotas with whom we were laboring were again in somewhat normal condition." However, as illustrated by the Hopkins family and hundreds of other Dakota families, the years after 1866 were anything but normal. The Dakota continued to be, according to John Williamson, "the banished Santees from Minnesota." They also suffered from poverty, isolation, and a federal policy that promoted divisions by continuing to privilege and reward "civilized" Christian Dakota, especially those who had served as scouts.

Overall, the years from 1866 to 1869 were challenging ones for the Dakota Oyate. During this period, the government established three reservations for Dakota: one near Niobrara (1866; the boundaries were not formally established until 1869), the second at Lake Traverse (1867), and the third at Devil's Lake (1867; now called Spirit Lake). In 1869, some Dakota families established a settlement near present-day Flandreau, South Dakota. The existence of these separate reservations, as well as scattered settlements in Dakota

Territory, Montana, and Canada, illustrates the permanent separation of the Dakota Oyate that had begun with their exile from Minnesota in the postwar period.

From these divergent locations, Dakota continued to endure challenges from the federal government, Protestant missionaries, and members of the public. Even three years later, many government officials still defined Dakota in terms of the U.S.-Dakota War and crafted policies based on a desire to punish and divide them. Protestant missionaries, meanwhile, supported Christian Indians, while neglecting those who did not embrace Christianity. However, the lives of even those Dakota who did not convert to Christianity intersected with Presbyterian and Episcopalian missionaries, who increasingly controlled aspects of Indian affairs. Members of the public remained fascinated with Dakota who passed through their towns on the way to their various reservations, but settlers chafed at living in close proximity to the so-called barbarous Indians of 1862. Dakota used all tools available to them—including literacy and Christianity—to survive these unfortunately familiar but no less challenging problems.

In spring 1866, the Camp Kearney prisoners and their families at Crow Creek finally received notice that they would be reunited near Niobrara in northeastern Nebraska. On February 27, President Johnson issued an executive order withdrawing from preemption and sale four townships on the Niobrara River; the government would purchase these lands for the Dakota. Government officials informed them that these townships had plenty of timber and at least two thousand acres of tillable land. Those who settled on the new reservation needed to adopt "civilization" and become farmers; they would be "watched and kept out of mischief" to make sure they achieved these goals. It is not surprising that most Dakota expressed skepticism about the government's plan. Even the ABCFM missionaries understood their cynicism, commenting that "it is not strange that, after their frequent and bitter disappointments, they were somewhat skeptical as to the intentions of the government." Indeed, from the beginning, the government's Niobrara plan had serious flaws: the townships needed to be purchased from settlers and were not guaranteed by treaty.

Although the Dakota did not yet have a defined reservation, on April 10,

1866, 247 Dakota—177 male prisoners and 70 women and children—boarded the steamboat *Pembina* on the first leg of their journey from Davenport to Nebraska. After a four-day layover in St. Louis, they transferred to the *Dora* and continued up the Missouri River. They made one additional stop in St. Joseph, Missouri, before arriving at their destination in the middle of May, only to find that their Crow Creek relatives had not left Dakota Territory.

Many aspects of the prisoners' relocation repeated the transfer of their families to Crow Creek three years previously. First, despite their purported freedom, they traveled on steamers under military escort. Second, several of the prisoners were extremely weak and ill from their years of imprisonment. On April 11, one day after the steamship left Iowa, forty-eight-year-old Iparte, who had been sick for several days prior to his departure, died. Guards stopped the boat and buried him in a shallow grave in Louisiana, Missouri, far from any of his kin. This journey was reminiscent of their relatives' removal from Fort Snelling to Crow Creek, when guards had buried a small child in a wood yard near Burlington, Iowa.

Third, in spring 1863, the public's anger at the Dakota had immediately transformed to fascination as the steamers passed from Minnesota into Missouri. Tourists gathered to view the Indians along the riverbanks and during their stops. The public's desire to see the now-freed Dakota prisoners had not waned three years later. Upon reaching St. Louis, the *Pembina* had a four-day layover during which citizens gathered to view the Dakota in their temporary camp and during a visit to "Cutley's Gallery." As they walked through the streets of St. Louis, the "tall wild looking Indians [and] . . . some three or four rather good-looking squaws" attracted "considerable curiosity." Again, as in Davenport, the Dakota men and women capitalized on the public's interest by selling souvenirs, including bows and arrows, pipes, and beadwork the women had made during their time on the *Pembina*.

In perhaps the strangest encounter during the Dakota's stay in St. Louis, W. T. Church, a white spiritualist, dragged several Dakota men to one of his séances. For more than half a century, Church and a Sioux named Nimwaukee, reportedly seven feet tall, toured the Midwest and East Coast holding séances. Newspaper articles across the United States reported on these séances in detail; many included stereotypical descriptions of Nimwaukee. During a séance in Indiana, Nimwaukee reportedly "stalked with heavy tread on the floor and spoke in guttural tones and broken English." In Harrisburg, Pennsylvania, he "gave vent to a deep guttural koo-o-o-o!" The journalist was scandalized that "Nimwaukee parades before them without pantaloons." However, the reporter reasoned that his lack of pants probably did not make a difference, "as the room is perfectly dark." At least one paper questioned Church's use of Nimwaukee, calling him a "spiritual prisoner" used solely "for the amusement of the pale faces." When Church and Nimwaukee happened to be in St. Louis during the Dakota's layover, Church impressed several of the "head men of the Sioux" to attend his séance for the "purpose of holding a conference with Nimwaukee in his natural tongue." Given the public's fascination with Dakota, it stands to reason that Church earned considerable fees for that particular séance despite his questionable reputation.

Once the *Dora* left St. Louis, the released prisoners stopped in St. Joseph, as their relatives had done three years earlier on their way to Crow Creek. During the *Dora*'s short layover, the St. Joseph *Morning Herald and Daily Tribune* informed "the curious who want to see the native Americans, male and female en masse, who live and roam in the wilderness, can satisfy themselves by paying a visit to the *Dora*." Although some of the newspaper articles called the released Indians uncivilized, most reports described them as "meek and humble now, from their long imprisonment." After supposedly "luxuriating on Uncle Sam's rations" for three years in the "beautiful surroundings of Camp Kearney," Dakota had adopted "civilization," and "most of them profess Christianity." These changes meant that the "reformed" Indians would set "to house-keeping in good shape" once they reached Nebraska.

The minute the *Dora* passed into Nebraska, however, descriptions of Dakota immediately shifted. The purportedly submissive Indians of Iowa and Missouri rhetorically transformed once again into fearsome warriors intent on murdering innocent settlers. W. A. Burleigh, a congressional delegate from Dakota Territory who happened to live near Niobrara, strongly protested against the residence of these "hostile savages" who would "seek revenge, by a system of robbery, rapine, and murder, upon our unprotected citizens only known to barbarians." These Indians would endanger "the lives of our people and [destroy] our Territory." Another article reported that "the turning loose of so large a body of lawless savages, who are believed to deserve the penalty of confinement for life, is received with great alarm by the people of the frontier." Once again, the press used words such as "hostile," "savage," and "dangerous" to describe Dakota. They could commit "atrocities and out-rages" at any time. Several articles rehashed the "bloody scenes of the past," which stoked fear in the present. When Dakota were guarded by soldiers, imprisoned, or living on an isolated reservation, tourists and even school-children treated them as harmless objects of fascination. However, when they settled on lands near settlers without guards, these same people once again became terrifying impediments to civilization.

The freed prisoners attempted to ignore the controversy surrounding their residence in Nebraska and instead concentrated on reuniting with their Crow Creek families. Unfortunately, the Davenport contingent arrived at Nebraska in the middle of May only to find their relatives missing. Agents had failed to provide a promised steamer to relocate the families, which meant that women, children, and the elderly needed to walk more than 130 miles to the new reservation. The released prisoners could not wait to see their loved ones and walked north from Nebraska, meeting their relatives somewhere between Niobrara and Crow Creek. When the families reunited, they experienced "a strange blending of widely different emotions." Stephen Riggs described this range of feelings: "Many wives looked in vain for their former husbands; they had gone to the spirit land. So there was wailing. Some returned to find their women the wives of other men. But to the greater part, on both sides, there were causes of rejoicing." The Dakota returned to Nebraska to try to rebuild their families. A few months later, about three hundred Dakota (mainly the families of scouts) who had lived in Minnesota also arrived in Ne-braska. The government had appropriated $10,000 for their relocation, money that Stephen Riggs called "a useless expenditure," because these families had lived in Minnesota without creating any trouble for several years.

By summer 1866, about 1,300 Dakota lived in Nebraska. This number was low given the number of Dakota reported three years previously in the areas now drawn together at Niobrara: approximately 400 Dakota had been impris-oned in Davenport; around 1,300 had been transferred to Crow Creek; and roughly 300 Dakota had resided in Minnesota over the last three years, for a total of close to 2,000 Dakota. While this is an extremely rough estimate, it means that more than 600 Dakota were absent from the new reservation. Cer-tainly, some were living in other areas, including Dakota Territory, Montana, and Canada. However, a large percentage of families knew that their relatives were not missing but dead: they had passed away over the last three years due to the horrible conditions across multiple locations. Families had left behind hundreds of graves at Crow Creek, especially of children, and they could not visit the unmarked graves of their male relatives in Davenport.

In addition to mourning the loss of their kin, families struggled to survive in Nebraska. John Williamson did not have any positive words about their new reservation: "I had hoped to find this such a place that the Indians might permanently locate; but on arriving here, I am surprised to find the whole reserve almost barren of wood." He predicted that "the Dakota might not remain long." In addition to poor resources, the Dakota experienced conflict with local settlers. The settlers complained that the government "greatly wronged them in bringing these Indians here as it destroys the value of the place as a town site and depreciates the value of their property." They responded by impeding the sale of land, demanding "more than the Government would be likely to pay" for the townships. Some of the settlers valued their lots at more than a thousand dollars each. As the standoff over land continued, other charges flew back and forth between the settlers and the Dakota. The Dakota complained that the settlers' cattle ate their crops; the settlers countered that the Dakota stole their timber. Dakota were also blamed for breaking into a small store and stealing most of the goods. Samuel Hinman, however, "ascertained that [the crime] was done by vagabond whites." Thomas Williamson also defended the Dakota, reporting that "the only pilfering I have heard them charged with is taking lumber from unoccupied houses and this chiefly to make coffins in which to bury their dead." Many of the deaths were likely caused by consumption, which the former prisoners brought with them from Davenport.

Conflicts over land led to numerous relocations over the next several years. During the fall of 1866, the Indian agent ordered Dakota families to move to a new site about four miles east of Niobrara at the mouth of Bazile Creek. In February 1867, the Dakota had to move again, this time several miles to another location called Breckenridge. That October brought a ten-mile relocation farther down the Niobrara River. The boundaries of what was eventually called the Santee Sioux Reservation were not firmly established until the summer of 1869. One superintendent characterized this final location as "the roughest and least valuable tract of country I have seen in Nebraska." Each of these removals required the agent to oversee the breaking of new lands for farms, the construction of agency buildings, and the relocation of more than a thousand Dakota. In an understatement, a government official admitted that "these successive locations cannot have failed to impress the Indians with the uncertainty of their tenure in this new home." The constant moves would "completely demoralize and discourage them." The relocations, as well as conditions on the reservation, led to a sharp decline in population at Niobrara. In 1868, a reservation census counted 1,300 Dakota; by 1870, that number had declined to about a thousand, primarily because of relocations and, more tragically, a high mortality rate.

As in the years immediately before and after the U.S.-Dakota War, Protestant missionaries continued to play a prominent role on the new reservation. Even before Dakota families arrived in Nebraska, the ABCFM missionaries and Samuel Hinman had requisitioned a large, unused hotel for their purposes. Hinman quickly established an Episcopal church and school. In July 1866, just six weeks after families arrived from Crow Creek, Thomas Williamson, Stephen Riggs, and a Dakota preacher named John B. Renville established the Pilgrim Presbyterian Church. Using methods pioneered at Camp Kearney and Crow Creek, the ABCFM selected several Dakota men to be elders and other church leaders, including Robert Hopkins.

In Nebraska, the missionaries continued to enforce a strict definition of what it meant to become and remain a Christian, as they had done at Camp Kearney and Crow Creek. For example, the ministers still required congregants to renounce all Dakota medicine and ceremonies even as sickness and deaths continued. John Williamson complained that some Christian Dakota returned to "heathen practices in times of sickness, calling in the conjuror or medicine man. One woman was admonished for having in her possession a medicine sack, which she was directed to destroy at once." Other church members also angered the missionaries by attending "suppers and dances . . . gotten up by white men." While the missionaries called these dances "a disgrace to humanity," the Dakota obtained food and even pay, which helped supplement their poor diets and lack of clothing, as some had done at Camp Kearney. They also helped their sick relatives.

When families reunited, many also returned to their previous polygamous marriages. Indeed, Stephen Riggs lamented that the number of plural marriages actually increased in Nebraska due to the gender imbalance created by the war and its aftermath. The missionaries, ignoring the reason for the increased number of polygamous marriages, continued to order all Christian men with two or more wives to choose only one; the other wives and their children were to be cast off. These put-away wives struggled to survive without husbands, just as they had done during the forced separation from their male kin at Crow Creek. While some Dakota ended their polygamous marriages, others resisted the missionaries' decree; as Riggs noted, "the adjustment of their marital relations is a work of considerable difficulty."

Some Dakota men chose not to cast away their wives, throw away their medicine sacks, or give up dancing, which led to their suspension from the Presbyterian and Episcopal churches. The refusal of some to give up key cultural and religious practices, many of which had helped them survive the harsh conditions after the war, provides further evidence of the tenuous nature of at least some of the conversions as well as the missionaries' strict requirements for Dakota Christians.

While the missionaries focused most of their time and efforts on promoting Christianity, they increasingly inserted themselves directly into federal Indian policy in order to reward or protect their converts, whom they still called friendly or loyal Indians. In February 1865, Congress authorized $7,500 "for the relief of certain friendly Indians of the Sioux Nation, in Minnesota." The commissioner of Indian affairs, D. N. Cooley, selected Bishop Whipple to determine who would receive payment. In 1866, Whipple's resulting report—which included extensive testimony from Thomas and John Williamson, Riggs, and Hinman—was deemed "just and equitable to all concerned" and used to distribute the funds to "the friendly Sioux who performed acts of bravery in rescuing white captives or signalized in some marked manner their friendship for the whites."

It is not surprising that the thirty-six names on Whipple's final list were mainly Christian Dakota who had served as scouts, including John Other Day, Taopi, Paul Mazakutemani, Simon Anawangmani, several Renvilles, and Lorenzo Lawrence. Whipple's report did not initially assign specific rewards to each person; a government official actually divided the funds among Whipple's names. The resulting rewards were extremely unequal: Other Day collected $2,500, while Anawangmani, Mazakutemani, Taopi, and Lawrence each received $500. Robert Hopkins was paid $150, while the bottom eleven names on the list received only $50. Bishop Whipple complained about the amounts, writing that "it is a great wrong that Other Day shall receive five times the reward of men whose fidelity was equally great." The bishop's influence only went so far, however, and the amounts stood. Although government officials did not always heed Whipple's advice, after 1866 missionary involvement in Indian affairs increased, because bureaucrats sought their opinions and advice as so-called Indian experts.

Of course, Dakota men and women realized that the missionaries increasingly played a role in government distributions, and some undoubtedly cultivated ties to them for this reason. As they had done from Davenport and Crow Creek, many wrote letters to the missionaries from Niobrara asking for their support. Hinman noted that his Dakota students at Niobrara continued to "excel in writing." In a letter to Hinman, for example, Wapaha informed the reverend that he was "yet always holding fast to the Great Spirit." He hoped that Hinman would "help me." Hinman received another letter, filled with descriptions of poverty and sickness on the writer's reservation: "We are going fast to destruction . . . men are dying here every day." The writer asked Hinman if "there was any hope for his people." In 1867, one of the ABCFM's native catechists (likely Robert Hopkins) wrote a letter to Thomas Williamson informing him of the conditions on the reservation. "They are so weak, from want of food," he wrote, "that they can do little work."

Dakota writers also penned letters to nonmissionaries. From Nebraska, Tawahinkpeduta wrote two letters—one to a hospital steward and another to his wife, whom he had met at Camp Kearney. The *Davenport Daily Gazette* published translations of the letters. Before printing them, however, the article praised the author's "excellent" penmanship and the "general style" of the letters, editorializing that "their imprisonment was, at least in some respects, advantageous for them" because they learned to read and write. While the newspaper's summary comments focused on the supposed benefits of imprisonment, Tawahinkpeduta likely had a different goal: he wanted to publicize the poor conditions in Nebraska and perhaps find a market to again sell Dakota goods in Davenport. He wrote: "The country that we are in is very poor and we have hard work to get along. There seems to be no way of earning anything." He remembered how much money he had earned selling items in Davenport and wished he had the same opportunities in Nebraska.

At the same time that Dakota like Tawahinkpeduta struggled to survive in ever-shifting locations near Niobrara, many Sisseton and Wahpeton remained in Dakota Territory unattached to a reservation. In 1867, a hand-picked delegation—headed by the former head of the Dakota scouts, Gabriel Renville—traveled to Washington, D.C., to negotiate a treaty. On February 19, 1867, the delegates signed a treaty creating two reservations: one for the Sisseton and Wahpeton at Lake Traverse, located mostly in present-day northeastern South Dakota, the second one for the Sisseton, Wahpeton, and Cut Head band of Yanktonai at Devil's Lake (now Spirit Lake) in North Dakota. Government officials called these reservations a reward for those Sisseton and Wahpeton who had "in part remained loyal to the Government and furnishing scouts and soldiers to service against their own people." Despite the fact that the government promoted these treaties as a positive development (as, indeed, it did with all treaties), many Sisseton and Wahpeton did not sign or support the document. Stephen Riggs called the treaties "a great swindle" evidently "made in the interests of [former chief of the scouts] J. R. Brown." These treaties "contributed to the extreme factionalism that later plagued the Sisseton-Wahpeton group."

The divisions further increased when government officials and Bishop Whipple directly inserted themselves into the newly established Lake Traverse tribal government. Many of the former scouts settled on the Lake Traverse Reservation and chose Simon Anawangmani as their chief. The government, however, appointed Gabriel Renville "chief of the Sissetons for his efficient aid of whites." During the distribution of annuities, Bishop Whipple followed government orders and would only "talk with the one whom your Great Father has made chief," that is, Gabriel Renville. Paul Mazakutemani strongly protested: "We are Dakotas, and . . . We want to have a chief from among ourselves. . . . Why did the Americans do this without our consent?"

Despite his close ties to the government, Gabriel Renville could do little to ameliorate the poor economic conditions at the Lake Traverse Reservation. The problem was compounded by none other than Joseph Brown, who allegedly continued his fleecing of the Dakota by stealing the reservation's rations and cattle. The Lake Traverse agent, Benjamin Thompson, charged that Brown appropriated the Dakota's cattle for his own use. Although Brown seemed to focus most of his attention on the Lake Traverse Reservation, residents at the Devil's Lake Reservation also suffered. In both locations, grass-hoppers destroyed all their crops, promised government rations failed to appear due to graft, and hunters risked "being treated as hostile" if they left the reservations to hunt buffalo. Conditions became so severe that several families used their tipis to make moccasins and clothing, which left them without shelter.

As they had done from Davenport and Crow Creek and most recently Nebraska, literate Dakota penned letters to the missionaries and government officials, informing them of the difficult conditions on the two new reservations and asking for remediation. Stephen Riggs received dozens of letters from men and women "in the Dakota language" referencing the conditions and asking for missionary aid. John Renville wrote Riggs that "the Indians are trying to be patient and submissive but say they don't think there is any virtue bearing starvation for themselves and their families." He heard "children crying for food and could not get it." Renville offered to travel to Washington with the missionaries to plead the Dakota's case.

Stephen Riggs and Thomas Williamson agreed with Renville about the need to take action and also contemplated traveling to Washington to inform government officials about conditions on the reservations. Before they could make a trip east, however, Bishop Whipple wrote letters to the commissioner of Indian affairs detailing the dire conditions on the Sisseton and Wahpeton reservations. Congress responded to these letters by putting the bishop— reportedly without his knowledge or consent—in charge of distributing food, clothing, and medicine on both reservations for 1867 and 1868. Although he did not want to travel to Dakota Territory, Whipple finally acquiesced and agreed to purchase and distribute the supplies. When handing them out, he enforced a treaty provision that stated that "every able-bodied man must work" to receive them. "If you are idle," he warned, "you must starve." Of course, the treaty defined labor for the men as working in agriculture, cutting timber, and constructing homes and, for the women, as performing domestic work. Whipple reported that despite some initial anger at this provision, his enforcement of the labor policy led to them all "working like beavers." During a trip to the reservations after Whipple's distributions, however, Thomas Williamson reported that the majority of Dakota still faced weakness from starvation.

Whipple's control over the distribution of supplies again illustrates the missionaries' evolving relationship with the government. During their first decades proselytizing to Dakota in Minnesota, between 1830 and 1860, most missionaries resolutely refused to meddle in Indian policy; indeed, their national boards actively discouraged any criticism of government officials or policy. As such, if they disliked a specific government program or a specific agent, they voiced their displeasure only in private correspondence. In the years following the war, from 1862 to 1866, the missionaries publicly protested the harsh conditions at Crow Creek and Davenport and supported Christian Dakota. However, they stopped short of inserting themselves into the management of Indian affairs and focused instead on supporting Christian and "civilized" Indians. From 1866 to 1869, however, Bishop Whipple in particular was directly involved in carrying out government Indian policy. His actions served as a precursor to President Ulysses Grant's decision to give Indian affairs entirely over to missionary organizations in the 1870s. While Whipple received some criticism from missionary circles for "accepting the secular appointment of the charge of the Dakota Indians," O. H. Browning, the secretary of the interior, defended Whipple, stating that he was "much better qualified to make a selection [for the Dakota] than I" and lauding the bishop for "his valuable counsel and assistance in the management of Indian Affairs."

In 1869, the ABCFM missionaries also inserted themselves into the establishment of a "civilized" farming community in Dakota Territory. The creation of this new settlement further divided the already fragmented Dakota. In the early spring, twenty-five families with strong ties to the ABCFM missionaries left the Santee Sioux Reservation "to take homesteads and become citizens." They formed their new community on the Big Sioux River, near present-day Flandreau, South Dakota. Many of the Dakota homesteaders were former Camp Kearney prisoners who had become and remained Christians. John Williamson stated that "the germs of this movement are to be found in the resolves for a new life made by these men when in prison."

Their decision to settle on homesteads near Flandreau was based on a small clause in the 1868 Treaty of Fort Laramie. Although the Fort Laramie treaty mainly involved Oglala, Miniconjou, and Brulé Lakota as well as Yanktonai and Arapaho, several Santee Dakota representatives also signed the document. The treaty promised that if Indians "did not get a tract of land on a reservation established for them, any man over 18 years of age could take a homestead on public land of 160 acres." Because the government failed to allot land on the reservation near Niobrara, the families decided to claim homesteads in Dakota Territory.

Despite the clause in the Fort Laramie treaty authorizing allotments, the Flandreau settlement brought "opposition from the government and their own chiefs." Non-Dakota landowners also complained about their new neighbors, contesting the allotments "on the ground that Indians were not citizens." The ABCFM missionaries, especially John Williamson, stepped in to support the newly formed community. Most important, Williamson helped Flandreau residents navigate conflicts with white settlers and the government. He even traveled to Washington and met with President Grant to plead for his support of the community. After that meeting, officials ruled that if the Flandreau homesteaders "permanently and wholly" dissolved all tribal connections, then they could "exercise the rights and assume the obligations of citizens." With Williamson's support, the Flandreau Dakota "executed a document renouncing their tribal ties and all benefits due them as members of their tribe." In 1870, those who could afford the fourteen-dollar fee "were finally given titles to their land." In 1871, John Williamson established a Presbyterian church with a membership of forty-seven. From its small beginnings, the community grew over the next several years, with approximately four hundred men, women, and children leaving Niobrara to settle permanently near Flandreau. Beginning in the mid-1870s, John Williamson served as U.S. special Indian agent to Flandreau. As such, he joined his rival Bishop Whipple as part of the growing missionary-government alliance.

The existence of the Flandreau community, as well as the three reservations at Devil's Lake, Lake Traverse, and Niobrara, illustrates the permanent division of the Dakota Oyate that came after 1866 despite promises of reunification. At each of these locations, Dakota men, women, and children continued to suffer from disease, poverty, and factionalism. Local homesteaders in Nebraska and Dakota Territory no longer demanded to see the exotic Dakota, nor did they clamor to purchase their bows and arrows or other handmade items; instead, settlers once again viewed their Native American neighbors as dangerous impediments to civilization. Settlers accused them of stealing land, appropriating timber, and robbing stores. These accusations led to continued moves and the loss of additional land over the next several decades, even after relocation to seemingly permanent reservations. Even D. N. Cooley, a former commissioner of Indian affairs, admitted that the relocations and subsequent suffering were unjust. "The only offense of which many of them appear to have been guilty," Cooley conceded, "is that of being Sioux Indians."

Still, collectively and individually, Dakota struggled to survive when faced with continued divisions and challenges. After 1866, many Dakota turned to the same tools they had relied on to help them navigate the postwar years. Some continued or established ties to missionaries; indeed, cultivating ties to missionaries became ever more significant as religious leaders like Henry Whipple and John Williamson increasingly became involved in the administration of Indian affairs. Dakota men and women also used literacy to write letters publicizing the poor conditions on the reservations and asking for aid. At least some converts continued to protest the missionaries' strict definition of what it meant to become and remain a Christian, especially with regard to polygamous marriages and healing ceremonies.

These methods of protest, however, could not remedy the problems and conflicts that defined the years following the Dakota's supposed reunification. After 1866, the Dakota Oyate remained divided, Minnesota stayed out of reach for all but a handful of Dakota, and many still faced starvation and illnesses. Protestant missionaries remained committed to "civilizing" and Christianizing all Dakota, as they had since their arrival in Minnesota in the early 1830s. The missionaries, however, increasingly wielded political power as the control of Indian affairs shifted to Christian organizations.

EPILOGUE

The postwar odyssey of Robert Hopkins Çaske and his family included imprisonment, separation from kin, illness, starvation, and death. While the Hopkinses' experience was not universal, especially due to their close ties to the ABCFM missionaries, their lives intersected with many of the key events and tragedies of the postwar period. Thus, it is fitting that this book ends, just as it began, with Robert Hopkins Çaske and his family.

In the late 1860s, after the permanent exile and division of the Dakota Oyate, Robert and Sarah continued their longstanding affiliation with the ABCFM missionaries. They traveled frequently, visiting ABCFM missionaries, their families, and various mission stations in Minnesota, Dakota Territory, and Nebraska. Despite her active travels, Sarah continued to suffer terribly from the consumption she had contracted during her years at Crow Creek. In 1867, Jane Huggins Holtsclaw, a second-generation missionary, reported that "Chaske and Sarah are at Dr. [Williamson's home] . . . Sarah had an alarming cough but hopes to get well." In August 1869, Stephen Riggs met Sarah at a camp meeting. Despite Sarah's optimism two years previously that her health would improve, her sickness had worsened. According to Riggs, "Sarah was standing on the brink of the river. . . . For nearly two years she had been walking 'in the valley and shadow of death.'" Riggs feared her name would soon be "written in heaven." On October 14, 1869, at Fort Wadsworth, Dakota Territory, Sarah Hopkins lost her battle with consumption. Stephen Riggs directly linked her death to events that followed the U.S.-Dakota War, including her exile from Minnesota, her time at Crow Creek, and her extended separation from Robert during his imprisonment. All these events contributed to her "continued decline." Her mother, Catherine Totidutawin, added her beloved daughter's illness and death to the suffering she and her family had endured over the last six years. "In this life upon this earth I have lived very long," she wrote, "and have much hardship."

After Sarah's death, Robert remained affiliated with the Presbyterian Church. While the records are scattered and fragmented, his name appeared in various missionary and government sources that located him across the western states and territories, including the Santee Sioux Reservation in Nebraska, the Lake Traverse Reservation, the Flandreau settlement in present-day South Dakota, and Wolf Point and Box Elder, Montana. Certainly, some of his numerous relocations—for example, to Nebraska—resulted from government-mandated removals designed to permanently settle the Dakota outside Minnesota. Bob Hopkins, the couple's great-great-grandson, recalls that some of his ancestors moved to Montana to escape danger from the bounties that were being paid for Dakota scalps in Minnesota. Many of the subsequent relocations were related to Robert's continuing missionary work. Over the course of several decades, he worked as a teacher and church elder at various locations in Nebraska, Dakota Territory, and ultimately Montana. He continued to teach and preach to the widely scattered Dakota, as he had done in the Davenport prison. While he was not an ordained minister, he wrote that he visited "from house to house through a church community, and praying with them." In 1899, church leaders lauded Robert for his dedication to Christianity, commenting that his "influence for good can surely be counted upon."

In the early 1870s, a few years after Sarah's death, Robert married a Dakota woman named Susan Hapan (born in 1851). They had a son, Moses, in 1872, and another son, Smith, in 1878. According to Bob Hopkins, their family also grew to include two daughters, Winnie and Sarah, who only lived into their early twenties. It is not known if the girls were their biological daughters or if they were adopted into the family. Traditionally, extended families had always played an important role in raising and caring for children. Contemporary Lakota author Virginia Driving Hawk Sneve writes that grandparents and "the mother's sisters or the father's brothers willingly took parentless children into their homes." Thus, the love of children "was not confined to the biological parents, but within the extended family." Caring for the children of kin became even more important after the war, when hundreds of children lost their mothers and fathers through death and separation. It is possible that the Hopkinses' girls were adopted into the family after losing their own mother and father. On the Lake Traverse Reservation, Catherine Totidutawin raised five-year-old Nani, who likely had lost her immediate family as well.

By 1881, Robert Hopkins and his family resided in Wolf Point, Montana, where he worked as a helper and teacher for the local Presbyterian mission. A visitor noted that although Robert was "now advanced in years, he still retains his physical vigor and cheerful heart." At the mission school, Robert focused on teaching students to read and write in the Dakota language, as he had done at Camp Kearney and after his release from prison. In 1887, his tenure as a teacher briefly ended when "policemen" burst into his school three times and arrested most of the children, forcing them to attend the government boarding school at Poplar Creek, some twenty miles away. At the boarding school, teachers punished students for speaking anything other than English and forced them to adopt "civilized" ways. By 1891, Robert had returned to teaching some of the children after the boarding school burned down. Perhaps the local agent's positive evaluation of Robert contributed to the reopening of the school; he called Hopkins "an Indian man of good standing among the Indians as well as the whites."

Robert and Sarah and then Susan passed their affiliation with the ABCFM and Christianity to their sons. After the war, Samuel attended the Crow Creek ABCFM school. In 1866, aged twelve at the time, he lived with Thomas Williamson and his family, studying reading, writing, English, and of course religion. Literacy had always been important to the extended Hopkins family, and Robert and Sarah wanted their son to continue his education. In 1873, Robert sent a letter to the faculty of Beloit College in Wisconsin, stating his "desire . . . to the extent of your ability, [to] teach my son." Supported by his father's letter and the ABCFM, Samuel earned the Fowler Scholarship for Indians and spent at least a year, 1873, at the college. In 1889, he became an ordained Presbyterian minister; he also worked as a teacher. Like his father, Samuel lived an itinerant existence, traveling between scattered churches and schools and frequently moving between reservations in North and South Dakota. In the late 1880s, he settled in Peever, South Dakota, on the Lake Traverse Reservation. At least three of his children attended the

Carlisle Indian Industrial School in Pennsylvania. Meanwhile, according to *Iapi Oaye*, the ABCFM's English-Dakota newspaper, Moses settled in Poplar Creek, Montana, on the Fort Peck Reservation (established in 1871). Moses belonged to the Presbyterian Church, but he did not become a minister.

Because their immediate and extended family remained scattered across the West, Robert and Susan often visited their relatives on the different reservations. In 1888, they visited the Devil's Lake Reservation in the summer, stopping at Fort Berthold in western North Dakota on their way home to Montana. They also frequently traveled between the Flandreau settlement in South Dakota and Montana. In 1891, the family reunited for a double wedding in Montana. Moses Hopkins married Sarah Ptanhawin, and Joseph Hopkins, Robert's nephew, wed Mary Canduhupawin. Edwin J. Lindsey, a white minister married to Thomas Williamson's granddaughter, performed the ceremony. The day before the wedding service, Robert and Reverend Lindsey sat around the dinner table. The conversation centered on Minnesota and the 1862 war. Robert mentioned that he had known Lindsey's grandparents and parents in Minnesota and had rescued them—and a young Lindsey—during the war. He told Lindsey that "your life was saved. I helped to save it. You are to me as one of my own children."

The war, however, had taken Robert away from Minnesota, creating a new itinerant reality that defined the last fifty years of his life. Although he eventually rebuilt his family in Montana, he never forgot Minnesota. According to Hopkins family history, when he passed away on November 14, 1908, reportedly in Ascension, South Dakota, Robert Hopkins's last request was to be taken home and buried in his homeland. According to great-great-grandson Bob Hopkins, Robert Hopkins was laid to rest in Minnesota. After suffering imprisonment in Davenport, isolation from his family at Crow Creek, and movement across several western states, Robert Hopkins had finally returned to his homeland.

Of course, the Hopkins family's story and the Dakota's story in general do not end in the late nineteenth or early twentieth centuries. The hardships that individuals and their communities faced in the 1860s still reverberate into the present day, as do efforts to rectify some of the tragedies that took place more than 150 years ago. For example, while Robert Hopkins was buried in his homeland, those hanged in Mankato or buried at Camp Kearney were not;

to this day, efforts persist to repatriate their remains to Minnesota. Similarly, Dakota communities are working to repatriate objects stolen or taken from them following the war. Many Dakota also still struggle with the historical trauma that stems from knowing that their ancestors were put on display for amusement, treated like vermin that needed to be exterminated, separated from their families, and exiled from their homeland.

Some initial closure has been gained by a few successful repatriations. In 2000, the remains of Dakota leader Marpiya Okinajin, He Who Stands in the Clouds, were finally returned to his homeland of Minnesota. His reburial took place 138 years after his execution at Mankato. Like those of the other thirty-seven men, Marpiya Okinajin's remains had a tragic history. His body was dug up by grave robbers and given to William Mayo, father of the brothers who later founded the Mayo Clinic. Reportedly, the brothers learned anatomy from the skeleton. Later, a "Dr. Sheardown" removed a piece of skin from the body and sent it to "G. S. Knapp" of Chicago. Over the years, Marpiya Okinajin's body was further desecrated and divided; his skull was found on display at the Mayo Clinic, and the piece of skin was somehow transferred to the Grand Rapids Public Museum in Michigan. Under the Native American Graves Protection and Repatriation Act, Marpiya Okinajin was finally laid to rest in the Mdewakanton Ehdakupi Wanagi Makoce (Mdewakanton Repatriation Burial Site) in the Lower Sioux Indian Community, Morton, Minnesota. As of the writing of this book, only two of the other men hanged at Mankato have been repatriated and reburied alongside Marpiya Okinajin. A fourth skeleton may have been displayed in the home of a Mankato doctor; efforts to repatriate these remains have been unsuccessful.

Like Marpiya Okinajin, White Dog was imprisoned, tried, and executed in Mankato. Just before his execution, White Dog gave an intricately designed catlinite pipe to a Lieutenant King, one of his captors (see fig. 1). By the 1880s, the pipe had been transferred to a private collection in Boston. In 2018, it was put up for auction over the strong objections of members of Dakota communities, who regard the pipe as a sacred object. The auction continued despite the protests. Eventually, the pipe was sold to an anonymous buyer for just shy of $40,000 (approximately $20,000 more than the initial estimate of its worth), who promised to return the pipe to the Dakota Oyate. While the pipe was returned to the Lower Sioux Indian Community, other items discussed in this book, such as the tipi stolen at Whitestone Hill, a child's doll also taken during the punitive expeditions, and objects purchased or stolen from families at Fort Snelling, remain in private collections and museums or have been lost over subsequent generations.

These two examples encapsulate the Dakota's enduring historical suffering as well as their long and continuing history of resistance and resilience. For Dakota and all Native Americans, the United States is not a postcolonial society; the past is still felt in the present. Native activists and scholars fight to acknowledge, confront, and decolonize their painful past, just as their ancestors fought to survive after 1862. Until all Americans acknowledge and understand the Dakota Oyate's traumatic history, the past will remain contested ground.

NOTES

Introduction

1, He married Wawiyohiyewin: Stephen R. Riggs, *Tah-Koo Wah-Kań; or, The Gospel among the Dakotas*, 179.

1, By 1860: Sarah-Eva Ellen Carlson, "They Tell Their Story: The Dakota Internment at Camp McClellan in Davenport, 1862–1866," 266.

2, Hopkins wrote: Robert Hopkins and Alexander Huggins to David Greene, June 22, 1848, mss. 244: no. 34, ABCFM Papers, Minnesota Historical Society, St. Paul, Minn., hereafter cited as ABCFM Papers; Robert Hopkins to Selah Treat, December 26, 1848, mss. 244: no. 141, ABCFM Papers. The Minnesota Historical Society has typed transcripts of selected ABCFM Papers related to the ABCFM's Dakota Mission. The originals are held at Harvard University.

2, "grandfather intimidated him": John Williamson, "Robert Hopkins Ta."

2, In 1862 . . . "great deal of energy": Riggs, *Tah-Koo Wah-Kań*, 347.

2, a young photographer: Adrian Ebell traveled from Chicago to Minnesota to photograph Indians in 1862; the timing of his arrival also allowed him to photograph the war. See Alan R. Woolworth, "Adrian J. Ebell, Photographer and Journalist of the Dakota War of 1862."

2, The image shows . . . Dakota dress: For a discussion of Ebell's photograph of Robert Hopkins and his family, see Curtis A. Dahlin, "Between Two Worlds."

2, "a very good one" . . . all of whom were male: Stephen Riggs to Selah Treat, March 3, 1869, reel 769, Papers of the American Board of Commissioners for Foreign Missions, 1827–1929, Wheaton College, Billy Graham Center, Wheaton, Ill., hereafter cited as Papers of the ABCFM.

3, Upon hearing . . . "be able to save": "Accounts of Dakota Conflict compiled at Camp McClellan by Thomas S. Williamson," January 11, 1864, Williamson Family Papers, Augustana College, Rock Island, Ill.

3, Stephen Riggs offered another explanation . . . "separated from his wife and boys": Riggs, *Tah-Koo Wah-Kań*, 348, 374.

5, thousands of pages: The U.S.-Dakota War of 1862 has received extensive coverage. Janet Dean comments on the "flood of words" and the "sheer volume of printed pages devoted to memorializing" it. William Lass's historiography analyzes thirteen different books about the war while noting that many more articles and books were published, including more than "25 articles about the background, nature, and effects of the war" published in the journal *Minnesota History* alone. See Janet Dean, "Nameless Outrages: Narrative Authority, Rape Rhetoric, and the Dakota Conflict of 1862," 94–95, and William E. Lass, "Histories of the U.S.-Dakota War of 1862." For other articles and books detailing the historiography of the war, see Kenneth Carley, *The Dakota War of 1862: Minnesota's Other Civilization*; Kellian Clink, "Historiography of the Dakota Conflict"; and John Hunt Peacock Jr., "An Account of the Dakota-US War as Sacred Text: Why My Dakota Elders Value Spiritual Closure over Scholarly 'Balance,'" which also provides information on translation. Several recent articles and book chapters cover the postwar period. See, for example, Colette A. Hyman, *Dakota Women's Work: Creativity, Culture, and Exile*, and Waziyatawin, *What Does Justice Look Like? The Struggle for Liberation in Dakota Homeland*.

5, "devote much time": David Martínez, "Remembering the Thirty-Eight: Abraham Lincoln, the Dakota, and the U.S. War on Barbarism," 24.

6, "explains a great deal": Colette A. Hyman, "Survival at Crow Creek, 1863–1866," 149–150.

6, "Dakota people remain": Waziyatawin, "Colonial Calibrations: The Expendability of Minnesota's Original People," 452.

6, historians began to stress: John Isch, *The Dakota Trials: Including the Complete Transcripts and Explanatory Notes on the Military Commission Trials in Minnesota, 1862–1864*, 1.

6, the larger history: Steven C. Schulte, "American Indian Historiography and the Myth of the Origins of the Plains Wars," 438; Brad Tennant, "The 1864 Sully Expedition and the Death of Captain John Feilner," 183.

6, "military campaigns": Roy W. Meyer, *History of the Santee Sioux: United States Indian Policy on Trial*, 136.

6, "history of all": Charles Eastman, *The Indian To-day: The Past and Future of the First American*, 28.

7, "the narrative of American history": Ned Blackhawk, *Violence over the Land: Indians and Empires in the Early American West*, 5.

7, In recent years: For a historiography of changing interpretations of Native American and First Nations history, especially the growing focus on agency and resistance, see John Munro, "Interwoven Colonial Histories: Indigenous Agency and Academic Historiography in North America."

7, "grave injustices": David Martínez, *Dakota Philosopher: Charles Eastman and American Indian Thought*, 129.

8, "single point of view": Gwen N. Westerman, "Treaties Are More than a Piece of Paper: Why Words Matter," 297.

8, legacy of "genocide": Waziyatawin, "Colonial Calibrations," 451.

8, "Dakota descendants": Peacock, "An Account of the Dakota-US War as Sacred Text," 197.

8, "not something that can be forgotten": Gary L. Roberts, *Massacre at Sand Creek: How Methodists Were Involved in an American Tragedy*, 1.

8, "the most innocent victims": Margaret D. Jacobs, "Genocide or Ethnic Cleansing? Are These Our Only Choices?" 447. Colette Hyman and Waziyatawin have authored several books and articles that reference the experience of Dakota women. See Hyman, "Survival at Crow Creek," and Waziyatawin, *What Does Justice Look Like?*

9, Protestant missionaries: Several Catholic priests proselytized to Dakota both before and after the war, especially at Fort Snelling and Mankato. However, Catholic missionaries were not at Camp Kearney or Crow Creek, although they would eventually establish missions across Dakota Territory in the late nineteenth century. For these reasons, I have not covered Catholic missionaries in this book.

10, colonize . . . "Indigenous Peoples": Waziyatawin and Michael Yellow Bird, eds., *For Indigenous Eyes Only: A Decolonization Handbook*, 2.

10, Indeed, Waziyatawin argues: Waziyatawin, *What Does Justice Look Like?* 83.

10, "ethnocide": Waziyatawin, *Remember This! Dakota Decolonization and the Eli Taylor Narratives*, 7. See also Waziyatawin, *What Does Justice Look Like?* 29.

10, "more subtle and insidious expressions": Jacobs, "Genocide or Ethnic Cleansing?" 445.

10, "the wounds of colonialism . . . culture": Michelle M. Jacob, *Yakama Rising: Indigenous Cultural Revitalization, Activism, and Healing*, 4, 12. There is a growing body of scholarship on the colonization and decolonization of indigenous peoples in the United States and around the world. For a summary of decolonization studies among Native American historians, see J. Kēhaulani Kauanui, ed., *Speaking of Indigenous Politics: Conversations with Activists, Scholars, and Tribal Leaders*, and Susan A. Miller, "Native America Writes Back: The Origin of the Indigenous Paradigm in Historiography" and "Native Historians Write Back: The Indigenous Paradigm in American Indian Historiography." For a further introduction to global indigenous decolonization, see Maori educator Linda Tuhiwai Smith's *Decolonizing Methodologies: Research and Indigenous Peoples*. Current decolonization efforts extend not only to history but to museums and numerous other public sites; for example, see Amy Lonetree, *Decolonizing Museums: Representing Native America in National and Tribal Museums*. See Waziyatawin and Yellow Bird, eds., *For Indigenous Eyes Only*, for a manual on implementing decolonization at the community level. For information on missionaries and colonization, see Robert Craig, "Christianity and Empire: A Case Study of American Protestant Colonialism and Native Americans," and George E. Tinker, *Missionary Conquest: The Gospel and Native American Cultural Genocide*.

10, missionary children: Children affiliated with many ABCFM missions also became missionaries when they reached adulthood. The six sons of Peter and Fanny Gulick, ABCFM missionaries in Hawaii, worked as missionaries after finishing their schooling. Myron Eells, the son of ABCFM Oregon missionaries Cushing and Myra Eells, established his own mission on the Skokomish Reservation on the Olympic Peninsula in Washington Territory. See Patricia Grimshaw, "'Christian Woman, Pious Wife, Faithful Mother, Devoted Missionary': Conflicts in Roles of American Missionary Women in Nineteenth-Century Hawaii," 511; Mary Zwiep, "Sending the Children Home: A Dilemma for Early Missionaries," 61; and http://nwda.orbiscascade.org/ark:/80444/xv32708.

12, Minnesotans . . . could not be trusted: Throughout the nineteenth century, Sioux were portrayed as violent and dangerous in popular culture. Specifically in Minnesota, most settlers developed a "relationship of fear, misunderstanding, and often hatred" of Dakota prior to the war. See Erik K. Clabaugh, "The Evolution of a Massacre in Newspaper Depictions of the Sioux Indians at Wounded Knee, 1876–1891," 41, 44; John M. Coward, *The Newspaper Indian: Native Identity in the Press, 1820–90*, 133, 191; and Bruce M. White, "Stereotypes of Minnesota's Native People," 100.

12, The Dakota's postwar experiences: Ned Blackhawk, "Look How Far We've Come: How American Indian History Changed the Study of American History in the 1990s," 15.

12, "intentionally altered or destroyed": Renato Rosaldo, *Culture and Truth: The Remaking of Social Analysis*, 69.

12, tourists' fantasies: For a discussion of Native Americans at world's fairs, see Robert W. Rydell, *All the World's a Fair: Visions of Empire at American International Expositions, 1876–1916*. For general information on Wild West shows, see Joy S. Kasson, *Buffalo Bill's Wild West: Celebrity, Memory, and Popular History*, and Paul Reddin, *Wild West Shows*. For specific information on Indians in the Wild West shows, see Linda Scarangella McNenly, "Foe, Friend, or Critic: Native Performers with Buffalo Bill's Wild West Show and Discourses of Conquest and Friendship in Newspaper Reports." Christina Welch, in "Savagery on Show: The Popular Visual Representation of Native American Peoples and Their Lifeways at the World's Fairs (1851–1904) and in Buffalo Bill's Wild West (1884–1904)," discusses both world's fairs and Wild West shows as creating similar images of Native Americans.

12, turn the situation to their advantage: For example, see Andrew Denson, "Muskogee's International Fairs: Tribal Autonomy and the Indian Image in the Late Nineteenth Century."

14, "kill the Indian in him": Richard Henry Pratt, quoted in Isabel C. Barrows, ed., *Proceedings of the National Conference of Charities and Correction*, 46.

1. War, Trials, Execution, and Exile, 1862–1863

17, In October 1862 . . . captured by Dakota warriors during the war: John Isch, *The Dakota Trials: Including the Complete Transcripts and Explanatory Notes on the Military Commission Trials in Minnesota, 1862–1864*, 196–197.

18, "strong excitement . . . it really was": Thomas Williamson to Selah Treat, November 21, 1862, mss. 310: no. 224, ABCFM Papers.

18–19, "a very strong appeal": Stephen Riggs to Mary Riggs, November 13, 1862, Stephen R. Riggs and Family Correspondence, Concerning Lac qui Parle Mission and Other Matters, Minnesota Historical Society, St. Paul, Minn., hereafter cited as Stephen R. Riggs and Family Correspondence.

19, save settlers: Stephen R. Riggs, *Tah-Koo Wah-Kaŋ: or, The Gospel among the Dakotas*, 349.

19, "their innocency": Stephen R. Riggs, *Mary and I: Forty Years with the Sioux*, 180.

19, "no guarantee of safety": Thomas Williamson to Stephen Riggs, October 25, 1862, Stephen R. Riggs and Family Papers, Minnesota Historical Society, St. Paul, Minn.

19, Approximately 2,300 Dakota: Michael A. Eggleston, "Fighting the Sioux," 38.

19, The Mdewakanton: The Dakota are part of the Oceti Śakowiŋ (the Seven Council Fires), comprised of the Dakota (Mdewakanton, Wahpekute, Wahpeton, and Sisseton) in Minnesota, the Nakota (Yankton and Yanktonai) in Nebraska and eastern Dakota Territory, and the Lakota (Teton) in western Dakota Territory. The Council Fires were linked by kinship, linguistics, and geographic proximity. See Ronald G. Stover, "A Graphic Representation of the Minnesota Dakota Diaspora," 32, and Thomas D. Peacock and Donald R. Day, "Nations within a Nation: The Dakota and Ojibwe of Minnesota," 140.

19, By 1862, they had lost: John Bell, "The Sioux War Panorama and American Mythic History," 285.

19, The treaties: Sources provide different numbers of acres lost through the treaties of 1851 and 1858. Waziyatawin places the number at between 24 and 35 million acres. She notes that originally Dakota lands included approximately 54 million acres; today, Dakota people occupy about .006 percent of their original land base. See *What Does Justice Look Like? The Struggle for Liberation in Dakota Homeland*, 34–35, 61.

20, Settlers eager for: Scott W. Berg, "Lincoln's Choice," 33.

20, In 1850, Minnesota: "Annual Message of Governor Ramsey to the Legislature of Minnesota, January 9, 1862," 18, https://www.leg.state.mn.us/docs/NonMNpub /oclc18189672.pdf.

20, "they were starving": Hannah Frazier, quoted in Virginia Driving Hawk Sneve, *Completing the Circle*, 55.

20, traders notoriously: Gary Clayton Anderson, "Myrick's Insult: A Fresh Look at Myth and Reality," 199.

20, "one cent": Bishop Henry Whipple, "The Duty of Citizens Concerning the Indian Massacre," September 1862, box 41, volume 3, letterbook 3, Henry B. Whipple Papers, Minnesota Historical Society, St. Paul, Minn.

20, In the summer of 1862: Gwen N. Westerman and Bruce M. White, *Mni Sota Makoce: The Land of the Dakota*, 193.

20, "no rations for them": Winifred W. Barton, *John P. Williamson: A Brother to the Sioux*, 48.

20, In January 1862 . . . routinely ignored: George E. H. Day to Abraham Lincoln, January 1, 1862, Abraham Lincoln Papers at the Library of Congress, series 1, General Correspondence, 1833–1916, National Archives and Records Administration, Washington, D.C., hereafter cited as Abraham Lincoln Papers.

21, they must "follow": Stephen R. Riggs, trans., "Narrative of Paul Mazakoote-mane," 84.

21, In June 1861 . . . the *Favorite*: *Pioneer and Democrat*, June 15, 1861.

21, During his year-long tour . . . only a few hours: Arthur Sterry, "A Short Visit to an Indian Reservation," [1861], Arthur Sterry Journal, Minnesota Historical Society, St. Paul, Minn.

22–23, "asymmetrical": John Hunt Peacock Jr., "An Account of the Dakota-US War as Sacred Text: Why My Dakota Elders Value Spiritual Closure over Scholarly 'Balance,'" 193.

23, approximately four hundred: The number of settlers who died during the war depends on the source cited and remains controversial. The 1862 *Annual Report of the Commissioner of Indian Affairs* (hereafter cited as *ARCIA*) claimed that 382 settlers were killed during the war (66). In the 1863 *ARCIA*, the Dakota's agent, Thomas J. Galbraith, listed 644 citizens and 93 soldiers killed during the war, for a total of 737 (294). Thomas Williamson "carefully inquired of persons well acquainted in the counties which suffered the most" and put the number at about 600; Thomas Williamson to Walter S. Griffith, April 10, 1863, mss. 310: no. 228, ABCFM Papers. Today, most historians mention 500 deaths, but 400 to 800 also appear in some sources. Legal scholar Carol Chomsky gives the precise number of 464: 77 American soldiers, 29 citizen-soldiers, and 358 settlers; see "The United States–Dakota War Trials: A Study in Military Injustice," 21. Most sources focus on the number of soldiers and settlers killed and rarely mention Dakota deaths. David A. Nichols reminds us that "it was characteristic of the time that few bothered to calculate Indian casualties"; see "The Other Civil War: Lincoln and the Indians," 8.

23, In the first two weeks: Riggs, *Tah-Koo Wah-Kań*, 305; Gary Clayton Anderson and Alan R. Woolworth, eds., *Through Dakota Eyes: Narrative Accounts of the Minnesota Indian War of 1862*, 1.

23, Taopi . . . "three missionaries": "Story of Lorenzo Lawrence," Lorenzo Lawrence Papers, Minnesota Historical Society, St. Paul, Minn.

23, Joseph LaFramboise: *ARCIA* (1863), 404.

23, John Other Day . . . "out of danger": "The Sioux War," *Continental Monthly* 3 (January–June 1863): 198.

23, more than 1,200 Dakota: H. H. Sibley to John Pope, October 30, 1862, in U.S. War Department, *The War of the Rebellion: A Compilation of the Official Records of the Union and Confederate Armies*, volume 13, series 1, 708, hereafter cited as *The War of the Rebellion*.

23, more than 2,000: H. H. Sibley to John Pope, October 5, 1862, *The War of the Rebellion*, 712; John Pope to H. W. Halleck, October 9, 1862, *The War of the Rebellion*, 722; "Samuel J. Brown," 23.

23, Sibley informed those . . . would receive protection: H. H. Sibley to "those of Half-Breeds and Sioux Indians who have not been concerned in the murder and outrages upon the white settlers," September 13, 1863, *The War of the Rebellion*, 632.

23, "to make war": H. H. Sibley to Ma-za-ka-tame and Wa-ke-nan-nan-te, September 24, 1862, *The War of the Rebellion*, 667.

23, Those who surrendered: Barton, *John P. Williamson*, 58.

24, Sibley informed Ta-tanka-nazin . . . "white people": H. H. Sibley to Ta-tanka-nazin, September 24, 1862, *The War of the Rebellion*, 667.

24, Ta-tanka-nazin must have questioned . . . passed away in 1871: "Particulars of the Death of 'Standing Buffalo,'" *Sacramento Daily Union*, August 19, 1871.

24, Wakandayamani . . . four years: Wakandayamani, quoted in http://usdakota war.org/history/aftermath/immediate-consequences/dakota-immediate -aftermath.

24, Sibley informed Charles Flandreau . . . "of suspected characters": H. H. Sibley to Charles Flandreau, September 28, 1862, *The War of the Rebellion*, 688.

24, "new developments": H. H. Sibley to John Pope, September 30, 1862, *The War of the Rebellion*, 694.

24, Sibley set up . . . put them in irons: "Samuel J. Brown," 25.

24, Sibley ordered: John Pope to H. W. Halleck, October 9, 1862, *The War of the Rebellion*, 722. See also Paul Finkelman, "I Could Not Afford to Hang Men for Votes: Lincoln the Lawyer, Humanitarian Concerns, and the Dakota Pardons," 418.

24, Sibley noted that . . . consumption: H. H. Sibley to John Pope, October 11, 1862, *The War of the Rebellion*, 728.

25, In the weeks: Colette Routel, "Minnesota Bounties on Dakota Men during the U.S.-Dakota War," 9.

25, Other Dakota families: Stover, "A Graphic Representation of the Minnesota Dakota Diaspora," 37.

25, These newspapers: Chuck Lewis, "Frontier Fears: The Clash of Dakotas and Whites in the Newspapers of Mankato, Minnesota, 1863–1865," 39; Charles Lewis, "Wise Decisions: A Frontier Newspaper's Coverage of the Dakota Conflict," 52.

25, strong negative emotions: David Martínez, "Remembering the Thirty-Eight: Abraham Lincoln, the Dakota, and the U.S. War on Barbarism," 16.

25, "quiet . . . fury": William Dole, quoted in House Executive Document 1/5, 37th Congress, 3d Session, 1862, 171.

25, "peaceful . . . avocations": Thomas Galbraith, quoted in *ARCIA* (1863), 290.

26, "cruelty": "Removal of the Minnesota Indians to Dakota," *Dakotian*, May 19, 1863.

26, "backward": William E. Lass, "Histories of the U.S.-Dakota War of 1862," 45.

26, "Indians were predisposed": Isaac V. D. Heard, *History of the Sioux War and Massacres of 1862 and 1863*, 31.

26, "feel they have been wronged" . . . "rather than reason": Harriet E. Bishop McConkey, *Dakota War Whoop: or, Indian Massacres and War in Minnesota of 1862-'3*, 127, 125.

26, "every man or woman" . . . "biped tigers": "The News," *St. Cloud Democrat*, September 4, 1862.

26, "Red Fiends" . . . "Hell Hounds": "Peace with the Sioux," *St. Cloud Democrat*, November 13, 1862; "Boston Philanthropy," *St. Cloud Democrat*, December 4, 1862; "Latest Abercrombie Murders," *St. Cloud Democrat*, October 2, 1862.

26, "beasts of prey": Sylvia D. Hoffert, "Gender and Vigilantism on the Minnesota Frontier: Jane Grey Swisshelm and the U.S.-Dakota Conflict of 1862," 343–344. See also Sylvia D. Hoffert, "Jane Grey Swisshelm and the Negotiation of Gender Roles on the Minnesota Frontier," and "Jane Grey Swisshelm, Elizabeth Keckley, and the Significance of Race Consciousness in American Women's History."

27, "wild beasts": "The News," *St. Cloud Democrat*, September 4, 1862.

27, "hunt them. . . crucifiers of infants": "Editorial Correspondence," *St. Cloud Democrat*, March 5, 1863. See also "The Lecture of Mrs. Swisshelm," *St. Cloud Democrat*, January 29, 1863.

27, "persecute a war" . . . "that is the word": "Let the Sioux Race Be Annihilated," *Weekly Pioneer and Democrat*, September 12, 1862.

27, "ruthless assassins" . . . "homes and property": "What Shall Be Done with the Sioux? Letter from Gov. Ramsey to President Lincoln," *New York Times*, November 9, 1862.

27, "borders of the state": "Extra Session. Message of Governor Alexander Ramsey to the Legislature of Minnesota, Delivered September 9, 1862," 12, https://www .leg.state.mn.us/docs/NonMNpub/oclc18189672.pdf.

27, "the horrible massacres" . . . "maniacs or wild beasts": John Pope to H. H. Sibley, September 28, 1862, *The War of the Rebellion*, 685–686.

27, "poison": Thomas Galbraith, quoted in *ARCIA* (1863), 294.

27, "small-pox": "The Dakota Rebellion. No. 2," *St. Paul Daily Press*, December 7, 1862.

27, $25 for every five: "Let the Sioux Race Be Annihilated," *Weekly Pioneer and Democrat*, September 12, 1862.

27, "offer a bounty . . . quickest manner": "Scalps," *St. Cloud Democrat*, September 11, 1862.

28, A company called . . . "vermin": *Mankato Weekly Record*, September 12, 1862. Also quoted in Charles Lewis, "Wise Decisions," 59.

28, "the recent atrocities" . . . "out of the State": Thomas Galbraith, quoted in *ARCIA* (1863), 409.

28, "starve, as they choose": "Nothing but Extermination Will Do," *Goodhue Volunteer*, December 3, 1862.

28, Advocates of removal . . . fishhooks: "The Sioux War," *St. Cloud Democrat*, November 6, 1862.

28, "'far beyond our borders'": Mary Riggs to Stephen Riggs, November 5, 1862, Stephen R. Riggs and Family Correspondence.

28, Most prominently, missionaries: Protestant missionaries were not the only Minnesotans to defend some of the Dakota. Sarah Wakefield, for example, defended Chaska, We-Chank-Wash-ta-don-pee, at his trial. She reported that he had protected her and her children throughout the war. Despite her testimony, the commission found Chaska guilty and sentenced him to hang. See Sarah F. Wakefield, *Six Weeks in the Sioux Tepees: A Narrative of Indian Captivity*.

28, "wicked white men": Thomas Williamson to Selah Treat, September 8, 1862, mss. 310: no. 222, ABCFM Papers.

28, "a hangman . . . grave": John P. Williamson to Selah Treat, November 5, 1862, mss. 310: no. 156, ABCFM Papers.

28–30, "future generations": Riggs, *Mary and I*, 205.

30, "a red skin": Henry Whipple to H. M. Rice, November 29, 1862, box 41, volume 3, letterbook 3, Henry B. Whipple Papers.

30, "their late reservation": Thomas Williamson to Selah Treat, December 1, 1862, mss. 310: no. 226, ABCFM Papers.

30, "wicked men": Thomas Williamson to Walter S. Griffith, April 10, 1863, mss. 310: no. 228, ABCFM Papers.

30, "some of our people" . . . "the Indian": Thomas Williamson, "The Indian Question," 624.

30, "bad policy": Stephen Riggs to his wife Mary, October 18, 1862, Stephen R. Riggs and Family Correspondence.

30, "wives, children, and friends" . . . "docile pupils": Henry Whipple to the Secretary of the Interior, April 21, 1863, box 41, volume 3, letterbook 3, Henry B. Whipple Papers.

30, "sentenced to death": Thomas Williamson to Selah Treat, November 21, 1862, mss. 310: no. 224, ABCFM Papers.

30, "There is no man" . . . "demand it": Henry Benjamin Whipple, *Lights and Shadows of a Long Episcopate: Being Reminiscences and Recollections of the Right Reverend Henry Benjamin Whipple*, 127–128.

30, "the innocent": Henry Whipple to H. M. Rice, November 29, 1862, box 41, volume 3, letterbook 3, Henry B. Whipple Papers.

31, "our beloved Christian Indians": Henry Whipple to Sibley, March 7, 1863, box 41, volume 3, letterbook 3, Henry B. Whipple Papers; Whipple to Hinman, November 4, 1862, box 41, volume 4, letterbook 4, Henry B. Whipple Papers.

31, "not supporting extermination": Diane Wilson, *Beloved Child: A Dakota Way of Life*, 34. Wilson's quote actually references Richard Henry Pratt and his Carlisle Indian Industrial School in the latter part of the nineteenth century, but the sentiment applies equally to missionaries.

31, General Sibley: Roy W. Meyer, *History of the Santee Sioux: United States Indian Policy on Trial*, 136; Barton, *John P. Williamson*, 59.

31, conflict of interest: Routel, "Minnesota Bounties on Dakota Men during the U.S.-Dakota War," 9.

31, On September 28 . . . "other outrages": Maeve Herbert, "Explaining the Sioux Military Commission of 1862," 771.

31, Those found guilty: H. H. Sibley to John Pope, September 28, 1862, *The War of the Rebellion*, 687.

31, While Sibley conceded . . . "my justification": H. H. Sibley to Charles E. Flandreau, September 28, 1862, *The War of the Rebellion*, 688.

31, When the trials ended . . . 69 were acquitted: Peacock, "An Account of the Dakota-US War of 1862 as Sacred Text," 194. See also Chomsky, "The United

States–Dakota War Trials," 7. For a list of the Dakota prisoners and their sentences, see "Names of the Condemned Dakota Men" in the *American Indian Quarterly*. Fourteen Ho-Chunk men were also tried; thirteen were acquitted, and one was sent to Camp Kearney.

31, If Sibley had executed: Waziyatawin, "Colonial Calibrations: The Expendability of Minnesota's Original People," 464.

31, "incompetent": Thomas Williamson to Selah Treat, November 21, 1862, mss. 310: no. 224, ABCFM Papers.

31, Bishop Whipple . . . "a military commission": *Spirit of Missions* 28, no. 3 (March 1863): 52.

31, Whipple wrote: Meyer, *History of the Santee Sioux*, 138–139.

32, Stating that . . . guilty until proven innocent: John Williamson to Selah Treat, November 5, 1862, mss. 310: no. 156, ABCFM Papers.

32, The defendants: John A. Haymond argues that in 1862 it was not a statutory requirement of military courts to provide defense counsel; see *The Infamous Dakota War Trials of 1862: Revenge, Military Law and the Judgment of History*, 79. However, John Williamson, commenting at the time, *believed* that the Dakota defendants should have been provided counsel. See John Williamson to Selah Treat, November 5, 1862, mss. 310: no. 156, ABCFM Papers.

32, The prisoners . . . used against them: Finkelman, "I Could Not Afford to Hang Men for Votes," 425.

32, hearsay evidence: John Williamson to Selah Treat, November 5, 1862, mss. 310: no. 156, ABCFM Papers; *Missionary Herald* 59, no. 1 (January 1863): 15–16; Routel, "Minnesota Bounties on Dakota Men during the U.S.-Dakota War," 9.

32, "forbid all justice": Henry Whipple to Sibley, March 7, 1863, box 41, volume 3, letterbook 3, Henry B. Whipple Papers.

32, 363 cases: Haymond, *The Infamous Dakota War Trials of 1862*, 85.

32, try one white man for murder: John Williamson to Selah Treat, November 5, 1862, mss. 310: no. 156, ABCFM Papers.

32, only a few minutes: Haymond, *The Infamous Dakota War Trials of 1862*, 84. See also Riggs, *Tah-Koo Wah-Kań*, 333.

32, The commission also applied . . . could not use this defense: Riggs, *Tah-Koo Wah-Kań*, 334.

32, Finally . . . or an animal: Isch, *The Dakota Trials*, 514.

32, "five dollars": Thomas Williamson to John Smith, November 13, 1862, reel 764, Letters Received by the Office of Indian Affairs, 1824–1870, St. Peter's Agency, 1862–1865, National Archives and Records Administration, Washington, D.C.

32, Federal law: Daniel W. Homstad, "Lincoln's Agonizing Decision," 28.

32, As such, Pope . . . guilty of rape: Janet Dean argues that "many white westerners joined in activating a stereotype of Indian male sexual aggression to silence reformist objections from the East." See "Nameless Outrages: Narrative Authority, Rape Rhetoric, and the Dakota Conflict of 1862," 104.

32, rape and murder: Herbert, "Explaining the Sioux Military Commission of 1862," 783.

32–33, He ordered the reviewers: Nichols, "The Other Civil War," 11.

33, all 303: Charles Lewis, "Wise Decisions," 62.

33, "condemned by the military court": Alexander Ramsey to Abraham Lincoln, November 10, 1862, *The War of the Rebellion*, 787.

33, "executed without exception": John Pope to Abraham Lincoln, November 11, 1862, *The War of the Rebellion*, 788.

33, pardoning any Dakota: Chomsky, "The United States–Dakota War Trials," 29.

33, "Tapaytatanka . . . the Agency": Jane L. Williamson to Stephen R. Riggs, November 14, 1862, Abraham Lincoln Papers.

33, "government and people": Stephen R. Riggs to Abraham Lincoln, November 17, 1862, Abraham Lincoln Papers.

33, "rescued white captives": Bishop Henry Whipple, "The Duty of Citizens Concerning the Indian Massacre," September 1862, box 41, letterbook 3, Henry B. Whipple Papers.

33, He wrote Lincoln . . . "deserve hanging": Henry H. Sibley to Abraham Lincoln, February 16, 1863, Abraham Lincoln Papers.

33, Sibley also wrote . . . "war of races": Henry Sibley to Henry Whipple, December 7, 1862, box 3, folder 4, Henry B. Whipple Papers.

33, "Indians in future": "The Sioux Indians," *St. Cloud Democrat*, December 4, 1862.

34, prisoners and their guards: Gabriel Renville, "A Sioux Narrative of the Outbreak in 1862, and of Sibley's Expedition in 1863," 609–610.

34, "insane": Riggs, *Mary and I*, 209.

34, On December 4 . . . "released on parole": "The Minnesotians Attempting to Take the Law into Their Own Hands," *Sunbury American*, December 13, 1862.

34, "lie down": Riggs, *Tah-Koo Wah-Kan*, 360.

34, "It was a sad sight": *Annual Report of the American Board of Commissioners for Foreign Missions* (1863), 147, hereafter cited as *Annual Report of the ABCFM*.

34, "stones and sticks": John Williamson to Selah Treat, November 28, 1862, mss. 310: no. 157, ABCFM Papers.

34, At Henderson . . . "beating them": "Samuel J. Brown," 26.

34, "so furious": Mary Renville to Stephen Riggs, January 10, 1863, Stephen R. Riggs and Family Papers.

35, One newspaper article . . . "not been seen for years": "Buffaloes Have Lately Been Shot . . . ," *Semi-Weekly Wisconsin*, April 21, 1863; "Game," *St. Cloud Democrat*, December 4, 1862.

35, An article . . . "murderers from justice": "The Indians," *Goodhue Volunteer*, December 10, 1862.

35, Legal historian . . . "American history": Finkelman, "I Could Not Afford to Hang Men for Votes," 408–409.

35–36, Historian David Martínez . . . "kangaroo courts": Martínez, "Remembering the Thirty-Eight," 6.

36, Other historians . . . desired compromise: For articles discussing the challenges Lincoln faced while making his decision, see Berg, "Lincoln's Choice"; Herbert, "Explaining the Sioux Military Commission of 1862"; Homstad, "Lincoln's Agonizing Decision"; and Nichols, "The Other Civil War."

36, "anxious to not act": Abraham Lincoln, *The Collected Works of Abraham Lincoln*, volume 5, 551.

36, On December 26: Charles Lewis, "Wise Decisions," 48. For a lengthy description of the mass execution, see "Execution of the Indians in Minnesota: Their Confessions of Guilt—Descriptions of the Parting Scenes—The Execution," *New York Times*, January 4, 1863.

36, Approximately 1,400 soldiers: In 1862, Mankato's population was around 1,500; see Charles Lewis, "Wise Decisions," 48. If the reported crowd of more than 4,000 is correct, this meant that many people traveled from other areas around Minnesota to witness the spectacle of the hangings. For example, William Mayo (father of the founders of the Mayo Clinic) traveled from Le Sueur to Mankato to view the executions; see Scott W. Berg, *38 Nooses: Lincoln, Little Crow, and the Beginning of the Frontier's End*, 238.

36, a "prolonged cheer": "Execution of the Indians in Minnesota: Their Confessions of Guilt—Descriptions of the Parting Scenes—The Execution," *New York Times*, January 4, 1863.

36, After the hangings: "Execution of Thirty-Eight Sioux Indians. At Mankato, Minnesota. December 26, 1862." This document, published in 1896, contains a series of copied newspaper articles; see https://babel.hathitrust.org/cgi/pt?id =uc1.31175035167082;view=1up;seq=1.

36–37, Spectators could . . . so-called scientific study: Berg, *38 Nooses*, 242, 240; Meyer, *History of the Santee Sioux*, 130.

37, "had the honor": "Relics," *St. Cloud Democrat*, June 11, 1863.

37, lithographs of the mass execution: Charles Lewis, "Wise Decisions," 71.

37, The popularity . . . "doomed ones": "Fatal Friday," *St. Cloud Democrat*, January 8, 1863.

37, "awful interest": "The Execution of the Minnesota Indians," *Harper's Weekly*, January 17, 1863.

37–38, "physical and cultural differences" . . . "white supremacy": Amy Lonetree,

Decolonizing Museums: Representing Native America in National and Tribal Museums, 12–13.

38, Today, tribal activists: For information on repatriation efforts, see ibid.; James Riding In, "Decolonizing NAGPRA"; and Devon A. Mihesuah, ed., *Repatriation Reader: Who Owns American Indian Remains?*

38, repatriated to the Dakota Oyate: Waziyatawin, *Remember This! Dakota Decolonization and the Eli Taylor Narratives,* 7.

38, 138 years after his execution: "Dakota Warrior's Remains Buried with Honor near Redwood Falls," *Post Bulletin,* May 5, 2014.

38, prisoners in Mankato: Chomsky, "The United States–Dakota War Trials," 37. See also J. R. Brown and G. D. Redfield to Abraham Lincoln, January 7, 1863, Abraham Lincoln Papers.

38, One week, rumors flew . . . "fever and ague": Stephen R. Riggs, "Sketches of the Dakota Mission."

38, Mahpiyatowin . . . Fort Snelling: Anderson and Woolworth, eds., *Through Dakota Eyes,* 55.

38–39, A woman . . . "any kind of food": "Starved to Death," *Daily Democrat and News,* February 27, 1863.

39, A military census: Colette A. Hyman, "Survival at Crow Creek, 1863–1866," 151.

39, pulmonary consumption: Joseph R. Brown, "Report of the prisoners and employees for the Month of March, 1863," March 31, 1863, reel 2, Joseph R. and Samuel J. Brown and Family Papers, Minnesota Historical Society, St. Paul, Minn.

39, In the months: "Report Exhibiting the number of prisoners in the Military prison at Mankato during the month of March 1863," March 31, 1863, and "Report exhibiting the final disposition of the Indian prisoners held in confinement at Mankato," April 1863, reel 2, Joseph R. and Samuel J. Brown Papers.

39, On February 16: Treaties had always been made with Native Americans for their lands. By enacting legislation to remove Dakota people from Minnesota, the government set a precedent for ending the treaty system, which would formally happen following the Civil War. See Meyer, *History of the Santee Sioux,* 141. The Dakota's agent, Thomas Galbraith, explicitly called for the United States to abandon the treaty system. See *ARCIA* (1863), 296.

39, Congress also established: Lass, "Histories of the U.S.-Dakota War of 1862," 46; "Minnesota's Uncivil War," Minnesota Public Radio, September 26, 2002, http://news.minnesota.publicradio.org/features/200209/23_steilm_1862-m/part5.shtml.

39, "made an unprovoked": Act of February 16, 1863, chapter 37, 12 Stat., 652, in George P. Sanger, ed., *The Statutes at Large, Treaties, and Proclamations of the United States of America from December 5, 1859, to March 3, 1863.*

39, On February 21: Act of February 21, 1863, chapter 53, 12 Stat., 658–660, in ibid.

39, This would be another: Hyman, "Survival at Crow Creek," 152. See also William E. Lass, "The Removal from Minnesota of the Sioux and Winnebago Indians." Lass argues that one of the main motives for removing the Ho-Chunk was that settlers coveted their lands. Linda M. Waggoner also discusses the re-moval of the Ho-Chunk from Minnesota; see "Sibley's Winnebago Prisoners: Deconstructing Race and Recovering Kinship in the Dakota War of 1862."

39, On March 3: Act of March 3, 1863, chapter 119, 12 Stat., 819, in Sanger, ed., *The Statutes at Large*. See also Frances H. Relf, "Removal of the Sioux Indians from Minnesota," 420–421.

39, "very generally worded": Lass, "The Removal from Minnesota of the Sioux and Winnebago Indians," 354.

39, Legal scholar . . . "domestic law": Howard J. Vogel, "Rethinking the Effect of the Abrogation of the Dakota Treaties and the Authority for the Removal of the Dakota People from Their Homeland," 539, 542.

40, The Dakota's agent . . . "possible": See *ARCIA* (1863), 295.

40, "a good deal of anxiety": Stephen Riggs to Selah Treat, April 21, 1863, mss. 310: no. 30, ABCFM Papers.

40, great "difficulty": Riggs, trans., "Narrative of Paul Mazakootemane," 90.

40, "just beginning": Thomas Williamson to Stephen Riggs, October 25, 1862, Stephen R. Riggs and Family Papers.

2. Crow Creek, Dakota Territory, 1863–1866

41, seventy-two-year-old mother: Catherine Totidutawin, a Wahpeton Dakota, was born in 1791. She lived until the age of ninety-seven, passing away in 1888. See Elden Lawrence, *The Peace Seekers: The Indian Christians and the Dakota Conflict*, 69.

41, At Crow Creek . . . her little boy died: John Williamson wrote that "Sarah's babe has been very sick. She wants to know if Sammy's pony is still getting along well." The latter part of the quotation indicates that military officials confiscated all Dakota horses, even children's ponies. John Williamson to Jane Williamson, August 27, 1863, Thomas S. Williamson Papers, Minnesota Historical Society, St. Paul, Minn. Based on the information I have found, I am assuming that Sarah and Robert's second son died at Crow Creek. Williamson's letter and other let-ters state that the little boy was extremely ill. After Crow Creek, I have not found a child linked to Robert Hopkins on any census records that fit the time frame when the second son would have lived. Given the incomplete nature of these records, however, I cannot definitely state that he passed away at Crow Creek.

41, Sarah sadly reported . . . "having a hard time": Wawiyohiyewin to Stephen

Riggs, April 27, 1864, trans. Louis Garcia and Michael Simon, Stephen R. Riggs and Family Papers.

42, "The years" . . . "fastened itself upon her": Stephen R. Riggs, *Tah-Koo Wah-Kań; or, The Gospel among the Dakotas*, 184.

42, "very sorry": Mary Riggs, quoted in Maida Leonard Riggs, ed., *A Small Bit of Bread and Butter: Letters from the Dakota Territory, 1832–1869*, 249.

42, "soon covered with graves . . . mention of the name": John Williamson, quoted in Stephen R. Riggs, "Sketches of the Dakota Mission." See also Winifred W. Barton, *John P. Williamson: A Brother to the Sioux*, 77.

42, "uttered the name . . . graves": Virginia Driving Hawk Sneve, *Completing the Circle*, 37.

42, "a dark cloud": Riggs, "Sketches of the Dakota Mission." See also Barton, *John P. Williamson*, 72.

42, Ta-tanka-nazin (Standing Buffalo) . . . "reason to love it": Ta-tanka-nazin, quoted in Gwen N. Westerman, "Treaties Are More than a Piece of Paper: Why Words Matter," 308.

42, "spiritual practices": Diane Wilson, *Beloved Child: A Dakota Way of Life*, 74.

43, In the early morning hours: John Williamson to his Mother, May 13, 1863, Thomas S. Williamson Papers. The number of Dakota who traveled to Crow Creek varies among sources. For example, in his testimony to Congress, John Williamson put the number at 1,324 rather than 1,310. See U.S. Congress, *Conditions of the Indian Tribes. Report of the Joint Special Committee. Appointed under Joint Resolution of March 3, 1865, with an Appendix*, 413.

43, According to . . . throughout the trip: John Williamson to Thomas Williamson, May 9, 1863, Thomas S. Williamson Papers.

43, "where we are going": John Williamson to his Mother, May 13, 1863, Thomas S. Williamson Papers.

43, After departing . . . west and north: Colette A. Hyman, "Survival at Crow Creek, 1863–1866," 152.

43, into Dakota Territory: U.S. Congress, *Conditions of the Indian Tribes*, 413.

43, "find their way back": John Williamson to Stephen Riggs, June 18, 1863, Stephen R. Riggs and Family Papers.

43, "nearly as bad . . . only Indians": Barton, *John P. Williamson*, 73. See also John Williamson to his Mother, May 13, 1863, Thomas S. Williamson Papers.

43, "so crowded": U.S. Congress, *Conditions of the Indian Tribes*, 413.

43, "inhumanity of such crowding" . . . "*540 Indians*": Barton, *John P. Williamson*, 74, 73.

44, "picking on the Indians": John Williamson to Thomas Williamson, May 25, 1863, Thomas S. Williamson Papers.

44, The food was . . . "chance to cook": Barton, *John P. Williamson*, 75.

44, adequate medical supplies: William E. Lass, "The Removal from Minnesota of the Sioux and Winnebago Indians," 413. See also John Williamson to his Mother, May 9, 1863, Thomas S. Williamson Papers.

44, By the end of their journey: John P. Williamson to Thomas S. Williamson, May 20, 1863, Thomas S. Williamson Papers; John Williamson to Stephen Riggs, May 25, 1863, Stephen R. Riggs and Family Papers. Again, the numbers differ among sources. In his testimony to Congress, John Williamson stated that sixteen Dakota died on the way to Crow Creek. See U.S. Congress, *Conditions of the Indian Tribes*, 413.

44, By the time the steamer arrived: John Williamson to Thomas Williamson, June 3, 1863, Thomas S. Williamson Papers.

44, In one tragic instance: Frances H. Relf, "Removal of the Sioux Indians from Minnesota," 422.

44, after leaving Fort Snelling . . . charge the crowd: Lass, "The Removal from Minnesota of the Sioux and Winnebago Indians," 358.

44, An article . . . "inhabited this State": "Minnesota Indians," *Semi-Weekly Wisconsin*, May 19, 1863.

45, "relic collecting": Jean M. O'Brien, *Firsting and Lasting: Writing Indians Out of Existence in New England*, xxiv.

45, "many visitors" . . . "very unpleasant": John Williamson to his Mother, May 13, 1863, Thomas S. Williamson Papers.

45, staying almost a week: John Williamson to Thomas Williamson, May, 25, 1863, Thomas S. Williamson Papers.

45, "to see Nature" . . . "science of Indianery:" "The Sioux Indians," *Morning Herald*, May 13, 1863.

45, "it is very annoying . . . worth of observation": "The Sioux," *Morning Herald*, May 14, 1863.

45, On May 30 . . . reached Crow Creek: U.S. Congress, *Conditions of the Indian Tribes*, 396.

45–46, Crow Creek was situated: Lass, "The Removal from Minnesota of the Sioux and Winnebago Indians," 360. For an extensive description of the Crow Creek boundaries, see *ARCIA* (1863), 318.

46, "white people will never desire": *ARCIA* (1864), 410.

46, "never will have a sufficient number . . . their location": "The Winnebagoes and the New Reservation," *St. Paul Daily Press*, July 7, 1863.

46, "good soil": *ARCIA* (1863), 311.

46, "land not desired" . . . Dakota to survive: Barton, *John P. Williamson*, 74, 75.

46, "ghost land": *Missionary Herald* 60, no. 9 (September 1864): 262.

46, "looked in vain" . . . "grass roots": Barton, *John P. Williamson*, 75.

46, "Indians can never remain here": John Williamson, quoted in Lass, "The Removal from Minnesota of the Sioux and Winnebago Indians," 364.

46, "Pray for me": John Williamson to Thomas Williamson, n.d., partial letter, Thomas S. Williamson Papers.

46, Despite the poor prospects . . . peoples: Hyman, "Survival at Crow Creek," 154.

46, "government employees and property": *ARCIA* (1863), 319. See also Lass, "The Removal from Minnesota of the Sioux and Winnebago Indians," 363.

46, "one at a time": "The New Sioux and Winnebago Reservations," *St. Paul Daily Press*, October 15, 1863.

46, This stockade: Hyman, "Survival at Crow Creek," 153.

47, "some slab shanties": Edward Pond to his cousin, November 12, 1864, box 4, folder 4, Pond Family Papers, Minnesota Historical Society, St. Paul, Minn.

47, "poor ragged tents" . . . "sad havoc of them": Mary Pond to Rebecca Pond, April 3 1865, box 4, folder 7, Pond Family Papers.

47, When he initially arrived . . . "he gave it up": John Williamson to Thomas Williamson, June 9, 1863, Thomas S. Williamson Papers.

47, After talking with settlers . . . "want of rain": John Williamson to Thomas Williamson, June 3, 1863, Thomas S. Williamson Papers.

47–48, "quite confident": Martha Riggs to Alfred Riggs, July 1, 1863, Alfred L. Riggs Papers, Oahe Mission Collection, South Dakota Conference of the United Church of Christ Archives, Augustana University, Center for Western Studies, Sioux Falls, S.Dak.

48, completely failed: *Missionary Herald* 60, no. 9 (September 1864): 261.

48, "garden of Minnesota": *ARCIA* (1864), 39.

48, "was ill-suited": Hyman, "Survival at Crow Creek," 153.

48, Even if they wanted . . . "attention from the Government": Barton, *John P. Williamson*, 78, 80.

49, whooping cough: John Williamson to Thomas Williamson, June 18, 1863, Thomas S. Williamson Papers; John Williamson to Thomas Williamson, August 13, 1864, Thomas S. Williamson Papers.

49, her little boy: Riggs, *Tah-Koo Wah-Kaṅ*, 188.

49, illness and starvation: John Williamson to Stephen Riggs, July 22, 1863, Stephen R. Riggs and Family Papers.

49, "small children left": John Williamson to Stephen Riggs, September 26, 1863, Stephen R. Riggs and Family Papers. See also U.S. Congress, *Conditions of the Indian Tribes*, 413, and Wilson, *Beloved Child*, 32.

49, starvation and illness: Samuel Hinman to Bishop Whipple, March 25, 1864, box 3, Henry B. Whipple Papers.

NOTES * 195

49, inflammatory rheumatism: John Williamson to Thomas Williamson, July 8, 1865, Thomas S. Williamson Papers.

49, Historian . . . spoiled on the way: William E. Lass, "The 'Moscow Expedition.'"

49, "Agent Balcombe" . . . "starve to death": John Williamson to Thomas Williamson, n.d., probably late 1864, Thomas S. Williamson Papers.

49, "he likes it better": John Williamson to Stephen Riggs, February 11, 1865, Stephen R. Riggs and Family Papers.

49, "nothing but heads" . . . the following June: U.S. Congress, *Conditions of the Indian Tribes*, 405. See also Hyman, "Survival at Crow Creek," 154.

50, "thin clothing": John Williamson to Thomas Williamson, December 24, 1863, Thomas S. Williamson Papers; U.S. Congress, *Conditions of the Indian Tribes*, 407.

50, When Agent Balcombe . . . reservation staff: U.S. Congress, *Conditions of the Indian Tribes*, 407.

50, Wicahpewastewin . . . "their garments": Gary Clayton Anderson and Alan R. Woolworth, eds., *Through Dakota Eyes: Narrative Accounts of the Minnesota Indian War of 1862*, 264.

50, Wasuhiya-ye-dom . . . "depredations against the whites": U.S. Congress, *Conditions of the Indian Tribes*, 407, 416.

50, Moreover, Balcombe . . . attacks from the other: Lass, "The Removal from Minnesota of the Sioux and Winnebago Indians," 364.

51, "half rations": Samuel Brown to Joseph Brown, November 23, 1863, reel 2, Joseph R. and Samuel J. Brown and Family Papers.

51, David Faribault . . . "bread out of it": U.S. Congress, *Conditions of the Indian Tribes*, 405.

51, To combat . . . heated overnight: Barton, *John P. Williamson*, 79.

51, Dakota families . . . "decomposed meat": U.S. Congress, *Conditions of the Indian Tribes*, 414, 401–402.

51, "They give us soup" . . . "I am in trouble": Catherine Totidutawin to Stephen Riggs, April 27, 1864, trans. Louis Garcia and Michael Simon, Stephen R. Riggs and Family Papers.

51, Several years later . . . her week-old infant: U.S. Congress, *Conditions of the Indian Tribes*, 407–414.

52, On June 9 . . . women and children: John Williamson to Thomas Williamson, June 9, 1863, Thomas S. Williamson Papers.

52, By 1865: Waziyatawin, "Colonial Calibrations: The Expendability of Minnesota's Original People," 479.

52, "emphasized complementary contributions" . . . "adult sons": Hyman, "Survival at Crow Creek," 149.

52, "diminish the Dakota population": Waziyatawin, "Colonial Calibrations," 479.

For a discussion of colonialism, gender, reproduction, and Native American women, see the chapter "'Better Dead than Pregnant': The Colonization of Native Women's Reproductive Health," in Andrea Smith, *Conquest: Sexual Violence and American Indian Genocide.*

52, According to letters: Samuel Brown to Joseph Brown, August 19, 1863, reel 2, Joseph R. and Samuel J. Brown and Family Papers; Samuel Brown to his sister, September 2, 1863, reel 2, Joseph R. and Samuel J. Brown and Family Papers.

52, "Mazetouwin . . . ragged and dirty": Joseph Brown to "My dear daughter," February 13, 1864, reel 3, Joseph R. and Samuel J. Brown and Family Papers.

52, back to Crow Creek: Wawiyohewin to Stephen Riggs, April 27, 1864, trans. Louis Garcia and Michael Simon, Stephen R. Riggs and Family Papers.

52, hunting at Crow Creek: Unknown author to Stephen Riggs, April 27, 1863, Stephen R. Riggs and Family Papers.

52, "a man or a gun": John Williamson to Thomas Williamson, August 13, 1864, Thomas S. Williamson Papers.

52, "their principal food": *Missionary Herald* 60, no. 9 (1864): 261. See also Ramona Stately, "Pazahiyayewin and the Importance of Remembering Dakota Women."

52, "hanging from the trees": John Williamson to Stephen Riggs, July 26, 1864, Stephen R. Riggs and Family Papers. See also "The Grasshopper Scourg in Dakota," *Goodhue Volunteer*, August 24, 1864.

52, By early 1864 . . . "desert to the hostiles": Barton, *John P. Williamson*, 82.

53, In early February . . . hungry women and children: Williamson noted that "the progress was slow, as even the strong among them were enfeebled by hunger." See Barton, *John P. Williamson*, 82.

53, In an understatement . . . pulled by horses: John Williamson to his Mother, March 2, 1864, Thomas S. Williamson Papers; Sneve, *Completing the Circle*, 10.

53, little ammunition: Barton, *John P. Williamson*, 82. The missionaries reported that "they have been deprived of their arms and implements for hunting, with a very few exceptions, their horses, cattle and wagons were lost or have been disposed of." See *Missionary Herald* 59, no. 7 (1863): 204.

53, searching for buffalo: U.S. Congress, *Conditions of the Indian Tribes*, 408.

53, "hollow eyes" . . . "life-saving buffalo hunt": Barton, *John P. Williamson*, 84, 86.

53, "a *moral hero*": *Annual Report of the ABCFM* (1865), 148.

53, Williamson supported what: John Williamson wrote that "contrary to our usual course, we were compelled to advise as many of them as could do so, to scatter off, wherever there was any prospect of their picking up for a living." See *Missionary Herald* 60, no. 7 (1864): 203.

53, He rejoiced that: *Annual Report of the ABCFM* (1864), 142.

54, Indeed, Edward Pond: Edward Pond to his Cousin, May 2, 1864, box 4, folder 5, Pond Family Papers.

54, Williamson also hoped: *Missionary Herald* 60, no. 7 (July 1864): 204.

54, Wasuhiya-ye-dom offered . . . "the goods": U.S. Congress, *Conditions of the Indian Tribes*, 407.

54, Issuing another shameful charge: Samuel Hinman to Henry Whipple, June 8, 1863, box 3, folder 6, Henry B. Whipple Papers.

54, Because government agents . . . in flour: U.S. Congress, *Conditions of the Indian Tribes*, 408.

54, They "cut and hauled wood": Sneve, *Completing the Circle*, 59.

54, "water for all": Riggs, *Tah-Koo Wah-Kań*, 367.

54, in search of food and supplies: Wawiyohewin to Stephen Riggs, April 27, 1864, trans. Louis Garcia and Michael Simon, Stephen R. Riggs and Family Papers.

54, "in search of food": *Missionary Herald* 60, no. 4 (April 1864): 102.

55, "keep them alive": *Missionary Herald* 60, no. 7 (July 1864): 203.

55, Other women: John Williamson noted that "they have shown not only a willingness, but a strong desire to work; but there had been almost nothing which they could do." See *Annual Report of the ABCFM* (1864), 142.

55, At the fort: Hyman, "Survival at Crow Creek," 156; Sneve, *Completing the Circle*, 59.

55, For instance, Mazetouwin . . . "for a long time": Joseph Brown to "My dear daughter," February 13, 1864, reel 3, Joseph R. and Samuel J. Brown and Family Papers.

55, John Williamson testified . . . "for something to eat": U.S. Congress, *Conditions of the Indian Tribes*, 414–415, 405.

55, "foul licentiousness": *ARCIA* (1864), 415.

55–56, "the influence . . . they could get": Mary Francis Pond to Rebecca Pond, April 3, 1865, box 4, folder 7, Pond Family Papers.

56, "all is blasphemy": Samuel Hinman to Henry Whipple, June 8, 1863, box 3, folder 6, Henry B. Whipple Papers.

56, Despite this abuse . . . Camp Kearney: John Williamson to Thomas Williamson, January 5, 1865, Thomas S. Williamson Papers; John Williamson to Thomas Williamson, July 21, 1863, Thomas S. Williamson Papers.

56, kin in Davenport: *Missionary Herald* 60, no. 5 (May 1864): 138.

56, In January 1865: John Williamson to Thomas Williamson, January 24, 1865, Thomas S. Williamson Papers.

56, In 1865 . . . "clothing of any kind": John Williamson to Thomas Williamson, January 5, 1865, Thomas S. Williamson Papers; Benjamin Roberts to Robert Littler, June 19, 1863, record group 393, entry 236, part 3, lot 2, volume 59/55, Records of United States Army Continental Commands, 1821–1920, National Archives and Records Administration, Washington, D.C., hereafter cited as Records of U.S. Army Continental Commands.

56, "Kinship" . . . "provide assistance": Patricia C. Albers, "Sioux Kinship in a Colonial Setting," 254, 260.

56, "The ultimate aim . . . life itself": Ella Cara Deloria, *Speaking of Indians*, 25.

56, Scholar . . . "Dakota peoplehood": Christopher J. Pexa, "Transgressive Adoptions: Dakota Prisoners' Resistances to State Domination Following the 1862 U.S.-Dakota War," 33.

56–57, "social integration": Albers, "Sioux Kinship in a Colonial Setting," 254.

57, In January 1864 . . . "see to the matter": Samuel Brown to Joseph Brown, January 6, 1864, reel 3, Joseph R. and Samuel J. Brown and Family Papers.

57, "a desolate region": *Annual Report of the ABCFM* (1863), 15.

57, "the barest of existence": *Annual Report of the ABCFM* (1865), 142.

57, "great scarcity of provisions": *Missionary Herald* 60, no. 9 (September 1864): 261.

57–58, The ABCFM missionaries: For example, see *ARCIA* (1864), 415. Stephen Riggs "had a long talk the other day with Agent Galbraith about [Crow Creek] and also with Mr. Thompson. How is it possible that they should be kept there when they can't raise food?" Stephen Riggs to Selah Treat, September 15, 1863, mss. 310: no. 34, ABCFM Papers.

58, They reported that: *ARCIA* (1864), 420–422.

58, "deplorable . . . condition": Joseph Brown to Samuel Brown, March 18, 1864, reel 3, Joseph R. and Samuel J. Brown and Family Papers.

58, Whipple penned . . . "do my duty": Bishop Whipple to E. N. Biddle, November 24, 1863, E. N. Biddle Papers, Episcopal Diocese of South Dakota Collection, Augustana University, Center for Western Studies, Sioux Falls, S.Dak.

58, "while I lived": Samuel Hinman to Henry Whipple, June 8, 1863, box 3, folder 6, Henry B. Whipple Papers.

58, In January 1864: "Our Indian System," *Weekly National Intelligencer*, January 28, 1864.

58, That April . . . "scarcely a drop of rain in two years": "News on Our Own State," *Chatfield Democrat*, April 23, 1864.

58, Whipple indicted "the Nation itself": "The Case of the Sioux Indians: Interesting Letter from Bishop Whipple in Regard to Them," *New York Times*, December 14, 1862.

58, "beastly swine": "The Right of Confirmation . . . ," *Stillwater Messenger*, March 31, 1863.

58, All the missionaries' public writings: The ABCFM missionaries made several references to not sharing food with Dakota families. Edward Pond wrote that he had "plenty of good beef and pork some fruit and some other things. I do not think we shall starve unless we should pity the Indians so that we should give away all our food." Edward Pond to his Cousin, November 12, 1863, box 4, folder 4, Pond Family Papers.

58–59, The missionaries reminded: *ARCIA* (1864), 420–422.

59, "it is hard": Samuel Hinman to Henry Whipple, June 8, 1863, box 3, folder 6, Henry B. Whipple Papers.

59, "deserve better things": Samuel Hinman to Henry Whipple, January 6, 186[4], box 3, folder 9, Henry B. Whipple Papers.

59, "renounced their religion" . . . church at Crow Creek: *ARCIA* (1864), 420–422.

59, Their poor . . . "spiritual condition": *Missionary Herald* 60, no. 1 (January 1864): 12; *Missionary Herald* 61, no. 3 (March 1865): 70.

59, "physical trials" . . . "temptation": *Annual Report of the ABCFM* (1865), 142.

59, "give up their faith": *Missionary Herald* 61, no. 3 (March 1865): 70.

59, "best young men" . . . "teachers and preachers": John Williamson to Stephen Riggs, January 5, 1864, Stephen R. Riggs and Family Papers.

59, "liberated" . . . "a comfortable living": *ARCIA* (1864), 420–422.

59, "hunted down the Minnesota Sioux": Gary L. Roberts, *Massacre at Sand Creek: How Methodists Were Involved in an American Tragedy*, 186.

59, Largely in response . . . *Conditions of the Indian Tribes*: Harry Kelsey, "The Doolittle Report of 1867: Its Preparation and Shortcomings," 107.

60, Wasuhiya-ye-dom's testimony . . . "some other location": U.S. Congress, *Conditions of the Indian Tribes*, 406, 365.

60, Also in 1865 . . . "tribes I have seen": General Samuel Curtis to Secretary of the Interior James Harlan, October 4, 1865, box 1, folder 8, Samuel R. Curtis Papers, State Historical Society of Iowa, Des Moines, Iowa.

61, He suggested . . . on the reservation: General Samuel Curtis, [September 18, 1865], "orphaned pages," box 1, folder 8, Samuel R. Curtis Papers.

61, First, while farming remained challenging: For descriptions of the grasshopper infestations in South Dakota during this period, see Harold E. Briggs, "Grasshopper Plagues and Early Dakota Agriculture, 1864–1876," 53.

61, Second, a new agent . . . "low monotonous diet": Barton, *John P. Williamson*, 103.

61, Third, in November 1865 . . . "a source of tension": Hyman, "Survival at Crow Creek," 155. Soon after their arrival at Crow Creek, many Ho-Chunk began to leave their new reservation for the Omaha reservation in Nebraska. On March 8, 1865, the Ho-Chunk signed a treaty officially trading their portion of Crow Creek for a portion of the Omaha reservation. See Linda M. Waggoner, "Sibley's Winnebago Prisoners: Deconstructing Race and Recovering Kinship in the Dakota War of 1862," 43.

3. Camp Kearney Prison, Davenport, Iowa, 1863–1866

63, On May 3 . . . "all the stoves": Clifford Canku and Michael Simon, *The Dakota Prisoner of War Letters: Dakota Kaŝkapi Okicize Wowapi*, 41, 73.

64, The prison's commander . . . "careless about fires": Benjamin S. Roberts to J. F. Meline, October 22, 1863, record group 393, part 3, entry 263, volume 59/55, Records of U.S. Army Continental Commands.

64, "never enough heat" . . . "I am heartbroken": Canku and Simon, *The Dakota Prisoner of War Letters*, 81, 39.

64, in search of provisions: Wawiyohewin to Stephen Riggs, April 27, 1864, trans. Louis Garcia and Michael Simon, Stephen R. Riggs and Family Papers.

64, In spring 1864 . . . "the fight": "Information got from Indian Prisoners in Camp McClellan in reference to the Out Break," January 11, 1864, Williamson Family Papers, Augustana College, Rock Island, Ill.

64, In early fall 1864: Stephen Riggs to Selah Treat, September 26, 1864, reel 7, Papers of the ABCFM; Stephen Riggs to Henry Sibley, September 14, 1864, reel 12, Henry H. Sibley Papers, Minnesota Historical Society, St. Paul, Minn.

64, In September . . . "ten days ago": Stephen Riggs to Mary Riggs, September 12, 1864, Stephen R. Riggs Papers, Oahe Mission Collection, South Dakota Conference of the United Church of Christ Archives, Augustana University, Center for Western Studies, Sioux Falls, S.Dak.

64, Some contemporary authors: Curt Brown, "Minnesota History: Caught in the Middle of the Dakota War."

64, He immediately wanted: Stephen Riggs to Mary Riggs, September 12, 1864, Stephen R. Riggs Papers.

64–65, As he waited . . . "part of them get none": Thomas Williamson to Stephen Riggs, December 12, 1864, Stephen R. Riggs and Family Papers.

65, Finally, in March 1865: John Williamson to Thomas Williamson, March 8, 1865, Thomas S. Williamson Papers.

65, Missionary correspondence: Thomas Williamson to Stephen Riggs, December 5, 1864, Stephen R. Riggs and Family Papers.

65, He arrived . . . remaining family members: John Williamson to Thomas Williamson, March 8, 1865, Thomas S. Williamson Papers.

65, In April . . . happen next: "Report exhibiting the final disposition of the Indian prisoners held in confinement at Mankato," April 1863, reel 2, Joseph R. and Samuel J. Brown and Family Papers.

65, Winyan . . . "my heart is very sad": Canku and Simon, *The Dakota Prisoner of War Letters*, 3.

65, General Sibley stoked: Henry H. Sibley to Abraham Lincoln, February 16, 1864, Abraham Lincoln Papers.

65, Despite Sibley's professed desire: Stephen R. Riggs, *Tah-Koo Wah-Kaṅ; or, The Gospel among the Dakotas*, 369. See also Roy W. Meyer, *History of the Santee Sioux: United States Indian Policy on Trial*, 144.

65, Sibley, however, attempted: William E. Lass, "The Removal from Minnesota of the Sioux and Winnebago Indians," 356. See also Seth J. Temple, "Camp McClellan during the Civil War," 36.

65, Officials decided that: "Removal of the Condemned Indians from Mankato," *St. Cloud Democrat*, April 30, 1863.

65–66, Stephen Riggs agreed . . . "wailing in the camp": Stephen Riggs to Selah Treat, April 21, 1863, mss. 310: no. 30, ABCFM Papers.

66, To avoid angry citizens . . . men to Iowa: Lass, "The Removal from Minnesota of the Sioux and Winnebago Indians," 356.

66, On April 21: "The Indian Murderers at Post McClellan," *Daily Democrat and News*, April 27, 1863.

66, In the predawn hours . . . blankets: Meyer, *History of the Santee Sioux*, 143.

66, The *Missionary Herald* reported: *Missionary Herald* 61, no. 1 (January 1865): 11.

66, While the prisoners' departure: "The deportation was conducted so quietly that when the *Favorite* moved off, but few persons in Mankato knew that she had on board the execrated savages." See "Removal of the Condemned Indians from Mankato," *St. Cloud Democrat*, April 30, 1863.

66, "As the boat neared" . . . "mourned the dead": "Removal of the Condemned Indians," *Goodhue Volunteer*, April 29, 1863.

66, "peculiarly affecting": "The Indian Murderers at Post McClellan," *Daily Democrat and News*, April 27, 1863.

66–67, "probably for life": "Minnesota Indian Matters: The Mankato Murderers Sent to Iowa," *Chicago Tribune*, April 2, 1863.

67, At this time, President Lincoln . . . put on hold: See Walt Bachman, *Northern Slave/Black Dakota: The Life and Times of Joseph Godfrey*, 299.

67, "the first installment": Stephen R. Riggs, *Mary and I: Forty Years with the Sioux*, 217.

67, Two days after the prisoners arrived: "The Indian Murderers at Post McClellan," *Daily Democrat and News*, April 27, 1863.

67, An article in the . . . "better satisfied will be the people": "More Indian Barbarities in Minnesota," *Daily Democrat and News*, July 18, 1863.

67, Another article also suggested extermination: "More Indians," *Daily Democrat and News*, May 18, 1863.

68, "sight of the Indians": *Muscatine Daily Journal*, May 9, 1863, quoted in "Chapter 19—Camps at Davenport—Camp Kearney," "Iowa's Rendezvous Camps, 1861–1866," 558. This unpublished manuscript, held at the Davenport Public Library, contains transcriptions of primary source records related to the Davenport prison. Hereafter cited as "Iowa's Rendezvous Camps."

68, Bill Boldt . . . "through the woods": Bill Boldt, January 31, 1927, quoted in

"Sioux Indian Prison, Post McClellan, Davenport, IA, 1863–66," notebook 14: "The Sioux Prison at Camp McClellan, Davenport, Iowa," John Henry Hauberg Papers, Augustana College, Rock Island, Ill. This collection is available digitally at http://collections.carli.illinois.edu/cdm/compoundobject/collection/aug _hauberg/id/390/rec/1. See scans 101–102.

68, The public's fascination . . . "slightly sold": "Sold Again," *Daily Democrat and News*, May 11, 1863.

68, In June 1864: "Camp Kearney—The Indian Prisoners," *Daily Davenport Democrat*, February 19, 1866.

68, In June 1865: *Missionary Herald* 61, no. 5 (June 1865): 183.

68, When it closed . . . just fifteen: The handwritten list of prisoners can be found at http://www.accessgenealogy.com/native/sioux-indian-prisoners-confined-at -camp-kearney.htm.

68, Most of the prisoners: "The Indian Murderers at Post McClellan," *Daily Democrat and News*, April 27, 1863.

69, The rolls listed: Canku and Simon, *The Dakota Prisoner of War Letters*, xii.

69, For example: "The Indian Murderers at Post McClellan," *Daily Democrat and News*, April 27, 1863.

69, In December 1863: "Another Camp," *Daily Democrat and News*, December 3, 1863.

69, Following Pope's orders: "Camp Kearney," *Daily Democrat and News*, December 5, 1863.

69, At the relocated prison . . . surrounded the prison: "The Indian Murderers at Post McClellan," *Daily Democrat and News*, April 27, 1863.

69, Stephen Riggs complained: Riggs, *Mary and I*, 221.

69, "small" and "cheap": "Orders to Brig. General B. S. Roberts," December 1, 1863, record group 393, entry 3438, part 1, volume 2/2, Records of U.S. Army Continental Commands.

69, Commander Roberts took: Riggs, *Tah-Koo Wah-Kań*, 369–370.

69, Dakota prisoner Elias Ruban: Canku and Simon, *The Dakota Prisoner of War Letters*, 81. A requisition for wood illustrates the difference between Camp McClellan and Camp Kearney. In 1865, Camp McClellan received seventy-five cords of wood a month; Camp Kearney, thirty cords a month. See "Proposals," *Davenport Daily Gazette*, July 29, 1865.

69, Riggs observed that the barracks: Stephen Riggs to Thomas Williamson, November 11, 1863, Stephen R. Riggs Papers.

69, Moreover, the barracks were crowded: Sarah-Eva Ellen Carlson, "They Tell Their Story: The Dakota Internment at Camp McClellan in Davenport, 1862–1866," 261.

69, Initially, Roberts supplied: Orders to General Littler, May 12, 1863, record

group 393, entry 3436, part 1, lot 3, volume 4/4, page 486, Records of U.S. Army
Continental Commands.

69, The male prisoners subsisted: Brig. General B. S. Roberts to Captain Robert
Littler, June 19, 1863, record group 393, entry 236, part 3, lot 2, volume 59/55,
Records of U.S. Army Continental Commands.

69–71, Likewise . . . an adult: "Camp Kearney—The Indian Prisoners," *Daily
Davenport Democrat*, February 19, 1866.

71, At first . . . revoked their privileges: Stephen Riggs to Mary Riggs, September
12, 1864, Stephen R. Riggs Papers; Stephen Riggs to Mary Riggs, September 30,
1865, Stephen R. Riggs Papers.

71, In 1864 . . . "very hungry": Canku and Simon, *The Dakota Prisoner of War Letters*, 109, 81.

71, The women and children: Stephen Riggs to Henry Sibley, September 14, 1864,
reel 11, Henry H. Sibley Papers.

71, One of the guards . . . the tragedy: "Shooting an Indian," *St. Cloud Democrat*,
May 5, 1864.

71, Dangerous conditions: For references to illnesses at the prison, see Winifred W.
Barton, *John P. Williamson: A Brother to the Sioux*, 72, and Riggs, *Mary and I*,
221, 229.

71, According to Dakota prisoner. . . "it is terrible here": Canku and Simon, *The
Dakota Prisoner of War Letters*, 31.

71, Despite the rampant illnesses . . . "wishes them all dead": Stephen Riggs to
Selah Treat, November 7, 1863, mss. 310: no. 36, ABCFM Papers.

71, Thomas Williamson reported . . . "cannot hang them": Thomas Williamson to
Stephen Riggs, [1863], Stephen R. Riggs and Family Papers.

71, Twenty-seven inmates: "Ugh!" *Daily Democrat and News*, December 11, 1863.

71–72, By March . . . "rapidly": "Indians Dying Off," *Daily Democrat and News*,
March 11, 1864.

72, That April: Canku and Simon, *The Dakota Prisoner of War Letters*, 35.

72, When the prison: *Missionary Herald* 60, no. 5 (May 1864): 137; *Missionary Herald*
62, no. 1 (January 1866): 11; Barton, *John P. Williamson*, 72.

72, Historians have offered: According to an article in the *Daily Davenport Democrat*, the prison records were "kept in a very irregular manner." The article then
proceeds to give the number of prisoners and the number of deaths at given
dates, but these numbers are very hard to put together into a coherent whole. See
"Camp Kearney—The Indian Prisoners," *Daily Davenport Democrat*, February
19, 1866. John Hunt Peacock Jr., provides a range of between 250 and 407 prisoners; see "An Account of the Dakota-US War as Sacred Text: Why My Dakota
Elders Value Spiritual Closure over Scholarly 'Balance,'" 196.

72, Bill Boldt recalled . . . "nothing but bones": In the 1920s, Bill Boldt remembered the Indian graveyard as having "three or four rows" of unmarked graves just outside the camp. See "The Sioux Prison at Camp McClellan, Davenport, Iowa," John Henry Hauberg Papers, scans 104, 111.

72, In 1878: "Academy of Science," *Davenport Democrat*, July 27, 1878.

72, These skulls . . . Morton, Minnesota: "The Two Sides of Camp McClellan," 4–5, http://www.davenportlibrary.com/files/5213/2586/6624/Camp_McClellan _also_known_as_Camp_Kearney.pdf.

72–73, Commander Roberts stated . . . "women and children": Brig. General B. S. Roberts to Captain Robert Littler, June 19, 1863, record group 393, entry 236, part 3, lot 2, volume 59/55, Records of U.S. Army Continental Commands.

73, During one visit: Thomas Williamson to Stephen Riggs, August 18, 1863, Stephen R. Riggs and Family Papers.

73, In spring 1863: "The Indian Murderers at Post McClellan," *Daily Democrat and News*, April 27, 1863.

73, Another article: "The Condemned Indians from Minnesota," *Semi-Weekly Wisconsin*, May 5, 1863.

73, A journalist: "Big Eagle," *Daily Iowa State Register*, March 1, 1874.

73, She was described . . . "distinguished air": "The Indian Murderers at Post McClellan," *Daily Democrat and News*, April 27, 1863.

73, An article . . . "pearl . . . among swine": "Davenport, Iowa," *Daily Democrat and News*, October 10, 1865.

73, Echoing the wording: Levi Wagoner, "Camp McClellan and the Redskins," 20.

73, He assuredly wanted: "Davenport, Iowa," *Daily Democrat and News*, October 10, 1865.

73–75, General Roberts complained: Benjamin Roberts to Robert Littler, June 23, 1863, record group 393, entry 236, part 3, lot 2, volume 59/55, Records of U.S. Army Continental Commands.

75, He lamented: Benjamin Roberts to J. F. Meline, August 22, 1863, record group 393, entry 236, part 3, lot 2, volume 59/55, page 133, Records of U.S. Army Continental Commands.

75, Stephen Riggs confirmed: Stephen Riggs to "My own dear home," October 22, 1865, box 3, folder 8, Stephen R. Riggs Papers.

75, "their proper duties": Benjamin Roberts to Pickenpaugh, September 4, 1863, record group 393, entry 236, part 3, lot 2, volume 59/55, page 153, Records of U.S. Army Continental Commands.

75, A side trip: "Compliment to Capt. R. M. Littler," *Daily Democrat and News*, June 1, 1863.

75, Journalists traveled: "Our City," *Daily Davenport Democrat*, October 23, 1865.

75, Even Iowa's governor: "Personal," *Daily Democrat and News*, August 15, 1863.

75, These local citizens: Carlson, "They Tell Their Story," 262.

75, On May 6 . . . "*en masse*": "The Indian Prisoners," *Daily Democrat and News*, May 6, 1863.

75, Later, children . . . "nearly all": "Big Injun," *Evening Argus*, May 25, 1865.

75, Another boy remembered: "J. Ed Kuehl Was Born in Bettendorf Sixty Years Ago," *Davenport Democrat and Leader*, February 27, 1917.

75, More than sixty years: "Mr. and Mrs. O'Connor Celebrate Anniversary," *Daily Times*, September 24, 1925.

76, For those children: "Our Fourth of July Celebration," *Daily Democrat and News*, June 12, 1863; "Big Ingin," *Daily Democrat and News*, June 2, 1863.

76, His proposed float: Lady Liberty has long been used as a symbol of the United States, especially during the Civil War era. For example, Civil War currency was adorned with Lady Liberty. In 1863, Thomas Crawford's *Statue of Freedom*, a female representing freedom and liberty, was installed on top of the dome of the United States Capitol.

76, In June . . . "to bathe": "Not to Be Seen," *Daily Democrat and News*, June 22, 1863.

76, Two thousand people . . . "church at Ottawa": "Huge Excursion," *Daily Democrat and News*, June 25, 1863.

76–77, For example, subsequent commanders: Barton, *John P. Williamson*, 69.

77, Several prisoners: Riggs, *Tah-Koo Wah-Kań*, 370.

77, By August: Canku and Simon, *The Dakota Prisoner of War Letters*, xix; Stephen Riggs to Selah Treat, July 27, 1865, reel 769, Papers of the ABCFM.

77, This practice continued: Riggs, *Tah-Koo Wah-Kań*, 371.

77, Some men went out: Thomas Williamson to Stephen Riggs, December 24, 1863, Stephen R. Riggs and Family Papers.

77, On several occasions . . . "hoped-for release": Riggs, *Tah-Koo Wah-Kań*, 371–372.

77, Finally, Four Lightning: Canku and Simon, *The Dakota Prisoner of War Letters*, 13.

77–78, An anonymous "tax payer" . . . "in the field": "Editor Gazette," *Davenport Daily Gazette*, August 19, 1864.

78, Another unidentified "tax payer" . . . "our citizens": "The Indians," *Daily Democrat and News*, August 20, 1864.

78, "The confinement" . . . "afraid to hope": Riggs, *Mary and I*, 229.

78, On the first trip: Stephen Riggs to Mary Riggs, September 30, 1865, Stephen R. Riggs Papers.

78, In December: Stephen Riggs to Alfred Riggs, December 6, 1865, Alfred L. Riggs Papers.

78, In January . . . "its fall": Stephen Riggs to "Dear Ones at Home," January 25, 1866, box 3, folder 3, Stephen R. Riggs Papers.

78, The remaining three barracks: "Camp Kearney—The Indian Prisoners," *Daily Davenport Democrat*, February 19, 1866.

78, Some even treated them: A journalist described visitors at the prison "petting" the "animals." See Carlson, "They Tell Their Story," 262.

78, Local newspapers . . . "lots of fun": "What Next?" *Davenport Daily Gazette*, October 18, 1865; "Indian Races," *Daily Davenport Democrat*, October 17, 1865; "The *Democrat* Thinks . . . ," *Davenport Daily Gazette*, October 21, 1865.

78, The *Daily* . . . $100, and $50: "Indian Races," *Daily Davenport Democrat*, October 17, 1865.

79, Spectators watched: "The Races," *Daily Davenport Democrat*, October 20, 1865; "The Races," *Daily Davenport Democrat*, October 21, 1865.

79, An editorial . . . "a brute": "The *Democrat* Thinks . . . ," *Davenport Daily Gazette*, October 21, 1865.

79, "dignified" and an "excellent sport": "Good," *Daily Davenport Democrat*, October 21, 1865.

79, In March 1865: "Take Care of Them," *Daily Davenport Democrat*, March 20, 1865. See also "Should Be Stopped," *Davenport Daily Gazette*, March 20, 1865. The author in the *Gazette* complained about Indians "found rambling around the neighborhood, ostensibly in charge of a guard, but virtually as far from the guard as they can be and still be in sight."

79, Residents complained: "Talking Back," *Daily Davenport Democrat*, March 22, 1865.

79, They demanded: "Take Care of Them," *Daily Davenport Democrat*, March 20, 1865.

79, After both the guards . . . "Christian people": "Talking Back," *Daily Davenport Democrat*, March 22, 1865; "Indignation Meeting," *Daily Davenport Democrat*, March 22, 1865.

79, On the one hand: "Davenport, Iowa," *Daily Davenport Democrat*, October 10, 1865.

80, These continuing traumas: *Annual Report of the ABCFM* (1864), 144.

80, "Since they put me in prison . . . my heart is very sorrowful": Canku and Simon, *The Dakota Prisoner of War Letters*, 113.

80, Like their mothers: Peacock, "An Account of the Dakota-US War as Sacred Text," 197.

80, Beginning with their arrival . . . "clam shells": The prisoners actually started to make items for sale in 1863 from materials gathered by the women and children, but Commander Roberts stopped this by taking away their tools. See Stephen Riggs to Selah Treat, November 7, 1863, mss. 310: no. 36, ABCFM Papers.

80–81, In September 1864: Stephen Riggs to Thomas Williamson, September 12, 1864, box 3, folder 7, Stephen R. Riggs Papers.

81, The prisoners then added: Riggs, *Tah-Koo Wah-Kań*, 372.

81, They were so industrious: Thomas Williamson to Stephen Riggs, March 3, 1864, Stephen R. Riggs and Family Papers.

81, The prisoners also made . . . "four bits a piece": "Put Them Where They Belong," *Davenport Daily Gazette*, June 23, 1865.

81, Fifty years later: "J. Ed Kuehl Was Born in Bettendorf Sixty Years Ago," *Davenport Democrat and Leader*, February 27, 1917.

81–82, An article . . . bows and arrows: The article described a little boy's eye injury from the Dakota bows and arrows in graphic detail, which ended in the child's loss of sight in that eye. The boy's story "should be a warning to the children about our city, with whom bows and arrows have become immensely popular of late." See "Unfortunate Accident," *Daily Davenport Democrat*, April 9, 1866.

82, Stephen Riggs reported: Stephen Riggs to Thomas Williamson, July 7, 1865, box 3, folder 12, Stephen R. Riggs Papers.

82, The prisoners even sold: *Missionary Herald* 60, no. 5 (1864): 138.

82, After a brief visit: Thomas Williamson to Stephen Riggs, March 23, 1864, Stephen R. Riggs and Family Papers.

82, During a trip: Stephen Riggs to Mary Riggs, September 12, 1864, box 3, folder 7, Stephen R. Riggs Papers.

82, For example, a journalist . . . far from the truth: "For Friends at Home," *Cedar Falls Gazette*, July 8, 1864.

82, One Davenport citizen: "Ugh!" *Daily Democrat and News*, December 11, 1863.

82, Another article . . . "pale of civilization": "An Abomination," *Daily Davenport Democrat*, May 26, 1865.

83, Stephen Riggs noted . . . "white people": Stephen Riggs to Selah Treat, October 25, 1865, reel 769, Papers of the ABCFM.

83, For their efforts: Stephen Riggs to "My Dear Home," October 25, 1865, box 3, folder 3, Stephen R. Riggs Papers.

83, In September: Stephen Riggs to "My Dear Home," September 30, 1865, box 3, folder 8, Stephen R. Riggs Papers.

83, In December: Stephen Riggs to Thomas Williamson, December 12, 1865, box 3, folder 12, Stephen R. Riggs Papers.

83, Compensation aside: Stephen Riggs to "My Dear Home," October 25, 1865, box 3, folder 3, Stephen R. Riggs Papers.

83, When "Arnold the settler" . . . "dying": Stephen Riggs to Thomas Williamson, December 12, 1865, box 3, folder 8, Stephen R. Riggs Papers. Riggs translated *wapiya* as "to conjure the sick"; *wapiyapi* was "conjuring," while *wapiye* was "a conjurer, an Indian doctor." Of course, from Riggs's perspective, conjuring was a savage practice that needed to be given up prior to an acceptance of Christianity. See Stephen R. Riggs, *A Dakota-English Dictionary*, 533–534.

83–84, According to an article . . . $215 today: *Davenport Weekly Democrat*, September 28, 1905, quoted in "Iowa's Rendezvous Camps," 563. I used 1864 as the basis for my calculations. Of course, the financial market varied over the course of this study due to the ongoing Civil War: currency was worth more in 1863, fell in 1864, and fell again in 1865. For an online calculator of monetary equivalencies, see http://www.in2013dollars.com/1865-dollars-in-2015?amount=230.

84, According to historian . . . "signification systems": Stephanie Pratt, "Restating Indigenous Presence in Eastern Dakota and Ho-Chunk (Winnebago) Portraits of the 1830s–1860s," 18, 25–26.

84, However, the photographer: "Photographs of 'Big Eagle,'" *Daily Davenport Democrat*, June 28, 1864.

84, For example . . . $80: *Missionary Herald* 62, no. 5 (May 1866): 164.

84, Another week: Riggs, *Tah-Koo Wah-Kań*, 372.

84, In one month: Stephen Riggs to Thomas Williamson, March 26, 1863, box 3, folder 12, Stephen R. Riggs Papers.

84, Their profits: *Statistics of the United States, in 1860*, 512.

86, In June: Thomas Williamson to Stephen Riggs, June 12, 1864, Stephen R. Riggs and Family Papers.

86, Over the months . . . "cornmeal": *Missionary Herald* 60, no. 5 (May 1864): 138.

86, In 1865, Stephen Riggs . . . "back to their people": Stephen Riggs to Selah Treat, July 27, 1865, reel 769, Papers of the ABCFM.

86, In 1865, several prisoners: John P. Williamson to Thomas Williamson, January 24, 1865, Thomas S. Williamson Papers.

86, A prisoner called Joe: John Williamson to Stephen Riggs, July 5, 1864, Stephen R. Riggs and Family Papers.

86, Another prisoner entrusted: Colette A. Hyman, *Dakota Women's Work: Creativity, Culture, and Exile*, 115.

86, When John Williamson visited: John Williamson to Thomas Williamson, June 9, 1863, Thomas S. Williamson Papers.

87, Even Williamson . . . at Camp Kearney: Thomas Williamson to Abraham Lincoln, April 27, 1864, Abraham Lincoln Papers.

87, Because they were required: *Missionary Herald* 61, no. 3 (March 1865): 71.

87, The prison guards: Stephen Riggs to Mary Riggs, January 18, 1865, Stephen R. Riggs Papers.

87, Another time: *Missionary Herald* 62, no. 4 (April 1866): 102.

87, "spiritual condition": *Missionary Herald* 60, no. 1 (January 1864): 12; *Missionary Herald* 61, no. 3 (March 1865): 70.

88, In July 1863: *Missionary Herald* 59, no. 9 (September 1863): 264.

88, Roberts angrily claimed . . . "unauthorized by any authority": Benjamin Roberts, quoted in "Iowa's Rendezvous Camps," 561, 560.

88, Roberts also banned . . . "no amusements": Alfred Riggs to Mary Riggs, July 23, 1863, Alfred L. Riggs Papers.

88, Samuel Hinman reported: Samuel Hinman to E. N. Biddle, May 15, 1865, E. N. Biddle Papers.

88, An article filled . . . "reversal of the order": *Annual Report of the ABCFM* (1863), 15, 147. See also *Missionary Herald* 59, no. 9 (September 1863): 264.

88, In 1864 . . . cost of his trip: *Missionary Herald* 62, no. 6 (June 1866): 164. See Selah Treat to Thomas Williamson, January 25, 1864, ABCFM Indians, volume 23, page 282, ABCFM Papers.

88, That March . . . "effected very little": Barton, *John P. Williamson*, 104.

88, When he finally met: Stephen Riggs to Alfred Riggs, April 19, 1864, Alfred L. Riggs Papers.

88, Although Williamson ultimately failed: "Abraham Lincoln, Saturday, April 30, 1864, List of Sioux Indians pardoned by Lincoln," Abraham Lincoln Papers. See also Carlson, "They Tell Their Story," 267, and Thomas Williamson to Stephen Riggs, May 4, 1864, Stephen R. Riggs and Family Papers.

88, He also promised: *Annual Report of the ABCFM* (1864), 145.

88–89, Stephen Riggs admitted . . . "he was mistaken": Stephen Riggs to Alfred Riggs, March 30, 1864, Alfred L. Riggs Papers.

89, Riggs frequently admonished . . . "their families": Stephen Riggs to Thomas Williamson, January 20, 1864, box 3, folder 12, Stephen R. Riggs Papers.

89, According to Williamson: Thomas Williamson to Stephen Riggs, April 7, 1864, Stephen R. Riggs and Family Papers.

89, In spring 1864: Stephen Riggs to General H. H. Sibley, April 6, 1864, Stephen R. Riggs Papers; Stephen Riggs to Alfred Riggs, April 19, 1864, Alfred L. Riggs Papers.

89, Samuel Hinman wrote . . . "made my point": Samuel Hinman to E. N. Biddle, May 15, 1865, E. N. Biddle Papers.

89, One time . . . "hostility upon himself": Henry Benjamin Whipple, *Lights and Shadows of a Long Episcopate: Being Reminiscences and Recollections of the Right Reverend Henry Benjamin Whipple*, 133, 122–123, 167–168.

89, The newspaper: Stephen Riggs to Thomas Williamson, March 12, 1864, Stephen R. Riggs Papers.

89, A military commander: Joseph Brown to D. S. Scott, February 25, 1866, reel 4, Joseph R. and Samuel J. Brown and Family Papers.

90, Moses Many Lightning: Canku and Simon, *The Dakota Prisoner of War Letters*, 149.

90, Although President Andrew Johnson: *Annual Report of the ABCFM* (1865), 143.

4. Resilience, Resistance, and Survival: Literacy

91–92, Indeed, the ABCFM missionaries . . . "American customs and language": Stephen R. Riggs, *Tah-Koo Wah-Kań; or, The Gospel among the Dakotas*, 180, 181.

92, John Peacock . . . "the Dakota language": John Hunt Peacock Jr., "Lamenting Language Loss at the Modern Language Association," 140, and "Wanna Dakota unkiapi kte!" 65.

92, Others have offered . . . empowerment rather than oppression: For examples of Native American uses of literacy, see Kimberly M. Blaeser, "Learning 'the Language the Presidents Speak': Images and Issues of Literacy in American Indian Literature"; Kathleen J. Bragdon, "The Pragmatics of Language Learning: Graphic Pluralism on Martha's Vineyard, 1660–1720"; Jacqueline Emery, "Writing against Erasure: Native American Students at Hampton Institute and the Periodical Press," 189; Amy M. Goodburn, "Literacy Practices at the Genoa Industrial Indian School"; Sean P. Harvey, "Colonialism, Literacies, and Languages," 584; and Phillip H. Round, *Removable Type: Histories of the Book in Indian Country, 1663–1880*, 4.

93, As Gwen Westerman asserts: Gwen N. Westerman, "Treaties Are More than a Piece of Paper: Why Words Matter," 305.

93, Those in charge . . . take place in English: Even in the 1850s, federal policy demanded that all instruction for Indians be conducted in English. See Thomas Williamson to Selah Treat, November 18, 1858, mss. 244: no. 448, ABCFM Papers.

93, As Rufus Anderson: Rufus Anderson, *Memorial Volume of the First Fifty Years of the American Board of Commissioners for Foreign Missions*, 310.

93, In every instance: Riggs, *Tah-Koo Wah-Kań*, 402.

93, Missionaries were exhorted: Thomas Williamson to Selah Treat, May 27, 1863, reel 769, Papers of the ABCFM.

93, In his instructions: William Joseph Barnds, "The Ministry of the Reverend Samuel Dutton Hinman, among the Sioux," 396.

93, Reverend Hinman confirmed: "The Dakota Mission. Advent, 1864," E. N. Biddle Papers.

93–94, Steffi Dippold . . . "how to read": Steffi Dippold, "The Wampanoag Word: John Eliot's *Indian Grammar*, the Vernacular Rebellion, and the Elegancies of Native Speech," 546.

94, "central focus . . . importance of literacy": Susan Neylan, *The Heavens Are Changing: Nineteenth-Century Protestant Missions and Tsimshian Christianity*, 164, 228.

94, The missionaries proselytizing: James K. Beatty, "Interpreting the Shawnee Sun: Literacy and Cultural Persistence in Indian Country, 1833–1841," 248.

94, Surprisingly . . . new language: Riggs, *Tah-Koo Wah-Kań*, 409.

94, Alfred Riggs summarized . . . "their own language": *ARCIA* (1871), 268.

94, To teach literacy . . . respectively: For information on the translation of the Dakota language into written form, see Samuel Pond to Preston Hollister, March 28, 1835, Pond Family Papers; Riggs, *Tah-Koo Wah-Kań*, 414; and Stephen R. Riggs, *Mary and I: Forty Years with the Sioux*, 59–60.

94, After the Ponds created . . . basic literacy: For an extensive bibliography of the missionaries' religious translations, see *Collections of the Minnesota Historical Society* 3 (1870–1880): 37–42, and Riggs, *Tah-Koo Wah-Kań*, 414–416.

96, a hymnal: In her oral history, Samuel Hinman's daughter Mary lists the materials her father translated. She stated that his Dakota hymnal is used by Dakota Episcopal churches in South Dakota into the present day. See "Interview with Mary Myrick Hinman LaCroix," *Collections of the Minnesota Historical Society*, 31, 37, http://collections.mnhs.org/cms/web5/media.php?pdf=1&irn=10279601. For a complete list of Hinman's translations, see James Constantine Pilling, "Bibliography of the Siouan Languages," 36–38.

96, For example . . . ABCFM school: *Annual Report of the ABCFM* (1862), 166.

96, Bishop Whipple claimed: *Spirit of Missions* 27, no. 1 (January 1862): 8.

96, Government administrators . . . in English: For literature on English education for Native Americans, see Ruth Spack, *America's Second Tongue: American Indian Education and the Ownership of English, 1860–1900*, 24, 49–52, and "English, Pedagogy, and Ideology: A Case Study of the Hampton Institute, 1878–1900."

97, One official lectured: *ARCIA* (1868), 44.

97, For example . . . "Pandemonium": "Hanging Indians," *St. Cloud Democrat*, January 8, 1863.

97, At Camp Kearney . . . "ugh": "Presentation at Camp Kearney," *Davenport Daily Gazette*, December 9, 1864.

97, An article . . . "Injun here!": "General News," *Daily Democrat and News*, March 8, 1864.

97, Commander Benjamin Roberts: "Put to Work," *Daily Democrat and News*, June 3, 1863.

97, The agent at Crow Creek: *ARCIA* (1863), 323.

97–98, Adjunct General: "Iowa's Rendezvous Camps," 570.

98, General Alfred Sully . . . "on the lookout?": *ARCIA* (1865), 208.

98, In 1866 . . . "take them north": Joseph Brown to D. S. Scott, February 20, 1866, reel 4, Joseph R. and Samuel J. Brown and Family Papers.

98, Indeed . . . "in letters": Stephen Riggs to Selah Treat, February 20, 1863, mss. 310: no. 26, ABCFM Papers.

98, Observers . . . "pen and paper": Stephen Riggs to Selah Treat, March 26, 1863, mss. 310: no. 29, ABCFM Papers. See also *Missionary Herald* 59, no. 5 (May 1863): 149.

98, Likewise, at Fort Snelling: Riggs, *Tah-Koo Wah-Kań*, 344.

98, Even women . . . "all the Dakotas": Stephen Riggs to Selah Treat, March 26, 1863, mss. 310: no. 29, ABCFM Papers. See also *Missionary Herald* 59, no. 5 (May 1863): 149.

98, Education took hold: Riggs, *Tah-Koo Wah-Kań*, 345.

99, Riggs reported . . . higher-level texts: Stephen Riggs to Selah Treat, March 26, 1863, mss. 310: no. 29, ABCFM Papers.

99, The demand: Riggs, *Tah-Koo Wah-Kań*, 345.

99, The Episcopalians: "The Dakota Mission. Advent, 1864," E. N. Biddle Papers.

99, The missionaries admitted: Riggs, *Tah-Koo Wah-Kań*, 407.

99, For hours: "Indian Prisoners," *Mankato Weekly Record*, March 28, 1863, mss. 309: no. 182, ABCFM Papers.

99, In this way: Riggs, *Tah-Koo Wah-Kań*, 344.

99, These instructors: *Missionary Herald* 60, no. 1 (January 1864): 13. See also *Annual Report of the ABCFM* (1865), 144.

99, Thomas Williamson . . . "fluently": *Missionary Herald* 60, no. 5 (May 1864): 138.

100, In December 1863 . . . "not enrolled": John Williamson to Thomas Williamson, December 24, 1863, Thomas S. Williamson Papers.

100, Two years later: John Williamson to Thomas Williamson, July 8, 1865, Thomas S. Williamson Papers.

100, The Episcopalians: "The Dakota Mission. Advent, 1864," E. N. Biddle Papers.

100, The agent: John P. Williamson to Thomas S. Williamson, July 7, 1863, Thomas S. Williamson Papers. See also Winifred W. Barton, *John P. Williamson: A Brother to the Sioux*, 103.

100, Williamson admitted: John Williamson to Thomas Williamson, January 6, 1864, Thomas S. Williamson Papers.

100, Samuel Hinman also hired: "The Dakota Mission. Advent, 1864," E. N. Biddle Papers.

100, The missionaries boasted: Riggs, *Tah-Koo Wah-Kań*, 408.

100–101, According to . . . "other symbols": Westerman, "Treaties Are More than a Piece of Paper," 298.

101, When he first arrived . . . "information": Samuel W. Pond, *Dakota Life in the Upper Midwest*, 78.

101, Samuel Hinman . . . (love or goodness): J. W. Powell, ed., *Tenth Annual Report of the Bureau of Ethnology to the Secretary of the Smithsonian Institution, 1888–89*, 204.

101, Stephen Riggs explained . . . "a man's history": Stephen R. Riggs, "Sketches of the Dakota Mission."

101, They drew symbols: Westerman, "Treaties Are More than a Piece of Paper," 298.

101, Traders used picture writing: Samuel W. Pond, *Two Volunteer Missionaries among the Dakotas: or, The Story of the Labors of Samuel W. and Gideon H. Pond*, 76.

101, In a letter . . . "on the walls": Thomas Williamson to Gideon Pond, February 24, 1840, Pond Family Papers.

101, Samuel Pond also noted: Pond, *Two Volunteer Missionaries*, 191.

101, When translating: Riggs, "Sketches of the Dakota Mission," 41.

101, "had been a good school for them": Stephen Riggs to Henry Sibley, March 21, 1866, reel 12, Henry H. Sibley Papers.

101–2, Even the missionaries . . . "perhaps a husband": *Missionary Herald* 60, no. 9 (September 1864): 262.

102, In early March . . . the same number: Riggs, *Tah-Koo Wah-Kań*, 344. See also Stephen Riggs to Selah Treat, March 3, 1863, mss. 310: no. 27, ABCFM Papers.

102, In late March . . . over and over again: "Indian Prisoners," *Mankato Weekly Record*, March 28, 1863, mss. 309: no. 182, ABCFM Papers.

102, The letters that passed: Riggs, *Tah-Koo Wah-Kań*, 355.

102, Henihda . . . "help me in my distress": Louis Walker to Bishop Henry Whipple, November 12, 1862, box 3, folder 4, Henry B. Whipple Papers.

102, Capeduta: "Translation of some letters of the Dakotas in prison at Mankato," December 25, 1862, Thomas S. Williamson Papers.

102, "My boy" . . . released from prison: Sarah F. Marpihdagawin (Mrs. White Dog), December 4, 1863, box 3, folder 8, Henry B. Whipple Family Papers.

102, Mary Renville sent a letter: Mary Renville to Stephen Riggs, January 23, 1863, Stephen R. Riggs and Family Papers.

102, Before the establishment: John Williamson to Thomas Williamson, August 13, 1863, Thomas S. Williamson Papers.

102, To circumvent: John Williamson reported that he hired a man to "take our letters on condition we pay him 25 cents a month for a piece, which I am willing to do." See John Williamson to Thomas Williamson, July 21, 1863, Thomas S. Williamson Papers.

102–3, In July 1863: John Williamson to Thomas Williamson, July 21, 1863, Thomas S. Williamson Papers.

103, A month later: John Williamson to Thomas Williamson, August 27, 1863, Thomas S. Williamson Papers.

103, Also in 1863: John Williamson to Thomas Williamson, June 9, 1863, Thomas S. Williamson Papers.

103, In January 1864: *Missionary Herald* 60, no. 1 (January 1864): 13.

103, Each time: *Missionary Herald* 60, no. 9 (September 1864): 262.

103, In 1863: John Williamson to Thomas Williamson, July 21, 1863, Thomas S. Williamson Papers.

103, In May 1864: *Missionary Herald* 60, no. 5 (May 1864): 138.

103, In a visit: Stephen Riggs to Thomas Williamson, March 26, 1863, Stephen R. Riggs Papers.

103, One of the first things: John Williamson to Thomas Williamson, January 5, 1865, Thomas S. Williamson Papers.

103, "I rejoice . . . my family and my relatives": Elias Ohan Manyakapi to Stephen Riggs, April 1, 1865, Stephen R. Riggs and Family Papers.

103, In 1865 . . . "home in the spring": John Williamson to Thomas Williamson, January 5, 1865, Thomas S. Williamson Papers.

104, Waniyhiyewin dictated . . . "I always remember you": "Probably a letter from a Dakota woman interned at Fort Snelling asking Dr. Williamson about her husband in prison at Mankato. Letter dictated in Dakota and translated into English," [1863], Thomas S. Williamson Papers.

104, Sarah Marpihdagawin wrote . . . "again in this world": Sarah F. Marpihdagawin (Mrs. White Dog), December 4, 1863, box 3, folder 8, Henry B. Whipple Family Papers.

104, In 1865: Stephen Riggs to Mary Riggs, September 30, 1865, Stephen R. Riggs Papers.

104, Another Dakota prisoner . . . "this is terrible": Clifford Canku and Michael Simon, *The Dakota Prisoner of War Letters: Dakota Kaŝkapi Okicize Wowapi*, 99, 37.

104, Stephen Riggs summarized . . . "gloom over them": Stephen Riggs to Thomas Williamson, October 1863, Stephen R. Riggs Papers.

105, Likewise, the families: Stephen Riggs to Selah Treat, November 7, 1863, mss. 310: no. 36, ABCFM Papers.

105, In 1864 . . . "give me a talk": Thomas Williamson, translation of letter for Wiyaka at Camp Kearney, February 5, 1864, Thomas S. Williamson Papers.

105, At Crow Creek . . . "long unheard of friends": *Missionary Herald* 60, no. 9 (September 1864): 262.

105, Stephen Riggs reported: Stephen Riggs to Selah Treat, March 26, 1863, mss. 310: no. 29, ABCFM Papers.

105, Because they knew: "The Indian Prisoners," *Chicago Tribune*, April 7, 1863.

106, In an undated letter . . . "talk among the Indians": John Williamson to Thomas Williamson, [1863?], Thomas S. Williamson Papers.

106, An intriguing sentence: John Williamson to Thomas Williamson, August 13, 1864, Thomas S. Williamson Papers.

107, In a letter . . . "anyone on the subject": Joseph Brown to Gabriel Renville, May 16, 1864, reel 3, Joseph R. and Samuel J. Brown and Family Papers.

107, For Dakota, however, literacy: Barbara Monroe, *Plateau Indian Ways with Words: The Rhetorical Tradition of the Tribes of the Inland Pacific Northwest*, 76.

5. Resilience, Resistance, and Survival: Christianity

109, Following the war: Stephen Riggs to Selah Treat, November 7, 1863, mss. 310: no. 36, ABCFM Papers.

109–10, The missionaries noted . . . "public speaking": *Annual Report of the ABCFM* (1863), 144–145.

110, Robert was "the ruling spirit": *Missionary Herald* 59, no. 5 (May 1863): 150.

110, An article . . . "in the Sioux language": "The Indian Murderers at Post McClellan," *Daily Democrat and News*, April 27, 1863.

110, He also performed: Clifford Canku and Michael Simon, *The Dakota Prisoner of War Letters: Dakota Kaśkapi Okicize Wowapi*, xii.

110, Even the guards: Stephen Riggs to Selah Treat, November 7, 1863, mss. 310: no. 36, ABCFM Papers.

110, Stephen Riggs summarized: Stephen R. Riggs, *Mary and I: Forty Years with the Sioux*, 214.

110, For example . . . "as a son": *Missionary Herald* 59, no. 1 (January 1863): 15.

110, Once the missionaries . . . "at Boston": Stephen Riggs to Thomas Williamson, October 1, 1864, Stephen R. Riggs Papers.

110–11, In May 1863 . . . "those persons": Canku and Simon, *The Dakota Prisoner of War Letters*, 7.

111, According to Waziyatawin: Waziyatawin, *What Does Justice Look Like? The Struggle for Liberation in Dakota Homeland*, 121.

112, In the case . . . conversion experience: Thomas S. Williamson to Samuel Pond, April 4, 1845, Pond Family Papers.

112, As Stephen Riggs explained: Stephen Riggs to David Greene, September 27, 1839, mss. 141: no. 57, ABCFM Papers.

112, Riggs understood: *Missionary Herald* 45, no. 6 (June 1849): 212.

112, Although missionary publications: Riggs, *Mary and I*, 42; *Annual Report of the ABCFM* (1862), 167; *Missionary Herald* 59, no. 1 (January 1863): 10.

112, Years later . . . "three churches": John Williamson, "Robert Hopkins Ta."

113, Although the missionaries worked: *Annual Report of the ABCFM* (1862), 167.

113, In 1860 . . . "from the church": Diary, July 4, 1860, box 42, volume 4, Episcopal Church, Diocese of Minnesota, Bishop Henry B. Whipple Papers, Minnesota Historical Society, St. Paul, Minn.

113, The ABCFM missionaries . . . small congregation: "The Story of Nancy McClure: Captivity among the Sioux," 444.

113, After Catherine Totidutawin converted: Stephen R. Riggs, *Tah-Koo Wah-Kań: or, The Gospel among the Dakotas*, 179.

113, Because of these strong challenges: *Annual Report of the ABCFM* (1862), 169.

113, To their surprise . . . They counted 140 converts: *Annual Report of the ABCFM* (1863), 142, 145, 146, 148, 149.

113, The Episcopalians: Henry Benjamin Whipple, *Lights and Shadows of a Long Episcopate: Being Reminiscences and Recollections of the Right Reverend Henry Benjamin Whipple*, 133.

113, In addition: Mary Riggs to her Son, January 1, 1863, Stephen R. Riggs and Family Correspondence.

113, All these conversions: *Missionary Herald* 59, no. 3 (March 1863): 72.

113–14, Evangelicals were thrilled . . . "Christianity": *Annual Report of the ABCFM* (1863), 149, 150.

114, Thomas Williamson marveled: *Missionary Herald* 59, no. 7 (July 1863): 202.

114, While the ABCFM claimed: For example, the ABCFM reported four to five Roman Catholic and about ten Episcopalian converts, while three men, six women, and seven children remained unbaptized at Camp Kearney. See *Annual Report of the ABCFM* (1865), 144. In July 1863, an Episcopalian minister went to the Mankato prison and "found nine who had not come to us, whom he baptized." The minister did not speak Dakota and relied on a translator. See *Missionary Herald* 59, no. 7 (July 1863): 204.

114, In 1864: "The Dakota Mission. Advent, 1864," E. N. Biddle Papers.

114, Of all the missionaries: Riggs, *Tah-Koo Wah-Kan*, 345.

114, He asked . . . material aid: *Annual Report of the ABCFM* (1863), 146.

115, While acknowledging: Selah Treat to Stephen Riggs, November 20, 1863, ABCFM Indians, volume 23, page 267, ABCFM Papers.

115, John Williamson agreed . . . "rejoice in that": *Annual Report of the ABCFM* (1863), 149.

115, Most rejected Riggs's cynicism: *Missionary Herald* 62, no. 1 (January 1866): 11.

115, An article in the *Goodhue Volunteer*: "Confession of the Prisoners," *Goodhue Volunteer*, January 7, 1863.

115, An article in the *St. Cloud Democrat* . . . "more horrible than the last": "Editorial Correspondence," *St. Cloud Democrat*, May 14, 1863.

115–16, A reporter . . . "so celebrated": "Minnesota Indians," *Semi-Weekly Wisconsin*, May 19, 1863.

116, An article in the *Goodhue Volunteer* confirmed . . . "Indian war": "Removal of the Condemned Indians," *Goodhue Volunteer*, April 29, 1863.

116, An article in the *St. Cloud Democrat* scoffed . . . "everlasting punishment": "Removal of the Condemned Indians from Mankato," *St. Cloud Democrat*, April 30, 1863.

116, For their part: John Williamson to his mother, May 13, 1863, Thomas S. Williamson Papers.

116, One journalist commented . . . "morning and night: "Davenport Correspondence," *Cedar Falls Gazette*, May 1, 1863.

116, Another visitor attended . . . "as far as we could see": "The Indian Murderers at Post McClellan," *Daily Democrat and News*, April 27, 1863.

116–17, One visitor . . . "treachery and cruelty": "Ugh!" *Daily Democrat and News*, December 11, 1863.

117, Another observer accused: "Davenport, Iowa," *Daily Davenport Democrat*, October 10, 1865.

117, An 1866 article . . . "very rare": "Letter from Fort Garry," *St. Cloud Democrat*, May 17, 1866.

117, He also intensely disliked . . . "intolerable": Benjamin Roberts to J. F. Meline, August 22, 1863, record group 393, entry 236, part 3, lot 2, volume 59/55, page 133, Records of U.S. Army Continental Commands.

117, An article . . . "before morning": "Pow Wow," *Daily Davenport Democrat*, October 21, 1865.

117, While the missionaries witnessed: *Missionary Herald* 59, no. 9 (September 1863): 264.

117, In 1864 . . . "Rev. Riggs": Canku and Simon, *The Dakota Prisoner of War Letters*, 35, 101, 85, xxii.

118, In a letter . . . "daily prayers": Whipple, *Lights and Shadows*, 181, 135.

118, Stephen Riggs extolled: Riggs, *Tah-Koo Wah-Kán*, 375.

118, Bishop Whipple also discussed . . . "affection and respect": Whipple, *Lights and Shadows*, 176–177.

118, In particular . . . "Santee Indians": Samuel Dutton Hinman, *Journal of the Rev. S. D. Hinman: Missionary to the Santee Sioux Indians. And Taopi*, vii, 9.

119, In addition: Samuel Hinman to Joseph Brown, April 3, 1863, reel 2, Joseph R. and Samuel J. Brown and Family Papers.

119, Likewise, as discussed earlier: For example, see Canku and Simon, *The Dakota Prisoner of War Letters*, 41, 43, 81, 111.

119, He wrote a letter . . . Camp Kearney: Thomas Galbraith to Stephen Riggs, March 4, 1864, Stephen R. Riggs and Family Papers.

119, For example, Elias Ruban . . . "Dakota have done": Canku and Simon, *The Dakota Prisoner of War Letters*, 81, 208–209, 61, 165.

120, The missionaries themselves noted: *Missionary Herald* 59, no. 3 (March 1863): 72.

120, John Peacock likewise argues . . . "help getting released": John Hunt Peacock Jr., "An Account of the Dakota-US War as Sacred Text: Why My Dakota Elders Value Spiritual Closure over Scholarly 'Balance,'" 201.

120, Robert Hopkins wrote . . . "it is so": Canku and Simon, *The Dakota Prisoner of War Letters*, 151, 121.

120, Another prisoner . . . "all dying": Unknown author to Stephen Riggs, April 27, 1863, Stephen R. Riggs and Family Papers.

120, "pray for their families": *Missionary Herald* 59, no. 7 (July 1863): 204.

120, Beginning in 1860: Selah Treat to Stephen R. Riggs, December 25, 1869, Stephen R. Riggs Papers.

120, They accused . . . "the Dakotas": Riggs, *Tah-Koo Wah-Kaṅ*, 359.

120, Bishop Whipple scoffed: Whipple, *Lights and Shadows*, 61.

120–21, John Williamson stated . . . join his church: John Williamson to Thomas Williamson, April 6, 1863, Thomas S. Williamson Papers.

121, In 1863: John Williamson to Thomas Williamson, January 6, 1863, Thomas S. Williamson Papers.

121, The following year: "The Dakota Mission. Advent, 1864," E. N. Biddle Papers.

121, The ABCFM missionaries alleged: John Williamson to Thomas Williamson, January 24, 1865, Thomas S. Williamson Papers.

121, Likewise, Stephen Riggs complained . . . "compete with him": Stephen Riggs to Alfred Riggs, July 28, 1866, Alfred L. Riggs Papers.

121, In 1866, John Williamson grumbled . . . religious materials: John Williamson to Thomas Williamson, December 19, 1866, Thomas S. Williamson Papers.

121, Hinman wrote . . . "never will": Samuel Hinman to Bishop Whipple, January 6, 1864, folder 9, Henry B. Whipple Papers.

122, In 1864, families at Crow Creek . . . "next May": John Williamson to Thomas Williamson, January 6, 186[4], Thomas S. Williamson Papers.

122, Clifford Canku . . . "denominations": See Clifford Canku, http://www .usdakotawar.org/stories/contributors/dr-clifford-canku/1023.

123, Some Dakota men: Royal B. Hassrick, *The Sioux: Life and Customs of a Warrior Society*, 132–133.

123, Samuel Pond reported . . . "one wife at a time": Samuel W. Pond, *The Dakota or Sioux in Minnesota as They Were in 1834*, 139.

123, Bishop Whipple agreed: Whipple, *Lights and Shadows*, 44.

123, Stephen Riggs, however: Stephen R. Riggs, "The Dakota Mission," 120.

123, Thomas Williamson was somewhere: Thomas Williamson to David Greene, August 14, 1837, mss. 141: no. 2, ABCFM Papers.

123, Numbers aside: In the early years of the Dakota Mission, Thomas Williamson was conflicted about dissolving all polygamous marriages, because this broke up families. However, in the postwar period, I did not find any information that he continued to oppose breaking up these marriages; indeed, he—and his son John—always admonished those who remained in the marriages following the war.

123, ABCFM missionary: Moses Adams to Selah Treat, August 1, 1853, mss. 244: no. 81, ABCFM Papers.

123, Riggs linked polygamy: Riggs, *Tah-Koo Wah-Kaṅ*, xxix.

123, Because polygamy was: Stephen R. Riggs, *Dakota Portraits*, 533.

123, For example, when Catherine Totidutawin . . . "join the church": "Totidutawin Ta," *Iapi Oaye* 17 (October 1888): 10, 1, trans. Louis Garcia.

124, In the Mankato prison . . . "forsaking the other": Stephen Riggs to Thomas Williamson, April 4, 1863, box 3, folder 12, Stephen R. Riggs Papers.

124, After compiling his list: *Missionary Herald* 59, no. 5 (May 1863): 149–150.

124, Following Tunkaknamane's discharge: John Williamson to Stephen Riggs, January 15, 1866, Stephen R. Riggs and Family Papers.

124, John Williamson also informed . . . "the session": John Williamson to Thomas Williamson, December 19, 1866, Thomas S. Williamson Papers.

124, Similarly . . . "brought to order": Samuel Hinman to Sibley, January 23, 1866, reel 13, Henry H. Sibley Papers.

124, John Williamson asked . . . Crow Creek: John Williamson to Stephen Riggs, January 15, 1866, Stephen R. Riggs and Family Papers.

125, Williamson also informed . . . "write to them as such": John Williamson to Thomas Williamson, January 9, 1865, Thomas S. Williamson Papers.

125, Stephen Riggs complained: Stephen Riggs to Selah Treat, October 25, 1865, reel 769, Papers of the ABCFM.

125, When he reprimanded . . . "their conjuring": Stephen Riggs to "My Dear Home," September 30, 1865, box 3, folder 8, Stephen R. Riggs Papers.

125, After learning . . . "wrong customs": Stephen Riggs to Selah Treat, December 16, 1865, reel 769, Papers of the ABCFM.

125, The prisoners . . . "heal the sick": Stephen Riggs to Selah Treat, October 25, 1865, reel 769, Papers of the ABCFM.

125, Another prisoner . . . "any other way": Stephen Riggs to "My Dear Home," October 25, 1865, box 3, folder 3, Stephen R. Riggs Papers.

126, Indeed, he decided to submit . . . ban the practice: Stephen Riggs to Selah Treat, December 16, 1865, reel 769, Papers of the ABCFM.

126, Both the ABCFM: Stephen Riggs to Mary Riggs, July 30, 1866, Stephen R. Riggs Papers.

126, In 1866, at Crow Creek: *Annual Report of the ABCFM* (1866), 153.

126, Reverend Hinman: Whipple, *Lights and Shadows*, 128, 176, 177.

126, At Crow Creek: "The Dakota Mission. Advent, 1864," E. N. Biddle Papers.

126, The small number: Riggs, *Tah-Koo Wah-Kaṅ*, 368; Riggs, *Mary and I*, 223.

126, John Williamson also selected: Winifred W. Barton, *John P. Williamson: A Brother to the Sioux*, 77.

126, Likewise, Bishop Whipple: Whipple, *Lights and Shadows*, 189.

126, Two Dakota women: "The Dakota Mission. Advent, 1864," E. N. Biddle Papers.

126, The missionaries admitted: *Missionary Herald* 61, no. 8 (August 1865): 248–249.

126, Stephen Riggs commented: Stephen Riggs to Alfred Riggs, August 13, 1868, Alfred L. Riggs Papers.

126–27, Religious historian . . . "the indigent": Bonnie Sue Lewis, "Leadership in the Native Tradition: Dakota and Nez Perce Presbyterian Pastors," 154, 153.

127, Dakota preachers also chose: *ARCIA* (1866), 243. See also *Missionary Herald* 62, no. 4 (April 1866): 102.

127, Robert Hopkins: *Missionary Herald* 59, no. 7 (July 1863): 203.

127, Elden Lawrence: Elden Lawrence, *The Peace Seekers: The Indian Christians and the Dakota Conflict*, 70.

127, In addition to offering comfort: Thomas Williamson to John Williamson, June 27, 1863, Thomas S. Williamson Papers.

127, They appointed *Hoonkayape* . . . "before this people": John Williamson, quoted in Bonnie Sue Lewis, "Leadership in the Native Tradition," 161.

127, When the elders focused: Riggs, "Sketches of the Dakota Mission." Christopher J. Pexa notes that one of the missionaries' most important objectives was to supplant "traditional kinship ties and communal responsibilities." See "Transgressive Adoptions: Dakota Prisoners' Resistances to State Domination Following the 1862 U.S.-Dakota War," 39.

127–28, Stephen Riggs complained: "To the Presbytery of Dakota," [1864], Stephen R. Riggs and Family Papers.

128, John Williamson concurred: John Williamson to Thomas Williamson, August 4, 1863, Thomas S. Williamson Papers.

128, In 1863, he expelled: John Williamson to Thomas Williamson, December 24, 1863, Thomas S. Williamson Papers.

128, In 1865, he noted: *Missionary Herald* 61, no. 3 (March 1865): 70.

128, In 1866 . . . "at Class Meeting": John Williamson to Thomas Williamson, December 19, 1866, Thomas S. Williamson Papers.

128, The depleted 1866 rolls: John Williamson to Stephen Riggs, January 15, 1866, Stephen R. Riggs and Family Papers.

128, One military commander: Joseph Brown to D. S. Scott, February 25, 1866, reel 4, Joseph R. and Samuel J. Brown and Family Papers.

128, John Williamson complained: John Williamson, scrap of paper, n.d., Thomas S. Williamson Papers.

129, With all these different . . . "to be true": Peacock, "An Account of the Dakota-US War of 1862 as Sacred Text," 202.

129, Whether Dakota men and women converted . . . "continuing hardships": Michael D. McNally, "The Practice of Christianity," 835.

6. Resilience, Resistance, and Survival: The Dakota Scouts

131, In the postwar years . . . "take no prisoners": Mary Beth Faimon, "Ties That Bind: Remembering, Mourning, and Healing Historical Trauma," 240.

132, Into the present day . . . their own people: Ibid., 241; Waziyatawin, *What Does Justice Look Like? The Struggle for Liberation in Dakota Homeland*, 124.

132, Other historians . . . "selfish interests": Thomas W. Dunlay, *Wolves for the Blue Soldiers: Indian Scouts and Auxiliaries with the United States Army, 1860–90*, 5, 109. For additional information on the scouts, see Janne Lahti, "Colonized Labor: Apaches and Pawnees as Army Workers."

132, However, Curtis Dahlin: Curtis A. Dahlin, *The Fort Sisseton Dakota Scouts and Their Camps in Eastern Dakota Territory, 1863–1866*, 6, 213–216; "Dakota Scouts and Camps Focus of BCHS Talk," *Journal*, August 17, 2016.

133, As Major Joseph Brown: Joseph Brown to D. S. Scott, February 25, 1866, reel 4, Joseph R. and Samuel J. Brown and Family Papers. General Sibley appointed Joseph Brown chief of the scouts and chief guide for his 1863 expedition. In 1864, Sibley appointed Brown special military agent at Fort Wadsworth, relieving him of his position of chief of the scouts. However, Brown still continued to interact with and report on the scouts; he also had scouts assigned to him into 1866, even if he no longer held the title chief of the scouts. Brown's son Samuel also held various positions with the Dakota scouts. See Dahlin, *The Fort Sisseton Dakota Scouts*, 17–34.

133, In the weeks: See Brad Tennant, "The 1864 Sully Expedition and the Death of Captain John Feilner," 183, and Gary Clayton Anderson and Alan R. Woolworth, eds., *Through Dakota Eyes: Narrative Accounts of the Minnesota Indian War of 1862*, 268.

133, Henry Sibley warned: Henry Sibley to Abraham Lincoln, February 16, 1863, Abraham Lincoln Papers.

133–34, On the Minnesota frontier: "Diary of Lewis C. Paxson, Stockton, N.J., 1862–1865," 5.

134, The *Goodhue Volunteer* claimed: "Sioux Spies in Wright Co.," *Goodhue Volunteer*, June 17, 1863.

134, Another article . . . "within six miles of Minneapolis": "The Indian War," *Goodhue Volunteer*, July 15, 1863.

134, In July 1863: "Inconsistency," *St. Cloud Democrat*, July 9, 1863. Colette Routel notes that "fewer than 20 civilians and military personnel were killed by Dakota raids in Minnesota during the spring and summer 1863." See "Minnesota Bounties on Dakota Men during the U.S.-Dakota War," 20.

134, In 1864: *ARCIA* (1864), 260.

134, As late as 1865: *ARCIA* (1865), 196.

134, An article . . . "Indian trail": "The Indian War," *Goodhue Volunteer*, July 15, 1863.

134, Soldiers assigned to . . . turned out to be cattle: "Diary of Lewis C. Paxson," 16, 19.

134, Despite several erroneous reports: Roy W. Meyer, *History of the Santee Sioux: United States Indian Policy on Trial*, 134.

134, These raids increased tensions: "Inconsistency," *St. Cloud Democrat*, July 9, 1863.

134, At first . . . "the recent murders": "Secret Society against the Indians in Minnesota," *Daily Evening Bulletin*, January 22, 1863.

134, In October 1862: Samuel Hinman to Henry Whipple, October 17, 1862, box 3, folder 4, Henry B. Whipple Papers.

134, By summer 1863 . . . "Sioux scalp taken": "Scouts Wanted!" *St. Cloud Democrat*, July 9, 1863.

135, In September, "General Orders No. 60": "More Sioux Scalps Wanted," *St. Cloud Democrat*, September 24, 1863.

135, Legal historian: Routel, "Minnesota Bounties," 4.

135, Even at the time . . . "our common humanity": "Bounty for Sioux Scalps," *St. Paul Pioneer*, July 16, 1863.

135, Even critics . . . questionable legality and morality: "Bring Them In," *Goodhue Volunteer*, July 15, 1863.

135, Two weeks after: Routel, "Minnesota Bounties," 21.

135, One article . . . "kill them": "From St. Paul: Minnesota Indian Matters," *Chicago Tribune*, July 22, 1863.

135, Four scouts: Routel, "Minnesota Bounties," 24.

135, In February 1864 . . . "paid to Mr. Horner": "Another Scalp Received," *St. Cloud Democrat*, February 11, 1864.

135, On July 3, 1863 . . . "might see it": "Sioux Executed for Uprising, Fifty-Two Years Ago Today," *Minneapolis Sunday Tribune*, December 26, 1915.

136, In the following weeks: "'Little Crow or Not Little Crow?' That's the Question," *St. Paul Daily Press*, August 21, 1863.

136, In March 1864: See Gary Clayton Anderson, *Little Crow: Spokesman for the Sioux*, 177–178, and Routel, "Minnesota Bounties," 25–29.

136, As tensions grew: Waziyatawin, "Colonial Calibrations: The Expendability of Minnesota's Original People," 476.

136, He also wanted: Paul N. Beck, *Columns of Vengeance: Soldiers, Sioux, and the Punitive Expeditions, 1863–1864*, 50. And see Robert M. Utley, *Frontiersmen in Blue: The United States Army and the Indian, 1848–1865*, 270.

136, To achieve these goals: Tennant, "The 1864 Sully Expedition," 184. See also

Richard N. Ellis, "Political Pressures and Army Policies on the Northern Plains, 1862–1865," 45.

136, Pope hoped to "create": Tennant, "The 1864 Sully Expedition," 184.

136, These massacres resulted: Kim Allen Scott and Ken Kempcke, "A Journey to the Heart of Darkness: John W. Wright and the War against the Sioux, 1863–1865," 5.

136, Commanders and soldiers . . . "one Indian from another": *ARCIA* (1865), 209.

136, In September 1863 . . . bison meat: Frank Myers, *Soldiering in Dakota, among the Indians, in 1863-4-5*, 8.

136, With regard to Whitestone Hill . . . "the United States": Samuel Brown to Joseph Brown, November 13, 1863, reel 2, Joseph R. and Samuel J. Brown and Family Papers.

137, Before troops destroyed . . . "war trophies": "Indian Trophies," *Daily Democrat and News*, December 18, 1863.

137, In a bizarre development: "Presentation at Camp Kearney," *Davenport Daily Gazette*, December 9, 1864.

137, A "scientist" . . . "specimens" themselves: J. Pitcher to Henry Sibley, November 16, 1864, reel 12, Henry H. Sibley Papers; J. Pitcher to Henry Sibley, April 19, 1865, reel 13, Henry H. Sibley Papers.

137, These studies: Robert E. Bieder, "The Representations of Indian Bodies in Nineteenth-Century American Anthropology," 25.

137–38, Once again: Joseph Brown to Charley [Mix], March 12, 1864, reel 3, Joseph R. and Samuel J. Brown and Family Papers.

138, In July 1864: Myers, *Soldiering in Dakota*, 12.

138, Sully's troops: "Diary of Lewis C. Paxson," 42.

138, Also similar to Whitestone Hill: Waziyatawin, "Colonial Calibrations," 477; "Diary of Lewis C. Paxson," 42.

138, Battles like Whitestone Hill: Historian Richard Ellis writes that although Pope "repeatedly defeated the Indians in battle, he failed to crush them or to settle the Sioux problem." See "Political Pressures and Army Policies," 43. See also Doreen Chaky, *Terrible Justice: Sioux Chiefs and U.S. Soldiers on the Upper Missouri, 1854–1868*.

138–39, Stephen Riggs, who served: Stephen Riggs to Alfred Riggs, August 1863, Alfred L. Riggs Papers.

139, Historian Paul Beck agrees: Beck, *Columns of Vengeance*, 49.

139, By 1865: Utley, *Frontiersmen in Blue*, 262.

139, Indeed, in summer 1865: Ellis, "Political Pressures and Army Policies," 43.

139, General Sibley authorized . . . thirty men: Thomas W. Milroy, "Solomon Two Stars (We-cah-npe-no-pah): Peace Warrior," 62; Henry Sibley to Gabriel

Renville, February 17, 1863, reel 2, Joseph R. and Samuel J. Brown and Family Papers.

139, Stephen Riggs noted: Stephen Riggs to Selah Treat, October 1, 1863, reel 769, Papers of the ABCFM.

139, Other scouts belonged . . . Robertson families: For a list of 222 scouts, see Senate Executive Documents, 52d Congress, 2d Session, 1892–1893, 743–747.

139, Many scouts were older: Dahlin, *The Fort Sisseton Dakota Scouts*, 35.

139–40, Finally, according to Riggs: Stephen R. Riggs, *Mary and I: Forty Years with the Sioux*, 225.

140, After 1863 . . . more diverse: Other Native Americans also served as scouts. In 1864, the army recruited fifty-one Yanktonai; a small number of Ho-Chunk and Ponca served as well. Although these other scouts are not the focus of this chapter, many of same themes apply. For example, Yankton scouts were not paid until thirty years after their service. See "Alfred Sully's Company of Sioux Indian Scouts," Senate Document 298, 57th Congress, 1st Session, 1902, 1–9, and Micheal Clodfelter, *The Dakota War: The United States Army versus the Sioux, 1862–1865*, 16.

140, In 1864, Bishop Whipple . . . "ought to be discharged": Henry Whipple to General Sibley, August 26, 1864, reel 12, Henry H. Sibley Papers.

140, By 1865: Dahlin, *The Fort Sisseton Dakota Scouts*, 21.

140, Samuel Brown . . . "three more men": "Samuel J. Brown's Pocket Diary," May–July 1865, volume 2, reel 26, Joseph R. and Samuel J. Brown and Family Papers.

140, Certainly, as captives . . . lack of choice: Gwen Westerman is working on translating Dakota letters. In a February 28, 2016, press release, she describes translating a letter that stated that "every fourth man was chosen" as a scout from those held as prisoners. Westerman argues that this challenges the idea that all Dakota scouts were traitors, because these men did not have a choice. See http://www.mankatofreepress.com/news/local_news/grant-funds-book-of-th-century-dakota-letters/article_d5efdeaa-d594-11e5-81dc-836090d7d546.html.

140, Military commanders . . . "hold on them": John Williamson to Stephen Riggs, December 26, 1863, Stephen R. Riggs and Family Papers.

140–41, Perhaps due to their impressment . . . Gabriel Renville: Joseph Brown to Sibley, September 8, 1864, reel 12, Henry H. Sibley Papers.

141, In spring 1863 . . . "Little Crow": Stephen Riggs to Selah Treat, May 27, 1863, reel 769, Papers of the ABCFM.

141, In fall 1863 . . . "half dozen exceptions": Stephen Riggs to Thomas Williamson, October 31, 1863, Stephen R. Riggs Papers.

141, Gabrielle Renville . . . "release him for me": Gabriel Renville to Stephen Riggs, [November 1863], Stephen R. Riggs and Family Papers.

141, In 1864: Mark Diedrich, *Old Betsey: The Life and Times of a Famous Dakota Woman and Her Family*, 77.

141, In an 1865 letter . . . "I am always sad": Pay Pay to Whipple, [1865], box 4, folder 2, Henry B. Whipple Papers; Pay Pay to Whipple, September 10, 1865, box 4, folder 4, Henry B. Whipple Papers.

141–42, In 1865, Thomas Williamson: Thomas Williamson to Stephen Riggs, August 11, 1865, Stephen R. Riggs and Family Papers.

142, He forwarded Day . . . three sons: Thomas Williamson to Stephen Riggs, [1865] (located in 1866 papers, but misfiled), Stephen R. Riggs and Family Papers.

142, In addition: George Day to Stephen Riggs, October 27, 1865, Stephen R. Riggs and Family Papers.

142, Finally, however, Williamson reported: Thomas Williamson to Stephen Riggs, August 25, 1865, Stephen R. Riggs and Family Papers.

142, Thomas Williamson received . . . write them letters: Stephen Riggs to Thomas Williamson, March 12, 1864, box 3, folder 12, Stephen R. Riggs Papers.

142, Paul Mazakutemani: Mary Renville to Stephen Riggs, November 24, 1864, Stephen R. Riggs and Family Papers.

142–43, Scout Red Iron's commander: C. Rice to J. Brown, December 21, 1863, reel 2, Joseph R. and Samuel J. Brown and Family Papers.

143, Catherine Totidutawin wrote: Wawiyohiyewin to Stephen Riggs, April 27, 1864, trans. Louis Garcia and Michael Simon, Stephen R. Riggs and Family Papers.

143, In December 1863: Joseph Brown to Samuel Brown, December 13, 1863, reel 2, Joseph R. and Samuel J. Brown and Family Papers.

143, Approximately thirty: Stephen R. Riggs, *Tah-Koo Wah-Kań: or, The Gospel among the Dakotas*, 364.

143, Gabriel Renville's family: Joseph Brown to Gabriel Renville, January 31, 1864, reel 3, Joseph R. and Samuel J. Brown and Family Papers.

143, Joseph Brown's Dakota wife . . . in Minnesota: Stephen Riggs to Selah Treat, May 12, 1863, mss. 310: no. 31, ABCFM Papers.

143, Bishop Whipple moved: Henry Benjamin Whipple, *Lights and Shadows of a Long Episcopate: Being Reminiscences and Recollections of the Right Reverend Henry Benjamin Whipple*, 133–134.

143, Many of the families . . . "my brother and his family": Wawiyohiyewin to Stephen Riggs, April 27, 1864, trans. Louis Garcia and Michael Simon, Stephen R. Riggs and Family Papers.

143, In 1864: Stephen Riggs to Selah Treat, July 8, 1864, mss. 310: no. 41, ABCFM Papers.

143, The military clearly stated . . . "military commanders": Riggs, *Tah-Koo Wah-Kań*, 365.

143–44, Moreover, by 1865: Stephen Riggs to Selah Treat, June 15, 1865, mss. 310: no. 52, ABCFM Papers.

144, For many Dakota: *ARCIA* (1865), 542.

144, Joseph Brown reported: Robert H. Rose to R. C. Olin, October 30, 1864, *South Dakota Historical Society Collections* 8 (1916): 497.

144, They were called names: Joseph Brown to "Major," December 9, 1864, reel 3, Joseph R. and Samuel J. Brown and Family Papers.

144, In November 1864: R. C. Olin to William Pfaender, November 23, 1864, *South Dakota Historical Society Collections* 8 (1916): 514.

144, In part: "Samuel J. Brown's Pocket Diary," May–July 1865, volume 2, reel 26, Joseph R. and Samuel J. Brown and Family Papers.

144, In 1866 . . . "cost him his life": Henry Whipple to Henry Sibley, March 5, 1866, reel 13, Henry H. Sibley Papers.

144, Samuel Brown summarized . . . "chastisement from his own people": "Samuel J. Brown's Pocket Diary," May–July 1865, volume 2, reel 26, Joseph R. and Samuel J. Brown and Family Papers.

144, Joseph Brown was convinced . . . "this subject": Joseph Brown to William R. Marshall, January 18, 1866, reel 4, Joseph R. and Samuel J. Brown and Family Papers.

144–45, To solve this perceived crisis . . . incursions into Minnesota: Curtis Dahlin, in *The Fort Sisseton Dakota Scouts*, provides a detailed list and description of each of these eighteen small camps, including a map and chart. See pages 40–82.

145, Brown ordered . . . "drive them back": Henry Sibley to Gabriel Renville, October 15, 1863, reel 2, Joseph R. and Samuel J. Brown and Family Papers.

145, In April 1863: "Capture of One of Little Crow's Band," *St. Cloud Democrat*, April 23, 1863.

145, In May 1865: "Gabriel Renville," *St. Paul Daily Globe*, September 11, 1892.

145, Also in 1865 . . . "awfullest moment of his life": Amos E. Oneroad and Alanson B. Skinner, *Being Dakota: Tales and Traditions of the Sisseton and Wahpeton*, 20–21.

145, A newspaper article . . . "four of them": "Important Indian News," *St. Cloud Democrat*, June 1, 1865.

145, In addition to challenging: Alan R. Woolworth, "Dakota Indian Scouts on the Minnesota/Dakota Territory Frontier, 1863–1866," 76.

145, In 1865, a small hunting party . . . "the Dakota river": *ARCIA* (1865), 221.

146, In addition to patrolling . . . affiliation of villages: Dunlay, *Wolves for the Blue Soldiers*, 8.

146, Soldier Frank Myers commented: Myers, *Soldiering in Dakota*, 10.

146, In both summer campaigns: Beck, *Columns of Vengeance*, 81.

146, Sibley and Sully: *ARCIA* (1865), 205.

146, Throughout the summer campaigns: Beck, *Columns of Vengeance*, 101.

146, In July 1863 . . . "reports are true": "From St. Paul: Minnesota Indian Matters," *Chicago Tribune*, July 22, 1863.

146, In July 1864 . . . "ridge of land": Joseph Brown to "Major," July 29, 1864, reel 3, Joseph R. and Samuel J. Brown and Family Papers.

146, For example, Frank Myers . . . "make a treaty": Myers, *Soldiering in Dakota*, 14, 39.

146–47, In a letter . . . "not murdered the whites": Joseph Brown to Gabriel Renville, January 31, 1864, reel 3, Joseph R. and Samuel J. Brown and Family Papers.

147, Specifically, the scouts: Joseph Brown to Samuel Brown, February 15, 1864, reel 3, Joseph R. and Samuel J. Brown and Family Papers.

147, In February 1864 . . . "will be exterminated": Joseph Brown to Sisseton Chiefs, February 17, 1864, reel 3, Joseph R. and Samuel J. Brown and Family Papers.

147, Paul Mazakutemani . . . "what was good": Stephen R. Riggs, trans., "Narrative of Paul Mazakootemane," 87–88.

147, Despite this combination . . . "fire and sword": John M. [Corse?] to Joseph Brown, February 12, 1866, reel 4, Joseph R. and Samuel J. Brown and Family Papers.

147, For example, military correspondence . . . "a good stockade": Robert H. Rose to R. C. Olin, October 30, 1864, *South Dakota Historical Society Collections* 8 (1916): 497.

147, They hauled hay: Joseph Brown to A. S. Everest, February 28, 1865, reel 3, Joseph R. and Samuel J. Brown and Family Papers.

147, In 1864, Brown reported: Joseph Brown to "Major," September 1, 1864, reel 3, Joseph R. and Samuel J. Brown and Family Papers; Joseph Brown to Henry Sibley, February 25, 1864, *South Dakota Historical Society Collections* 8 (1916): 521.

147, They even planned: Robert H. Rose to R. C. Olin, October 30, 1864, *South Dakota Historical Society Collections* 8 (1916): 497.

147, The military also used: Riggs, trans., "Narrative of Paul Mazakootemane," 88.

147–48, This task: *ARCIA* (1865), 209.

148, Major Rose . . . "tomorrow morning": R. H. Rose to Samuel Brown, March 22, 1865, reel 3, Joseph R. and Samuel J. Brown and Family Papers.

148, When the scouts . . . "one more chance": Robert H. Rose to Samuel Brown, March 23, 1865, reel 3, Joseph R. and Samuel J. Brown and Family Papers.

148, In 1864, Brown was camping . . . "they were good Indians": Joseph Brown to "Major," July 29, 1864, reel 3, Joseph R. and Samuel J. Brown and Family Papers.

148, For example, in 1863, Chaska . . . He died: Beck, *Columns of Vengeance*, 128.

148–49, In another case . . . "trouble is there": John Williamson to Thomas Williamson, August 8, 1865, Thomas S. Williamson Papers.

149, For example, during the punitive expeditions: Henry H. Sibley, "Sketch of John Other Day," 101.

149, During the punitive expeditions: Myers, *Soldiering in Dakota*, 14.

149, When stationed on the frontier: Joseph Brown to Gabriel Renville, February 17, 1863, reel 2, Joseph R. and Samuel J. Brown and Family Papers.

149, When General Sibley appointed: Joseph Brown, [1863], reel 2, Joseph R. and Samuel J. Brown and Family Papers.

149, By 1865, however, after complaints: Joseph Brown to C. P. Adams, October 16, 1865, reel 3, Joseph R. and Samuel J. Brown and Family Papers.

149, One scout complained: Inkapadutah to Samuel Brown, March 1866, reel 4, Joseph R. and Samuel J. Brown and Family Papers.

149, The scouts . . . "Minnesota [River]": Joseph Brown to R. C. Olin, January 11, 1866, reel 4, Joseph R. and Samuel J. Brown and Family Papers.

149, Moreover, the military confiscated: R. C. Olin to R. Rose, November 5, 1864, *South Dakota Historical Society Collections* 8 (1916): 504.

150, Joseph Brown complained: Joseph Brown to John M. Corse, April 5, 1866, reel 4, Joseph R. and Samuel J. Brown and Family Papers.

150, The lack of rations . . . "properly appreciated": Joseph Brown to R. C. Olin, January 11, 1866, reel 4, Joseph R. and Samuel J. Brown and Family Papers.

150, The *St. Cloud Democrat* published . . . "bearer Brown": "From the Frontier," *St. Cloud Democrat*, March 30, 1865.

150, The *St. Paul Press* also received . . . "most of our readers": "Joseph and His Brethren," *St. Paul Press*, June 8, 1865.

150, Historians have confirmed: George Martin Smith, ed., *South Dakota: Its History and Its People*, 65.

150, The scouts were not reimbursed: See Section 27, Chapter 543, Laws 1891, 51st Congress, 2d Session, 431.

151, In 1863, for example: "Diary of Lewis C. Paxson," 22.

151, In 1865, a "deserter" . . . "movements of the troops": *ARCIA* (1865), 206, 208.

151, In 1865, at least five scouts . . . "engaging as scouts": Dahlin, *The Fort Sisseton Dakota Scouts*, 31, 180.

151, One of the most startling acts . . . escaped to Manitoba: For references to Henok and Wamdiokiya, see Riggs, *Mary and I*, 78; "A Word from Fort Ellice," *Iapi Oaye / The Word Carrier*, July 1, 1876; "From Manitoba," *Iapi Oaye / The Word Carrier*, March 1, 1877; "News from Manitoba," *Iapi Oaye / The Word Carrier*, February 1, 1880; and "Memorial Services at Hazelwood and Yellow Medicine," *Word Carrier*, July 1, 1903.

151–52, In December 1863 . . . "protection of the Government": General Sibley to Henok, December 1, 1863, reel 2, Joseph R. and Samuel J. Brown and Family Papers.

152, By 1866, however . . . kept the Sisseton from surrendering: Charles Crawford to Joseph Brown, January 30, 1866, reel 4, Joseph R. and Samuel J. Brown and Family Papers.

152, Upon reading this letter . . . his own benefit: Joseph Brown to Charles Crawford, February 3, 1866, reel 4, Joseph R. and Samuel J. Brown and Family Papers.

152, Some were treated as heroes: For example, after his death, Gabriel Renville was eulogized as "a fine specimen of the 'noble red man;' stately, dignified, reticent, intelligent, straightforward and manly in his bearing." See Samuel J. Brown, "Biographic Sketch of Chief Gabriel Renville," 617. For references to scouts supposedly taking plunder, see "Our Indian Scouts. . . ," *Goodhue Volunteer*, July 22, 1863.

7. Conflicts Continue, 1866–1869

155, The previous summer: Stephen Riggs to Selah Treat, July 8, 1864, mss. 310: no. 41, ABCFM Papers.

156, In 1866, Sarah's brother . . . accompanied him: Thomas Williamson to Selah Treat, July 6, 1866, mss. 310: no. 255, ABCFM Papers.

156, Also in 1867: Stephen R. Riggs, *Tah-Koo Wah-Kaṅ: or, The Gospel among the Dakotas*, 426.

156, During this trip . . . "to his people": *Missionary Herald* 63, no. 12 (December 1867): 387.

156, On March 20, 1868 . . . "write me a letter": Catherine Totidutawin to Jane Huggins Holtsclaw, March 20, 1868, trans. Alfred Riggs, Alexander G. Huggins and Family Papers, Minnesota Historical Society, St. Paul, Minn.

156–57, When government officials promised: "An Experiment of Faith: The Journey of the Mdewakanton Dakota Who Settled on the Bend in the River."

157, Stephen Riggs called Nebraska: *Missionary Herald* 62, no. 6 (June 1866): 164; Stephen R. Riggs, *Mary and I: Forty Years with the Sioux*, 230.

157, The Dakota continued: Winifred W. Barton, *John P. Williamson: A Brother to the Sioux*, 105.

158, In spring 1866 . . . tillable land: Roy W. Meyer, *History of the Santee Sioux: United States Indian Policy on Trial*, 155, 156.

158, Those who settled: "The Condemned Indians," *St. Paul Daily Press*, April 20, 1866.

158, Even the ABCFM missionaries: *Annual Report of the ABCFM* (1866), 154.

158–59, Indeed, from the beginning: Meyer, *History of the Santee Sioux*, 158.

159, First, despite their purported freedom: See "Those Indians," *Daily Davenport Democrat*, April 9, 1866.

159, On April 11 . . . far from any of his kin: *ARCIA* (1866), 234.

159, Upon reaching St. Louis: "The Condemned Indians," *St. Paul Daily Press*, April 20, 1866.

159, As they walked: "Indian Prisoners on the Streets," *Daily Missouri Republican*, April 15, 1866.

159, Again, as in Davenport: *ARCIA* (1866), 234; Meyer, *History of the Santee Sioux*, 157.

160, During a séance: "Exposure of a Medium," *Evansville Daily Journal*, April 30, 1866.

160, In Harrisburg . . . "perfectly dark": "The Hidden Hand," *Harrisburg Telegraph*, June 22, 1866.

160, At least one paper . . . "natural tongue": "The Condemned Indians," *St. Paul Daily Press*, April 20, 1866.

160, During the *Dora*'s short layover . . . "long imprisonment": "The River," *Morning Herald and Daily Tribune*, April 26, 1866.

160, After supposedly "luxuriating" . . . once they reached Nebraska: "Indians for Niobrara Valley," *Semi-Weekly Telegraph*, May 28, 1866.

160, W. A. Burleigh . . . "our Territory": *ARCIA* (1866), 229.

160–61, Another article reported . . . fear in the present: "The Indian Prisoners," *Daily Davenport Democrat*, May 18, 1866.

161, Unfortunately, the Davenport contingent . . . "widely different emotions": *Annual Report of the ABCFM* (1866), 155, 156.

161, Stephen Riggs described . . . "causes of rejoicing": Riggs, *Tah-Koo Wah-Kań*, 419–420.

161, The government had appropriated: *ARCIA* (1866), 228; Stephen Riggs to Selah Treat, March 12, 1867, mss. 310: no. 73, ABCFM Papers.

161, By summer 1866: Barton, *John P. Williamson*, 108.

162, Families had left behind: For example, in 1866 the commissioner of Indian affairs reported that three hundred Dakota had died at Crow Creek. See *ARCIA* (1866), 231.

162, John Williamson . . . "might not remain long": *Missionary Herald* 62, no. 8 (August 1866): 249.

162, The settlers complained: Thomas Williamson to Selah Treat, July 30, 1866, mss. 310: no. 256, ABCFM Papers.

162, They responded: *Missionary Herald* 62, no. 10 (October 1866): 294.

162, Some of the settlers: Thomas Williamson to Selah Treat, July 30, 1868, mss. 310: no. 256, ABCFM Papers.

162, Samuel Hinman, however, "ascertained": Samuel Dutton Hinman, *Journal of the Rev. S. D. Hinman: Missionary to the Santee Sioux Indians. And Taopi*, 8–9.

162, Thomas Williamson also defended: Thomas Williamson to Selah Treat, July 30, 1866, mss. 310: no. 256, ABCFM Papers.

162, Many of the deaths: Stephen Riggs to Mary Riggs, August 1, 1866, Stephen R. Riggs Papers.

162, During the fall of 1866 . . . Niobrara River: See *ARCIA* (1868), 246, and Barton, *John P. Williamson*, 118.

162–63, One superintendent . . . "this new home": Meyer, *History of the Santee Sioux*, 163, 158.

163, The constant moves: *ARCIA* (1868), 228.

163, The relocations . . . high mortality rate: Clyde A. Milner II, "Off the White Road: Seven Nebraska Indian Societies in the 1870s—A Statistical Analysis of Assimilation, Population, and Prosperity," 39–40.

163, Even before Dakota families arrived: Meyer, *History of the Santee Sioux*, 158.

163, In July 1866: *Missionary Herald* 63, no. 12 (December 1867): 388.

163, Using methods: "An Experiment of Faith."

163, John Williamson complained . . . "destroy at once": Barton, *John P. Williamson*, 112.

163, Other church members . . . at Camp Kearney: Hinman, *Journal of the Rev. S. D. Hinman*, 5.

163–64, Indeed, Stephen Riggs lamented: Stephen Riggs to Selah Treat, July 21, 1866, mss. 310: no. 66, ABCFM Papers.

164, The missionaries . . . at Crow Creek: Virginia Driving Hawk Sneve, *Completing the Circle*, 59, 61.

164, While some Dakota ended: Stephen Riggs to Selah Treat, August 1, 1866, reel 769, Papers of the ABCFM.

164, While the missionaries focused: *Missionary Herald* 62, no. 1 (January 1866): 11.

164, In February 1865, Congress authorized . . . "fidelity was equally great": *ARCIA* (1866), 235, 237, 239.

165, Hinman noted . . . "hope for his people": Hinman, *Journal of the Rev. S. D. Hinman*, 25, 36–37.

165, In 1867 . . . "can do little work": *Missionary Herald* 65, no. 5 (May 1867): 153.

165, From Nebraska, Tawahinkpeduta wrote . . . opportunities in Nebraska: "From the Indian Country," *Davenport Daily Gazette*, July 28, 1866.

166, Government officials called: Mary Beth Faimon, "Ties That Bind: Remembering, Mourning, and Healing Historical Trauma," 240.

166, Stephen Riggs called: Stephen Riggs to Selah Treat, March 12, 1867, mss. 310: no. 73, ABCFM Papers.

166, These treaties: Meyer, *History of the Santee Sioux*, 200.

166, The government: "Obituary, Gabriel Renville," *St. Paul Globe*, September 11, 1892.

166, During the distribution . . . "without our consent?": Stephen R. Riggs, trans., "Narrative of Paul Mazakootemane," 89.

166, The problem was compounded . . . for his own use: *ARCIA* (1867), 245.

166–67, In both locations: Meyer, *History of the Santee Sioux*, 200.

167, Conditions became so severe: *ARCIA* (1869), 323.

167, Stephen Riggs received: Stephen Riggs to Selah Treat, January 7, 1868, mss. 310: no. 82, ABCFM Papers.

167, John Renville wrote . . . plead the Dakota's case: John B. Renville to Stephen Riggs, n.d., mss. 309: no. 214, ABCFM Papers.

167, Stephen Riggs and Thomas Williamson agreed: Stephen Riggs to Selah Treat, January 7, 1868, mss. 310: no. 82, ABCFM Papers.

167, Before they could make . . . 1867 and 1868: *ARCIA* (1869), 326; Meyer, *History of the Santee Sioux*, 201–202.

167, Although he did not want . . . "working like beavers": Henry Benjamin Whipple, *Lights and Shadows of a Long Episcopate: Being Reminiscences and Recollections of the Right Reverend Henry Benjamin Whipple*, 286.

167, During a trip: *Missionary Herald* 65, no. 5 (May 1869): 153.

168, From 1866 to 1869 . . . "Indian Affairs": Whipple, *Lights and Shadows*, 290–291.

168, In 1869, the ABCFM missionaries . . . "when in prison": Barton, *John P. Williamson*, 138, 139.

168, The treaty promised: "An Experiment of Faith."

169, Despite the clause . . . support of the community: Barton, *John P. Williamson*, 139, 141.

169, After that meeting . . . "members of their tribe": Meyer, *History of the Santee Sioux*, 245.

169, In 1870: Barton, *John P. Williamson*, 141.

169, In 1871: "An Experiment of Faith."

169, From its small beginnings: Milner, "Off the White Road," 39.

169, Beginning in the mid-1870s . . . alliance: For references to John Williamson as U.S. special Indian agent to Flandreau, see "Local Laconics," *Daily Press and Dakotaian*, October 27, 1876, and "Proposals Wanted," *Daily Press and Dakotaian*, March 15, 1878.

169–70, Even D. N. Cooley . . . "being Sioux Indians": *ARCIA* (1867), 265. See also Bonnie Sue Lewis, *Creating Christian Indians: Native Clergy in the Presbyterian Church*, 58.

Epilogue

171, In 1867: Jane Holtsclaw to Hattie, November 4, 1867, Alexander G. Huggins and Family Papers.

171, In August 1869 . . . "written in heaven": Stephen Riggs to Selah Treat, September 10, 1869, mss. 310: no. 113, ABCFM Papers.

171, On October 14: George D. Crocker to Thomas Williamson, October 17, 1869, Stephen R. Riggs and Family Papers.

171–72, Stephen Riggs . . . "continued decline": Stephen R. Riggs, *Tah-Koo Wah-Kaṅ; or, The Gospel among the Dakotas*, 184.

172, Her mother . . . "much hardship": Catherine Totidutawin to Jane Huggins Holtsclaw, March 20, 1868, trans. Alfred Riggs, Alexander G. Huggins and Family Papers.

172, While the records are scattered . . . the Davenport prison: For references to Robert Hopkins at the Lake Traverse Reservation, see *Missionary Herald* 63, no. 12 (December 1867): 390; in Flandreau, https://www.facebook.com/permalink .php?id=113297675423815&story_fbid=560753754011536; and in Montana, "Notices of the Upper Dakota Mission," *Presbyterian Monthly Record* 33 (1882): 419, and "Mission News," *Word Carrier*, May 1, 1891, 19. Also phone call, Bob Hopkins, November 21, 2017.

172, While he was not an ordained minister: Robert Hopkins to the Faculty of Beloit College, April 2, 1873, trans. Stephen Riggs, folder 19, Beloit College Indian (Native American) Students Collection, Beloit College, Beloit, Wisc.

172, In 1899: "Good Will Notes," *Word Carrier*, June–July 1899, 27.

172, According to Bob Hopkins . . . the family: Phone call, Bob Hopkins, November 21, 2017.

172, Traditionally, extended families . . . "extended family": Virginia Driving Hawk Sneve, *Completing the Circle*, 42, 49.

173, A visitor noted: "Mission News," *Word Carrier*, May 1, 1891, 19.

173, In 1887, his tenure: *Eighteenth Annual Report of the Board of Home Missions of the Presbyterian Church in the United States of America* (1888), 15.

173, By 1891, Robert had returned: "From Poplar Creek," *Word Carrier*, December 1, 1891, 36.

173, Perhaps the local agent's: *ARCIA* (1884), 119.

173, In 1873, Robert sent: Robert Hopkins to the Faculty of Beloit College, April 2, 1873, trans. Stephen Riggs, folder 19, Beloit College Indian (Native American) Students Collection. See also Amy Lyn Rogel and Frederick A. Burnwell, "Mastering the Secret of White Man's Power: Indian Students at Beloit College, 1871–1884."

173, Supported by: "Indian Student Bills—Samuel Hopkins," December 1872–July 1873, folder 19, Beloit College Indian (Native American) Students Collection. Samuel's scholarship for three sessions of tuition paid, respectively, $10, $8.25, and $7.25. He owed about a dollar a session that his scholarship did not cover. Stephen Riggs served as his sponsor.

173–74, At least three: Many records of the Carlisle school, including those of several of Samuel Hopkins's children, have been digitized. See http://carlisleindian

.dickinson.edu/people/hopkins-samuel. Samuel Hopkins passed away on November 29, 1927. See "Rev. Samuel Hopkins Ta," *Iapi Oaye*, December 1927, 38.

174, Meanwhile, according to *Iapi Oaye*: For example, see *Iapi Oaye*, January 1, 1875, 2, and "Mission News," *Word Carrier*, May 1, 1891, 10.

174, In 1888, they visited: "Berthold Mission," *Word Carrier*, June 1888, 23.

174, In 1891, the family reunited: The *Word Carrier* reported that Joseph Hopkins helped his uncle, Robert Hopkins, with missionary work at the Wolf Point station. See "Former Pupils," *Word Carrier*, February 1, 1891, 7.

174, The day before . . . "my own children": "Mission News," *Word Carrier*, May 1, 1891, 19.

174, According to Hopkins family history: John Williamson, "Robert Hopkins Ta." While Williamson's obituary lists Hopkins's place of death as Ascension, South Dakota, Ascension historian Floyd DeCoteau did not find Robert Hopkins listed in the session books at Ascension Church, nor did he find a headstone or marker in the cemetery. E-mail from Floyd DeCoteau, March 18, 2018.

174, According to great-great-grandson: Phone call, Bob Hopkins, November 21, 2017.

175, In 2000, the remains of Dakota leader . . . Morton, Minnesota: "Dakota Warrior's Remains Buried with Honor near Redwood Falls," *Post Bulletin*, May 5, 2014. For a report on the repatriation of Marpiya Okinajin, see *Federal Register* 65, no. 100 (May 23, 2000), 33352. See also "Indian Warrior 'Comes Home,'" *St. Cloud Times*, July 17, 2000. In September 2018, the Mayo Clinic apologized for its role in the desecration of Marpiya Okinajin's body. It also created a scholarship in his name for meritorious Native American medical school candidates or students in the clinic's School of Health Sciences, graduate school, or nursing programs. See Matt McKinney, "In Hopes of Healing, Mayo Creates Scholarship as Apology for Misuse of Dakota Leader's Body."

175, A fourth skeleton: "Dakota Skeleton Was Displayed for Decades in Mankato Home," *Mankato Free Press*, November 26, 2014.

175, Like Marpiya Okinajin . . . a sacred object: "Minnesota Tribe Looks to Block Sale of U.S.-Dakota War Relic," *St. Cloud Times*, May 3, 2018.

175, The auction continued . . . the Dakota Oyate: "Pipe Finds Rightful Place," *Star Tribune*, May 9, 2018.

WORKS CITED

Archival Collections

Augustana College, Rock Island, Ill.
  John Henry Hauberg Papers
  Williamson Family Papers
Augustana University, Center for Western Studies, Sioux Falls, S.Dak.
  E. N. Biddle Papers, Episcopal Diocese of South Dakota Collection
  Alfred L. Riggs Papers, Oahe Mission Collection, South Dakota Conference of
    the United Church of Christ Archives
  Stephen R. Riggs Papers, Oahe Mission Collection, South Dakota Conference of
    the United Church of Christ Archives
Beloit College, Beloit, Wisc.
  Beloit College Indian (Native American) Students Collection
Davenport Public Library, Davenport, Iowa
  "Iowa's Rendezvous Camps, 1861–1866"
Minnesota Historical Society, St. Paul, Minn.
  ABCFM Papers
  Joseph R. and Samuel J. Brown and Family Papers
  Daily Journal of the Sibley Expedition, 1863, U.S. Army Continental Commands
  Diaries, Episcopal Church, Diocese of Minnesota, Bishop Henry B. Whipple
    Papers
  Alexander G. Huggins and Family Papers
  Lorenzo Lawrence Papers
  Pond Family Papers
  Stephen R. Riggs and Family Correspondence, Concerning Lac qui Parle
    Mission and Other Matters

Stephen R. Riggs and Family Papers
Henry H. Sibley Papers
Arthur Sterry Journal
Henry B. Whipple Papers
Thomas S. Williamson Papers, reel 1
National Archives and Records Administration, Washington, D.C.
Letters Received by the Office of Indian Affairs, 1824–1870, St. Peter's Agency, 1862–1865
Abraham Lincoln Papers at the Library of Congress, series 1, General Correspondence, 1833–1916
Records of United States Army Continental Commands, 1821–1920, record group 393
South Dakota Historical Society, Pierre, S.Dak.
South Dakota Historical Society Collections
State Historical Society of Iowa, Des Moines, Iowa
Samuel R. Curtis Papers
Wheaton College, Billy Graham Center, Wheaton, Ill.
Papers of the American Board of Commissioners for Foreign Missions, 1827–1929

Newspapers and Reports

Annual Report of the American Board of Commissioners for Foreign Missions, Boston, Mass.
Annual Report of the Commissioner of Indian Affairs, Boston, Mass.
ARTnews, New York, N.Y.
Cedar Falls Gazette
Chatfield Democrat
Chicago Tribune
Continental Monthly, New York, N.Y.
Daily Davenport Democrat
Daily Democrat and News, Davenport, Iowa
Daily Evening Bulletin, San Francisco, Calif.
Daily Iowa State Register, Des Moines, Iowa
Daily Missouri Republican, St. Louis, Mo.
Daily Press and Dakotaian, Yankton, Dakota Territory
Daily Times, Davenport, Iowa
Dakotian, Yankton, Dakota Territory
Davenport Daily Gazette
Davenport Democrat

Davenport Democrat and Leader
Evansville Daily Journal
Evening Argus, Rock Island, Ill.
Goodhue Volunteer, Red Wing, Minn.
Harper's Weekly, New York, N.Y.
Harrisburg Telegraph
Iapi Oaye, Dakota Mission
Iapi Oaye/The Word Carrier, Dakota Mission
Journal, New Ulm, Minn.
Mankato Weekly Record
Minneapolis Sunday Tribune
Missionary Herald, Boston, Mass.
Morning Democrat, Davenport, Iowa
Morning Herald, St. Joseph, Mo.
Morning Herald and Daily Tribune, St. Joseph, Mo.
Muscatine Daily Journal
New York Times
Pioneer and Democrat, St. Paul, Minn.
Post Bulletin, Rochester, Minn.
Presbyterian Monthly Record, Philadelphia, Pa.
Sacramento Daily Union
Semi-Weekly Telegraph, Great Salt Lake City, Utah
Semi-Weekly Wisconsin, Milwaukee, Wisc.
Spirit of Missions, Gambier, Ohio
Star Tribune, Minneapolis, Minn.
Stillwater Messenger
St. Cloud Democrat
St. Cloud Times
St. Paul Daily Globe
St. Paul Daily Press
St. Paul Globe
St. Paul Pioneer
St. Paul Press
Sunbury American
Vermont Chronicle, Bellows Falls, Vt.
Weekly National Intelligencer, Washington, D.C.
Weekly Pioneer and Democrat, St. Paul, Minn.
Word Carrier, Santee, Nebr.
Word Carrier of the Santee Normal Training School, Santee, Nebr.

Books and Articles

Albers, Patricia C. "Sioux Kinship in a Colonial Setting." *Dialectical Anthropology* 6, no. 3 (March 1982): 253–269.

Anderson, Gary Clayton. *Kinsmen of Another Kind: Dakota White Relations in the Upper Mississippi Valley, 1650–1862*. St. Paul: Minnesota Historical Society Press, 1997.

——. *Little Crow: Spokesman for the Sioux*. St. Paul: Minnesota Historical Society Press, 1986.

——. "Myrick's Insult: A Fresh Look at Myth and Reality." *Minnesota History* 48, no. 5 (Spring 1983): 198–206.

Anderson, Gary Clayton, and Alan R. Woolworth, eds. *Through Dakota Eyes: Narrative Accounts of the Minnesota Indian War of 1862*. St. Paul: Minnesota Historical Society Press, 1988.

Anderson, Rufus. *Memorial Volume of the First Fifty Years of the American Board of Commissioners for Foreign Missions*. Boston: The Board, 1861.

Bachman, Walt. *Northern Slave/Black Dakota: The Life and Times of Joseph Godfrey*. Bloomington, Minn.: Pond Dakota Press, 2013.

Barnds, William Joseph. "The Ministry of the Reverend Samuel Dutton Hinman, among the Sioux." *Historical Magazine of the Protestant Episcopal Church* 38, no. 4 (December 1969): 393–401.

Barrows, Isabel C., ed. *Proceedings of the National Conference of Charities and Correction*. Boston: Geo. H. Ellis, 1892.

Barton, Winifred W. *John P. Williamson: A Brother to the Sioux*. New York: Fleming H. Revell Company, 1919.

Beatty, James K. "Interpreting the Shawnee Sun: Literacy and Cultural Persistence in Indian Country, 1833–1841." *Kansas History* 31, no. 4 (Winter 2008–09): 243–259.

Beck, Paul N. *Columns of Vengeance: Soldiers, Sioux, and the Punitive Expeditions, 1863–1864*. Norman: University of Oklahoma Press, 2013.

Bell, John. "The Sioux War Panorama and American Mythic History." *Theatre Journal* 48, no. 3 (October 1996): 279–299.

Berg, Scott W. "Lincoln's Choice." *Quarterly Journal of Military History* 26, no. 2 (Winter 2014): 30–39.

——. *38 Nooses: Lincoln, Little Crow, and the Beginning of the Frontier's End*. New York: Pantheon, 2012.

Berkhofer, Robert F., Jr. *The White Man's Indian: Images of the American Indian from Columbus to the Present*. New York: Vintage, 1979.

Bieder, Robert E. "The Representations of Indian Bodies in Nineteenth-Century American Anthropology." In *Repatriation Reader: Who Owns American Indian Re-*

mains? ed. Devon A. Mihesuah, 19–36. Lincoln: University of Nebraska Press, 2000.

Blackhawk, Ned. "Look How Far We've Come: How American Indian History Changed the Study of American History in the 1990s." *OAH Magazine of History* 19, no. 6 (November 2005): 13–17.

———. *Violence over the Land: Indians and Empires in the Early American West.* Cambridge, Mass.: Harvard University Press, 2006.

Blaeser, Kimberly M. "Learning 'the Language the Presidents Speak': Images and Issues of Literacy in American Indian Literature." *World Literature Today* 66, no. 2 (Spring 1992): 230–235.

Bragdon, Kathleen J. "The Pragmatics of Language Learning: Graphic Pluralism on Martha's Vineyard, 1660–1720." *Ethnohistory* 57, no. 1 (Winter 2010): 35–50.

Briggs, Harold E. "Grasshopper Plagues and Early Dakota Agriculture, 1864–1876." *Agricultural History* 8, no. 2 (April 1934): 51–63.

Brown, Curt. "Minnesota History: Caught in the Middle of the Dakota War." *Star Tribune*, April 2, 2015.

Brown, Samuel J. "Biographic Sketch of Chief Gabriel Renville." *Collections of the Minnesota Historical Society* 10, no. 2 (1905): 614–618.

Canku, Clifford, and Michael Simon. *The Dakota Prisoner of War Letters: Dakota Kaśkapi Okicize Wowapi.* St. Paul: Minnesota Historical Society Press, 2013.

Carley, Kenneth. *The Dakota War of 1862: Minnesota's Other Civilization.* 2d ed. St. Paul: Minnesota Historical Society Press, 2001.

Carlson, Sarah-Eva Ellen. "They Tell Their Story: The Dakota Internment at Camp McClellan in Davenport, 1862–1866." *Annals of Iowa* 63, no. 3 (Summer 2004): 251–278.

Chaky, Doreen. *Terrible Justice: Sioux Chiefs and U.S. Soldiers on the Upper Missouri, 1854–1868.* Norman: University of Oklahoma Press, 2012.

Chomsky, Carol. "The United States–Dakota War Trials: A Study in Military Injustice." *Stanford Law Review* 43, no. 1 (January 1990): 13–98.

Clabaugh, Erik K. "The Evolution of a Massacre in Newspaper Depictions of the Sioux Indians at Wounded Knee, 1876–1891." *Atlanta Review of Journalism History* 12, no. 1 (Spring 2015): 38–64.

Clemmons, Linda M. *Conflicted Mission: Faith, Disputes, and Deception on the Dakota Frontier.* St. Paul: Minnesota Historical Society Press, 2014.

———. "'We Are Writing This Letter Seeking Your Help': Dakotas, ABCFM Missionaries, and Their Uses of Literacy, 1863–1866." *Western Historical Quarterly* 47, no. 2 (Spring 2016): 183–209.

———. "'The Young Folks [Want] to Go in and See the Indians': Davenport Citizens, Protestant Missionaries, and Dakota Prisoners of War, 1863–1866." *Annals of Iowa* 77, no. 2 (Spring 2018): 121–150.

Clink, Kellian. "Historiography of the Dakota Conflict." Presentation at the Northern Great Plains Conference, Grand Forks, N.Dak., October 2001.

Clodfelter, Micheal. *The Dakota War: The United States Army versus the Sioux, 1862–1865.* Jefferson, N.C.: McFarland and Company, 1998.

Coward, John M. *The Newspaper Indian: Native Identity in the Press, 1820–90.* Urbana: University of Illinois Press, 1999.

Craig, Robert. "Christianity and Empire: A Case Study of American Protestant Colonialism and Native Americans." *American Indian Culture and Research Journal* 21, no. 2 (1997): 1–41.

Dahlin, Curtis A. "Between Two Worlds." *Minnesota's Heritage* 5 (January 2012): 79–81.

————. *The Fort Sisseton Dakota Scouts and Their Camps in Eastern Dakota Territory, 1863–1866.* Roseville, Minn.: Curtis A. Dahlin, 2017.

Dean, Janet. "Nameless Outrages: Narrative Authority, Rape Rhetoric, and the Dakota Conflict of 1862." *American Literature* 77, no. 1 (March 2005): 93–122.

Deloria, Ella Cara. *Speaking of Indians.* New York: Friendship Press, 1944; reprint, Lincoln: University of Nebraska Press, 1998.

Denson, Andrew. "Muskogee's International Fairs: Tribal Autonomy and the Indian Image in the Late Nineteenth Century." *Western Historical Quarterly* 34, no. 3 (Autumn 2003): 325–345.

"Diary of Lewis C. Paxson, Stockton, N.J., 1862–1865." *Collections State Historical Society of North Dakota* 2 (1908): 1–64.

Diedrich, Mark. *Old Betsey: The Life and Times of a Famous Dakota Woman and Her Family.* Rochester, Minn.: Coyote Books, 1995.

Dippold, Steffi. "The Wampanoag Word: John Eliot's *Indian Grammar*, the Vernacular Rebellion, and the Elegancies of Native Speech." *Early American Literature* 48, no. 3 (January 2013): 543–575.

Dunlay, Thomas W. *Wolves for the Blue Soldiers: Indian Scouts and Auxiliaries with the United States Army, 1860–90.* Lincoln: University of Nebraska Press, 1987.

Eastman, Charles A. *The Indian To-day: The Past and Future of the First American.* New York: Doubleday, Page and Company, 1915.

Eggleston, Michael A. "Fighting the Sioux." *North and South* 14, no. 4 (November 2012): 38–47.

Ellis, Richard N. "Political Pressures and Army Policies on the Northern Plains, 1862–1865." *Minnesota History* 42 (Summer 1970): 43–53.

Emery, Jacqueline. "Writing against Erasure: Native American Students at Hampton Institute and the Periodical Press." *American Periodicals* 22, no. 2 (2012): 178–198.

"An Experiment of Faith: The Journey of the Mdewakanton Dakota Who Settled

on the Bend in the River." 2003, http://www.vondradev.com/wp-content
/uploads/2015/08/fsst_experiment_of_faith_2015.pdf.

Faimon, Mary Beth. "Ties That Bind: Remembering, Mourning, and Healing
Historical Trauma." *American Indian Quarterly* 28, nos. 1 and 2 (Winter/Spring
2004): 238–251.

Fear-Segal, Jacqueline, and Rebecca Tillett, eds. *Indigenous Bodies: Reviewing, Relocating, Reclaiming.* Albany, N.Y.: SUNY Press, 2013.

Finkelman, Paul. "I Could Not Afford to Hang Men for Votes: Lincoln the Lawyer,
Humanitarian Concerns, and the Dakota Pardons." *William Mitchell Law Review*
39, no. 2 (2013): 405–449.

Goodburn, Amy M. "Literacy Practices at the Genoa Industrial Indian School."
Great Plains Quarterly 19, no. 1 (January 1999): 35–52.

Graber, Jennifer. "Mighty Upheaval on the Minnesota Frontier: Violence, War, and
Death in Dakota and Missionary Christianity." *Church History* 80, no. 1 (March
2011): 76–108.

Grimshaw, Patricia. "'Christian Woman, Pious Wife, Faithful Mother, Devoted
Missionary': Conflicts in Roles of American Missionary Women in Nineteenth-
Century Hawaii." *Feminist Studies* 9, no. 3 (Fall 1983): 489–521.

Harvey, Sean P. "Colonialism, Literacies, and Languages." *Reviews in American
History* 41, no. 4 (December 2013): 583–591.

Hassrick, Royal B. *The Sioux: Life and Customs of a Warrior Society.* Norman: University of Oklahoma Press, 1988.

Haymond, John A. *The Infamous Dakota War Trials of 1862: Revenge, Military Law
and the Judgment of History.* Jefferson, N.C.: McFarland and Company, 2016.

Heard, Isaac V. D. *History of the Sioux War and Massacres of 1862 and 1863.* New
York: Harper and Brothers, 1863.

Herbert, Maeve. "Explaining the Sioux Military Commission of 1862." *Columbia
Human Rights Law Review* 40, no. 3 (Spring 2009): 743–798.

Hinman, Samuel Dutton. *Journal of the Rev. S. D. Hinman: Missionary to the Santee
Sioux Indians. And Taopi.* Philadelphia: McCalla and Stavely, 1869.

Hoffert, Sylvia D. "Gender and Vigilantism on the Minnesota Frontier: Jane Grey
Swisshelm and the U.S.-Dakota Conflict of 1862." *Western Historical Quarterly*
29, no. 3 (Autumn 1998): 342–363.

———. "Jane Grey Swisshelm, Elizabeth Keckley, and the Significance of Race
Consciousness in American Women's History." *Journal of Women's History* 13,
no. 3 (Autumn 2001): 8–33.

———. "Jane Grey Swisshelm and the Negotiation of Gender Roles on the Minnesota Frontier." *Frontiers: A Journal of Women Studies* 18, no. 3 (1997): 17–39.

Homstad, Daniel W. "Lincoln's Agonizing Decision." *American History* 36, no. 5
(December 2001): 28–37.

Hyman, Colette A. *Dakota Women's Work: Creativity, Culture, and Exile*. St. Paul: Minnesota Historical Society Press, 2012.

———. "Survival at Crow Creek, 1863–1866." *Minnesota History* 61, no. 4 (Winter 2008–09): 148–161.

Isch, John. *The Dakota Trials: Including the Complete Transcripts and Explanatory Notes on the Military Commission Trials in Minnesota, 1862–1864*. New Ulm, Minn.: Brown County Historical Society, 2013.

Jacob, Michelle M. *Yakama Rising: Indigenous Cultural Revitalization, Activism, and Healing*. Tucson: University of Arizona Press, 2013.

Jacobs, Margaret D. "Genocide or Ethnic Cleansing? Are These Our Only Choices?" *Western Historical Quarterly* 47, no. 4 (Winter 2016): 444–448.

Kasson, Joy S. *Buffalo Bill's Wild West: Celebrity, Memory, and Popular History*. New York: Hill and Wang, 2000.

Kauanui, J. Kēhaulani, ed. *Speaking of Indigenous Politics: Conversations with Activists, Scholars, and Tribal Leaders*. Minneapolis: University of Minnesota Press, 2018.

Kelsey, Harry. "The Doolittle Report of 1867: Its Preparation and Shortcomings." *Arizona and the West* 17, no. 2 (Summer 1975): 107–120.

Lahti, Janne. "Colonized Labor: Apaches and Pawnees as Army Workers." *Western Historical Quarterly* 39, no. 3 (Autumn 2008): 283–302.

Lass, William E. "Histories of the U.S.-Dakota War of 1862." *Minnesota History* 62, no. 2 (Summer 2012): 44–57.

———. "'The 'Moscow Expedition.'" *Minnesota History* 39, no. 6 (Summer 1965): 227–240.

———. "The Removal from Minnesota of the Sioux and Winnebago Indians." *Minnesota History* 38, no. 8 (December 1963): 353–364.

Lawrence, Elden. *The Peace Seekers: The Indian Christians and the Dakota Conflict*. Sioux Falls, S.Dak.: Pine Hill Press, 2005.

Lewis, Bonnie Sue. *Creating Christian Indians: Native Clergy in the Presbyterian Church*. Norman: University of Oklahoma Press, 2003.

———. "Leadership in the Native Tradition: Dakota and Nez Perce Presbyterian Pastors." *Journal of Presbyterian History* 77, no. 3 (Fall 1999): 153–166.

Lewis, Charles. "Wise Decisions: A Frontier Newspaper's Coverage of the Dakota Conflict." *American Journalism* 28, no. 2 (Spring 2011): 48–80.

Lewis, Chuck. "Frontier Fears: The Clash of Dakotas and Whites in the Newspapers of Mankato, Minnesota, 1863–1865." *Minnesota Heritage* 5 (January 2012): 36–53.

Lincoln, Abraham. *The Collected Works of Abraham Lincoln*. Ed. Roy P. Basler. Vol. 5. Springfield, Ill.: Abraham Lincoln Association, 1953.

Lonetree, Amy. *Decolonizing Museums: Representing Native America in National and Tribal Museums.* Chapel Hill: University of North Carolina Press, 2012.

Martínez, David. *Dakota Philosopher: Charles Eastman and American Indian Thought.* St. Paul: Minnesota Historical Society Press, 2009.

————. "Remembering the Thirty-Eight: Abraham Lincoln, the Dakota, and the U.S. War on Barbarism." *Wicazo Sa Review* 28, no. 2 (Fall 2013): 5–29.

McConkey, Harriet E. Bishop. *Dakota War Whoop: or, Indian Massacres and War in Minnesota of 1862–'3.* St. Paul: D. D. Merrill, 1863.

McKinney, Matt. "In Hopes of Healing, Mayo Creates Scholarship as Apology for Misuse of Dakota Leader's Body." *Star Tribune*, September 19, 2018.

McNally, Michael D. "The Practice of Christianity." *Church History* 69, no. 4 (December 2000): 834–859.

McNenly, Linda Scarangella. "Foe, Friend, or Critic: Native Performers with Buffalo Bill's Wild West Show and Discourses of Conquest and Friendship in Newspaper Reports." *American Indian Quarterly* 38, no. 2 (Spring 2014): 143–176.

Meyer, Roy W. *History of the Santee Sioux: United States Indian Policy on Trial.* Rev. ed. Lincoln: University of Nebraska Press, 1993.

Mihesuah, Devon A., ed. *Repatriation Reader: Who Owns American Indian Remains?* Lincoln: University of Nebraska Press, 2000.

Miller, Susan A. "Native America Writes Back: The Origin of the Indigenous Paradigm in Historiography." *Wicazo Sa Review* 23, no. 2 (Fall 2008): 9–28.

————. "Native Historians Write Back: The Indigenous Paradigm in American Indian Historiography." *Wicazo Sa Review* 24, no. 1 (Spring 2009): 25–45.

Milner, Clyde A., II. "Off the White Road: Seven Nebraska Indian Societies in the 1870s—A Statistical Analysis of Assimilation, Population, and Prosperity." *Western Historical Quarterly* 12, no. 1 (January 1981): 37–52.

Milroy, Thomas W. "Solomon Two Stars (We-cah-npe-no-pah): Peace Warrior." *Minnesota Archaeologist* 47, no. 2 (1988): 59–66.

Monroe, Barbara. *Plateau Indian Ways with Words: The Rhetorical Tradition of the Tribes of the Inland Pacific Northwest.* Pittsburgh: University of Pittsburgh Press, 2014.

Munro, John. "Interwoven Colonial Histories: Indigenous Agency and Academic Historiography in North America." *Canadian Review of American Studies* 44, no. 3 (Winter 2014): 402–425.

Myers, Frank. *Soldiering in Dakota, among the Indians, in 1863–4–5.* Huron, S.Dak.: Huronite Printing House, 1888.

"Names of the Condemned Dakota Men." *American Indian Quarterly* 28, nos. 1 and 2 (Winter/Spring 2004): 175–183.

Neel, Susan Rhoades. "Tourism and the American West: New Departures." *Pacific Historical Review* 65, no. 4 (November 1996): 517–523.

Neylan, Susan. *The Heavens Are Changing: Nineteenth-Century Protestant Missions and Tsimshian Christianity*. Montreal: McGill-Queen's University Press, 2003.

Nichols, David A. "The Other Civil War: Lincoln and the Indians." *Minnesota History* 44, no. 1 (Spring 1974): 3–15.

O'Brien, Jean M. *Firsting and Lasting: Writing Indians Out of Existence in New England*. Minneapolis: University of Minnesota Press, 2010.

Oneroad, Amos E., and Alanson B. Skinner. *Being Dakota: Tales and Traditions of the Sisseton and Wahpeton*. Ed. Laura L. Anderson. St. Paul: Minnesota Historical Society Press, 2005.

Peacock, John Hunt, Jr. "An Account of the Dakota-US War as Sacred Text: Why My Dakota Elders Value Spiritual Closure over Scholarly 'Balance.'" *American Indian Culture and Research Journal* 37, no. 2 (2013): 185–206.

———. "Lamenting Language Loss at the Modern Language Association." *American Indian Quarterly* 30, nos. 1 and 2 (Winter/Spring 2006): 138–152.

———. "Wanna Dakota unkiapi kte!" *Studies in American Indian Literatures* 18, no. 1 (Spring 2006): 57–72.

Peacock, Thomas D., and Donald R. Day. "Nations within a Nation: The Dakota and Ojibwe of Minnesota." *Daedalus* 129, no. 3 (Summer 2000): 137–159.

Pexa, Christopher J. "Transgressive Adoptions: Dakota Prisoners' Resistances to State Domination Following the 1862 U.S.-Dakota War." *Wicazo Sa Review* 30, no. 1 (Spring 2015): 29–66.

Pilling, James Constantine. "Bibliography of the Siouan Languages." Smithsonian Institution, Bureau of Ethnology, bulletin 5. Washington, D.C.: Government Printing Office, 1887.

Pond, Samuel W. *Dakota Life in the Upper Midwest*. St. Paul: Minnesota Historical Society Press, 1986.

———. *The Dakota or Sioux in Minnesota as They Were in 1834*. St. Paul: Minnesota Historical Society Press, 1986.

———. *Two Volunteer Missionaries among the Dakotas: or, The Story of the Labors of Samuel W. and Gideon H. Pond*. Boston: Congregational Sunday-School and Publishing Society, 1893.

Powell, J. W., ed. *Tenth Annual Report of the Bureau of Ethnology to the Secretary of the Smithsonian Institution, 1888–89*. Washington, D.C.: Government Printing Office, 1893.

Pratt, Stephanie. "Restating Indigenous Presence in Eastern Dakota and Ho-Chunk (Winnebago) Portraits of the 1830s–1860s." In *Indigenous Bodies: Reviewing, Relocating, Reclaiming*, ed. Jacqueline Fear-Segal and Rebecca Tillett, 17–30. Albany, N.Y.: SUNY Press, 2013.

Reddin, Paul. *Wild West Shows*. Urbana: University of Illinois Press, 1999.

Relf, Frances H. "Removal of the Sioux Indians from Minnesota." *Minnesota History Bulletin* 2, no. 6 (May 1918): 420–425.

Renville, Gabriel. "A Sioux Narrative of the Outbreak in 1862, and of Sibley's Expedition in 1863." *Collections of the Minnesota Historical Society* 10, no. 2 (1905): 595–613.

Riding In, James. "Decolonizing NAGPRA." In *For Indigenous Eyes Only: A Decolonization Handbook*, ed. Waziyatawin and Michael Yellow Bird, 53–66. Santa Fe, N.M.: School of American Research, 2005.

Riggs, Maida Leonard, ed. *A Small Bit of Bread and Butter: Letters from the Dakota Territory, 1832–1869*. South Deerfield, Mass.: Ash Grove Press, 1996.

Riggs, Stephen R. *A Dakota-English Dictionary*. Ed. James Owen Dorsey. Contributions to North American Ethnology, vol. 7. Washington, D.C.: Government Printing Office, 1890; reprint, St. Paul: Minnesota Historical Society, 1992.

———. *Dakota Grammar, Texts and Ethnography*. Ed. James Owen Dorsey. Contributions to North American Ethnology, vol. 9. Washington, D.C.: Government Printing Office, 1893.

———. "The Dakota Mission." *Collections of the Minnesota Historical Society* 3 (1870–1880): 115–128.

———. *Dakota Portraits*. St. Peter: Minnesota Free Press, 1858.

———. *Mary and I: Forty Years with the Sioux*. Chicago: W. G. Holmes, 1880; reprint, Minneapolis: Ross and Haines, 1969.

———. *Model First Reader—Wayawa Tokaheya*. Chicago: G. Sherwood and Company, 1873.

———, trans. "Narrative of Paul Mazakootamane." *Collections of the Minnesota Historical Society* 3 (1870–1880): 82–90.

———. "Sketches of the Dakota Mission." 1873, https://archive.org/details/sketchesofdakotaoorigg/page/no.

———. *Tah-Koo Wah-Kań; or, The Gospel among the Dakotas*. Boston: Congregational Sabbath-School and Publishing Society, 1869.

Roberts, Gary L. *Massacre at Sand Creek: How Methodists Were Involved in an American Tragedy*. Nashville: Abingdon Press, 2016.

Rogel, Amy Lyn, and Frederick A. Burnwell. "Mastering the Secret of White Man's Power: Indian Students at Beloit College, 1871–1884." Part 2, https://www.beloit.edu/archives/documents/archival_documents/masteringthesecret/.

Rosaldo, Renato. *Culture and Truth: The Remaking of Social Analysis*. Boston: Beacon Press, 1989.

Round, Phillip H. *Removable Type: Histories of the Book in Indian Country, 1663–1880*. Chapel Hill: University of North Carolina Press, 2010.

Routel, Colette. "Minnesota Bounties on Dakota Men during the U.S.-Dakota War." *William Mitchell Law Review* 40, no. 1 (October 2013): 1–77.

Rydell, Robert W. *All the World's a Fair: Visions of Empire at American International Expositions, 1876–1916.* Chicago: University of Chicago Press, 1984.

"Samuel J. Brown." *Annual Report of Charles G. Bennett, Secretary of the Senate.* 56th Congress, 2d Session, Document 23. Washington, D.C.: Government Printing Office, 1900.

Sanger, George P., ed. *The Statutes at Large, Treaties, and Proclamations of the United States of America from December 5, 1859, to March 3, 1863.* Boston: Little, Brown, 1863.

Schulte, Steven C. "American Indian Historiography and the Myth of the Origins of the Plains Wars." *Nebraska History* 61, no. 4 (December 1980): 437–446.

Scott, Kim Allen, and Ken Kempcke. "A Journey to the Heart of Darkness: John W. Wright and the War against the Sioux, 1863–1865." *Montana: The Magazine of Western History* 50, no. 4 (Winter 2000): 2–17.

Sibley, Henry H. "Sketch of John Other Day." *Collections of the Minnesota Historical Society* 3 (1870–1880): 99–102.

Smith, Andrea. *Conquest: Sexual Violence and American Indian Genocide.* Durham, N.C.: Duke University Press, 2015.

Smith, George Martin, ed. *South Dakota: Its History and Its People.* Vol. 3. Chicago: S. J. Clarke, 1914.

Smith, Linda Tuhiwai. *Decolonizing Methodologies: Research and Indigenous Peoples.* London: Zed Books, 1999.

Sneve, Virginia Driving Hawk. *Completing the Circle.* Lincoln: University of Nebraska Press, 1995.

Spack, Ruth. *America's Second Tongue: American Indian Education and the Ownership of English, 1860–1900.* Lincoln: University of Nebraska Press, 2002.

———. "English, Pedagogy, and Ideology: A Case Study of the Hampton Institute, 1878–1900." *American Indian Culture and Research Journal* 24, no. 1 (2000): 1–24.

Stately, Ramona. "Pazahiyayewin and the Importance of Remembering Dakota Women." In *In the Footsteps of Our Ancestors: The Dakota Commemorative Marches of the 21st Century*, ed. Waziyatawin, 192–195. St. Paul: Living Justice Press, 2006.

Statistics of the United States, in 1860. Washington, D.C.: Government Printing Office, 1866.

"The Story of Nancy McClure: Captivity among the Sioux." *Collections of the Minnesota Historical Society* 6 (1894): 439–460.

Stover, Ronald G. "A Graphic Representation of the Minnesota Dakota Diaspora." *Great Plains Sociologist* 24 (2014): 32–44.

Temple, Seth J. "Camp McClellan during the Civil War." *Annals of Iowa* 21, no. 1 (Summer 1937): 17–55.

Tennant, Brad. "The 1864 Sully Expedition and the Death of Captain John Feilner." *American Nineteenth Century History* 9, no. 2 (June 2008): 183–190.

Tinker, George E. *Missionary Conquest: The Gospel and Native American Cultural Genocide.* Minneapolis: Fortress Press, 1993.

U.S. Congress. *Conditions of the Indian Tribes. Report of the Joint Special Committee. Appointed under Joint Resolution of March 3, 1865, with an Appendix.* Washington, D.C.: Government Printing Office, 1867.

U.S. Department of War. *The War of the Rebellion: A Compilation of the Official Records of the Union and Confederate Armies.* Vol. 13, series 1. Washington, D.C.: Government Printing Office, 1885.

Utley, Robert M. *Frontiersmen in Blue: The United States Army and the Indian, 1848–1865.* Lincoln: University of Nebraska Press, 1981.

Vogel, Howard J. "Rethinking the Effect of the Abrogation of the Dakota Treaties and the Authority for the Removal of the Dakota People from Their Homeland." *William Mitchell Law Review* 39, no. 2 (2013): 538–581.

Waggoner, Linda M. "Sibley's Winnebago Prisoners: Deconstructing Race and Recovering Kinship in the Dakota War of 1862." *Great Plains Quarterly* 33 (Winter 2013): 25–48.

Wagoner, Levi. "Camp McClellan and the Redskins." *Annuals of Jackson County, Iowa*, no. 5 (1908): 19–21.

Wakefield, Sarah F. *Six Weeks in the Sioux Tepees: A Narrative of Indian Captivity.* Ed. June Namias. Norman: University of Oklahoma Press, 1997.

Waziyatawin [Angela Wilson]. "Colonial Calibrations: The Expendability of Minnesota's Original People." *William Mitchell Law Review* 39, no. 2 (2013): 450–485.

———, ed. *In the Footsteps of Our Ancestors: The Dakota Commemorative Marches of the 21st Century.* St. Paul: Living Justice Press, 2006.

———. *Remember This! Dakota Decolonization and the Eli Taylor Narratives.* Lincoln: University of Nebraska Press, 2005.

———. *What Does Justice Look Like? The Struggle for Liberation in Dakota Homeland.* St. Paul: Living Justice Press, 2008.

Waziyatawin and Michael Yellow Bird, eds. *For Indigenous Eyes Only: A Decolonization Handbook.* Santa Fe, N.M.: School of American Research, 2005.

Welch, Christina. "Savagery on Show: The Popular Visual Representation of Native American Peoples and Their Lifeways at the World's Fairs (1851–1904) and in Buffalo Bill's Wild West (1884–1904)." *Early Popular Visual Culture* 9, no. 4 (November 2011): 337–352.

Westerman, Gwen N. "Treaties Are More than a Piece of Paper: Why Words Matter." *Albany Government Law Review* 10 (2017): 293–317.

Westerman, Gwen N., and Bruce M. White. *Mni Sota Makoce: The Land of the Dakota.* St. Paul: Minnesota Historical Society Press, 2012.

Whipple, Henry Benjamin. *Lights and Shadows of a Long Episcopate: Being Reminiscences and Recollections of the Right Reverend Henry Benjamin Whipple.* New York: Macmillan, 1899.

White, Bruce M. "Stereotypes of Minnesota's Native People." *Minnesota History* 53, no. 3 (Fall 1992): 99–111.

Williamson, John. "Robert Hopkins Ta." Trans. Louis Garcia. *Iapi Oaye* 38, no. 1 (January 1909): 3.

Williamson, Thomas. "The Indian Question." *North American Review* 116, no. 239 (April 1873): 329–389.

Wilson, Diane. *Beloved Child: A Dakota Way of Life.* St. Paul: Minnesota Historical Society Press, 2011.

Woolworth, Alan R. "Adrian J. Ebell, Photographer and Journalist of the Dakota War of 1862." *Minnesota History* 54, no. 2 (Summer 1994): 87–92.

———. "Dakota Indian Scouts on the Minnesota/Dakota Territory Frontier, 1863–1866." *Minnesota's Heritage* 6 (July 2012): 60–77.

Zwiep, Mary. "Sending the Children Home: A Dilemma for Early Missionaries." *Hawaiian Journal of History* 24 (1990): 39–68.

INDEX

Page numbers in italics refer to figures

IOWA AND THE MIDWEST EXPERIENCE

*Transcendental Meditation in America:
How a New Age Movement Remade a
Small Town in Iowa*
by Joseph Weber

*What Happens Next? Essays on Matters
of Life and Death*
by Douglas Bauer

*Woman Suffrage and Citizenship in the
Midwest, 1870–1920*
by Sara Egge